9/97

Killer
Among Us

Killer
_____Among Us_____

Public Reactions to Serial Murder

Joseph C. Fisher

Westport, Connecticut
London

Library of Congress Cataloging-in-Publication Data

Fisher, Joseph C.
    Killer among us : public reactions to serial murder / Joseph C.
Fisher.
        p.   cm.
    Includes bibliographical references and index.
    ISBN 0–275–95558–3 (alk. paper)
    1. Serial murders—United States.   2. Victims of crimes—United
States—Attitudes.   3. Violent crimes—Psychological aspects.
I. Title.
HV6529.F57   1997
364.1'523—dc20   96–33198

British Library Cataloguing in Publication Data is available.

Library of Congress Catalog Card Number: 96–33198
ISBN: 0–275–95558–3

First published in 1997

Praeger Publishers, 88 Post Road West, Westport, CT 06881
An imprint of Greenwood Publishing Group, Inc.

Printed in the United States of America

The paper used in this book complies with the
Permanent Paper Standard issued by the National
Information Standards Organization (Z39.48–1984).

10 9 8 7 6 5 4 3 2 1

For Dorit

Contents

Tables and Figures

Preface

Between 1968 and 1974, I had the dubious distinction of living in two communities that were threatened by serial killers. The earlier of the two serial killings took place in the university towns of Ann Arbor and Ypsilanti, Michigan and involved the deaths of seven young women, the majority of whom were coeds at the University of Michigan and Eastern Michigan University. The latter occurred in Folly Beach, South Carolina and cost the lives of three teenage girls. Therefore, in many respects, research for *Killer Among Us* began nearly three decades ago when, as an incidental participant-observer in these two areas, I experienced firsthand the reactions of a terrified populace when confronted with a serial murderer in their midst.

Having gone through the experience twice, I became aware of a certain regularity in the behavior of the residents of both areas. Preoccupation with the killer—who he was, when and where he would strike next, who was at risk—was extreme, irrational, and all consuming. It seemed to dominate every social interaction and to creep into and control every conversation. But for me, the fascinating part of the drama was not the killer, his motivations or behavior, but rather the strategies the community adopted to deal with the pervasive, at times suffocating, atmosphere of fear. These strategies, in turn, seemed to progress through several identifiable stages, each emerging out of the one preceding.

For example, as discussed more fully in Chapter 3, the fact that the killer in Ann Arbor and Ypsilanti seemed to have the power to select victims at will and lure them to a violent death with open disdain for a massive manhunt mounted to stop him magnified the community's fear. Perhaps most unsettling for the community was the behavior of the victims; some of whom were reported to have gone willingly with their killer even though they may have known what lay ahead. This blind trust and the killer's exploitation of that trust seemed to have an eerie, supernatural quality. The killer had special powers and could therefore only be caught by those also so gifted. An appeal to the greatest psychic of the day, Peter Hurkos, for help in solving the crimes was the end result. An appeal to the supernatural is just one of several identifiable stages of collective psychological adaptation identified and developed in the present volume.

Chapter 1 recounts the factual details of the Folly Beach case. With respect to my personal experiences on Folly Beach, two incidents stand out in my memory. At one point during the investigation, police excavated bodies buried on the beach. At night, the floodlights illuminated the work site and were visible along the length of the island, and throughout the night, the distant double-clutching of earth-moving equipment could be heard as front-loaders cut continually deeper into the sand in search of more victims.

Compounding this constant reminder of what had happened on the island was the police blockade established on the only bridge leading to the mainland. As every Folly Beach resident knew, the killer was trapped with them on the island. Someone, living on the island and caught there, had murdered three young girls over the course of a year and had only by the slimmest of margins been prevented from killing three more.

Needless to say, the tension among the townspeople was palpable, as was a sense of intense isolation. For my part, I felt the need to talk to someone and to make some sort of social contact. My landlord, normally a gregarious man, had been curiously absent in the preceding few days, not working in his yard as usual. I wondered how he had weathered the night and if his concerns were similar to mine. As a long-time resident of the island, he might also have facts about the investigation that I did not.

So I walked across the street talk to him. No one was outside. I climbed the stairs to the second floor deck. The house was shut tight, even the windows were closed, an odd circumstance on what promised to be a hot April day. I knocked. The front door opened part way, the screen door stayed shut. We briefly said hello, but when I tried to engage him further by asking what he thought about the recently discovered bodies, he closed the door unceremoniously in my face with a force just short of a slam. I will never forget how totally alone I felt as I walked back to my house across the street.

Several days later a policeman arrived quite unexpectedly at the front door. He called through the screen and said he needed to ask me some questions about the dead girls. The abruptness of his presence and interrogation caught me off guard, as did the quick realization that I was a suspect in the crimes. For the briefest of moments, perhaps only a second or two, I experienced a flash of self-doubt so profound it left me shaken. I was in Ann Arbor too when the girls were killed. Could I be the one?

I went to the door, hoping my guilty thoughts were not reflected in my expression. The officer looked me up and down and immediately ruled me out as the murderer. When asked why I was a suspect, the police officer indicated that someone who had seen me driving through town had reported that I resembled the composite drawing then in circulation. Like the killer, I had curly hair and a mustache but fortunately not his identifying birthmark. I never quite got over the incident and how deeply it affected me. It was not until years later, after I began to study public reactions to serial murder, that I learned my feelings of self-doubt were by no means unique.

In the simplest terms then, *Killer Among Us* is a study of betrayal and of its consequences for the collective psychology and social intercourse of a community. This betrayal has a multiplicity of layers. The most obvious level is the killers' betrayal of the social contract when they live among us and periodically emerge to murder in violation of society's most sacrosanct moral and ethical canons. This primary form of betrayal represents the immediate threat to safety and initiates the progressive stages of mass psychological adaptation, the search for rational explanations, appeals to the supernatural, and transference.

Concomitant with the knowledge that the killer remains uncaught in the community, and therefore free to kill again at any time, is the belief that anyone could be the killer. Suspicion and mistrust of others grow, permeate, and eventually dominate social interaction. Symptoms of mistrust, such as the avoidance of friends and neighbors or the reporting of neighbors, friends, and even loved ones to police as suspects, are commonplace. If trust is the oil of social relations, suspicion is the grist. The inability to trust others at the time of greatest need is the principal mechanism behind the negative social consequences that attend serial murder cases; it is a more pervasive and fundamental betrayal of the social contract.

As the ultimate consequence of prejudice is self-hatred, so too the most profound manifestation of suspicion is self-doubt. Betrayal of self is, then, the final product of having a killer in our midst, a sense of suspicion so complete no one can be trusted—not the authorities, not neighbors, acquaintances, or friends, and in the end not even oneself. The deleterious effects of extreme suspicion and isolation on social cohesion and social relations represent another focus of this work.

With respect to methodology, *Killer Among Us* uses contemporary newspaper reports as a window through time to observe and recapture the thoughts, feelings, and actions of each community studied. This archival record of factual reports, which is often imperfect and inaccurate given the knowledge available at the time, as well as feature stories, editorials, and letters to the editor, are the raw data from which the characteristic stages of public reactions to serial murder are discerned and described.

As noted in Chapter 5, The Media and the Murderer, the information, pecuniary, and ego gratification needs of the public, press, and killer frequently converge to create a climate of media hysteria and an avalanche of reportage for the duration of the crimes. On a practical basis, there is no dearth of raw material available for research purposes; therefore, its simple accumulation can be a daunting task. In this regard, I was greatly assisted by a number of persons: Susan Warstadt assembled information on both the Jeffrey Dahmer and Jack the Ripper cases, Elizabeth Warstadt collected and summarized reports on Wayne Williams, by far the most voluminous case, Javeed Ismail researched the Son of Sam case, and the Boyce family, Elizabeth, Barbara, and Harry, compiled the newspaper history used to develop the John Norman Collins case. I am also indebted to John Cronin, Librarian for the *Boston Herald*, who provided access to the paper's clipping files and material on the Boston Strangler. Finally, I would like to thank Chief George Tittle for taking the time to discuss the Folly Beach murders with me.

I was fortunate as well to have the support and guidance of a number of persons during the preparation of the manuscript and prepublication review. For their encouragement I am indebted to Ellen Mugar, Louise and Patrick Grubb, and Sandy Fifield. Other friends and colleagues who offered assistance along the way include John Conklin, Barbara Shapiro, and Niko Pfund. The maps in Chapters 1, 4, and 7 were made possible through the auspices of Paul Ravenna of International Sailing Supply, makers of Waterproof Charts, and were expertly prepared by Bill Quantick; I am grateful to both.

I would like to express my appreciation to Ann and Donald Farber for their time and efforts on my behalf during the preparation of this book. At a critical juncture, their insightful critique of the work helped me reorganize the material and see my way clear to finish the manuscript. Finally, special thanks are due Nick Street, editor, and James Dunton, publisher, of Praeger, for their faith in the work and their patience and guidance during the publication process.

Although I was aided immeasurably by all of these individuals and undoubtedly could not have completed *Killer Among Us* without their help, the analysis and authorship contained herein are mine alone. I am solely responsible for the interpretation of events, representations, and descriptions of public sentiment, and for any omissions or errors of fact.

More than a quarter of a century has passed since my first exposure to a city brought to the brink of hysteria by a serial killer and the nascent formulation of the ideas and stages of community response that comprise the subject matter of this book. While I always wanted to write about my observations, the process of writing would never have begun without the steady encouragement of my wife Dorit. Nearly four years elapsed between the start of research and writing and the eventual publication of *Killer Among Us*. More than once during that period I lost faith in the endeavor and was ready to scrap the project. That I did not is testimony to Dorit's moral support.

Introduction

RICHARD RAYMOND VALENTI
Folly Beach, South Carolina (1973–1974)

"If I had to write a book, I couldn't write it. It's too sordid, too horrible."
—Robert Wallace, Circuit Court Solicitor
Charleston Evening Post, June 27, 1974

On Saturday, September 19, 1973, a young woman brought a man she had just met at a party to her North Charleston apartment. Suddenly, without warning or provocation, the man assaulted her. He tied and bound her to her bed after which he looked on in an aroused state. Refusing to struggle, she summoned her courage and confronted the attacker, "Well, if all you want's a piece of pussy come on. I got things to do and places to go."[1] The assailant lost his erection immediately and ran from the room.

Thinking her tormentor might be a sailor, the nineteen-year-old woman notified the military authorities at the nearby naval base. She was told to refer her complaint to the county sheriff's office. Instead she let the matter drop for almost a year.

Four months earlier on a Wednesday afternoon, May 23, 1973, thirteen-year-old Alexis Ann Latimer and her fourteen-year-old friend, Sherri Jan Clark, left the Latimer family cottage on Folly Beach. They did not return. (See Figure 1.1 for a map of the Folly Beach and Charleston, South Carolina area.)

Despite their expressed intention to take only a short walk on the beach, police concluded that the girls had run away from home. Mrs. Latimer would later bitterly recall, "The girls were reported missing immediately, but the police laughed at me. They thought I was just an overwrought mother."[2] She also stated that it was two weeks before the police began any kind of investigation or pursued any leads:

Someone had reported seeing the girls and it was over two weeks before the police went back and talked with them. They (the police) just assumed that she had run

Figure 1.1
Folly Beach and Charleston, South Carolina Area

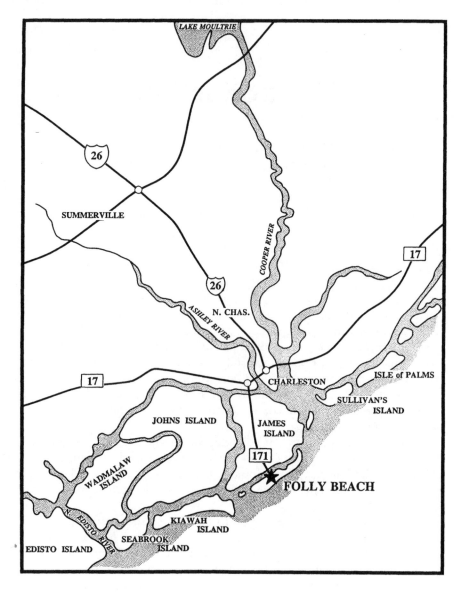

away. All it would have taken is a few phone calls to find out that they were not the runaway types.[3]

The police failed to act but at the same time admitted being mystified by the dual disappearance.

In nearby Charleston, the evening papers that day were dominated by a national political scandal and cover-up that was quickly unraveling. White House aide John Caulfield admitted knowing his offer of executive clemency extended to Watergate burglar James McCord was illegal. Justifying his actions, he stated he thought the clemency offer had originated with President Nixon. The president, in turn, denied any knowledge of the offer or that he had authorized it.

A short article inside the *Charleston News and Courier* described the hunt in McConnellsburg, Pennsylvania for the body of nineteen-year-old Richard Miller. The search was led by twenty-six-year-old mass murderer Wayne Coleman who confessed to killing Miller. Coleman and three fellow escapees from Wicomico Prison in Maryland had previously killed a family of six on a farm in Georgia. The ominous prospect of multiple murder in the local community was never considered, however. Neither of the two major Charleston papers mentioned the disappearance of the two teenagers on Folly Beach.

In subsequent months, the parents tried desperately to find the girls by printing and circulating leaflets and placing ads in the local paper. Mrs. Latimer even appealed to a Dutch psychic, Gerard Croiset, Jr., for any insight he could offer into the mystery. After examining pictures of the girls, the psychic told Mrs. Latimer that her daughter was dead and that she should search around the Coast Guard station at the north end of the island to find the body.

In early spring, February 12, 1974, police found a teenage girl bound, gagged, and tied to a tree behind the James Island Shopping Center, a few miles from Folly Beach. The rescued girl's attacker was not immediately found. About a week later on February 20, 1974, Mary Earline Bunch, age 16, disappeared on Folly Beach. She was last seen walking on Center Street, the main thoroughfare in town, headed for her house just two blocks away.

The news that week was filled with reports of crime, violent death, and kidnapping, but danger from social problems seemed to happen elsewhere, in places far away. The papers carried stories of

- the Patty Hearst kidnapping in California
- block patrols in New York City designed to curb crime
- a business executive, Reg Murphy, kidnapped in Atlanta
- the death of a fifth grader in a fire in Charlotte, North Carolina

• the start of a series of interracial shootings in San Francisco that would become known as the Zebra killings

Locally, there was considerable concern about the increased cost of haircuts, the Arab oil embargo, and the lines created at filling stations. On the day Mary Bunch failed to return home, there was even a report summarizing the recent Town Council meeting on Folly Beach during which the pros and cons of building a new playground were debated, and a decision was made to change the residential numbering system on the island. But again the strange disappearance of a teenager on Folly Beach was not reported in the Charleston papers.

Several weeks later, E. D. Pickerell, a retired naval base employee, took his dog for their customary exercise walk on the beach. Before long, the dog became preoccupied with one spot in the dunes and refused to go farther. On closer inspection Mr. Pickerell noticed blood and saw maggots burrowing out of the sand. Briefly he thought it odd that garbage would be buried on the beach, but just at that moment he was distracted when his dog began to chase several other dogs. Giving the matter no more thought, he continued walking. He had no reason to recall the incident until a month later.

On Friday, April 12, 1974, the Folly Beach Police were called to investigate an illegal surfing complaint. During the inspection an officer heard a call for help coming from below a vacant beachfront cottage. There he found three sixteen-year-old girls bound and gagged. One of the girls had been able to slip her gag just enough to summon help.

The girls told the officer they had come to the island from their hometown of Summerville to enjoy a day at the beach. Twenty minutes earlier while sunbathing, a man had approached them on the beach. Wielding a gun, he forced them to come with him. As if to reinforce his threat, he said that he had killed two policemen and would kill them too if they resisted. He brought them to an outdoor shower room under a vacant cottage where he tied them up, after which he left abruptly.

The girls were able to provide the police with an excellent description of their abductor, including several identifying characteristics and one distinctive, perhaps unique, feature. Slowed by the approaching weekend, the composite drawing did not begin to get wide circulation until the following week.

Suddenly, progressively, and with a chilling finality, the connections began to occur to everyone involved. Mr. Pickerell, in particular, started to reexamine an incident that did not quite make sense at the time. His dog's behavior and its possible connection to the escaped and missing girls continued to bother him, "After that I couldn't sleep. I thought, 'Well Gee-Menneli, that could have been a body.' "[4] But still he hesitated since, as he later explained, "So many times somebody will report something like this and people say to themselves, 'This guy hasn't got a full string of fish.' "[5] Eventually, his concern overcame the potential for embarrassment, and on

Tuesday he approached his long-time friend Folly Beach city manager John Wilbanks and told him about the place on the beach that affected his dog so strongly.

The two men went to the spot, less than a quarter of a mile from where the three girls were abducted, and began to dig with shovels. After a short time they uncovered what was thought to be a piece of clothing. Next the men contacted a local contractor who owned and operated a bulldozer. His first two passes through the sand with the heavy equipment found nothing. The men decided to make a final attempt before giving up, and on the third try a body was discovered.

The body, clad only in underwear, was buried in two feet of sand. A nylon clothesline like that used to restrain the three recently rescued girls was found tied around the hands and feet. Only the skeleton remained, and it was not immediately clear what sex it was or whether or not there had been a sexual assault. A comparison of dental records the following day positively identified the victim as Mary Earline Bunch.

Digging continued at the beach site through the night and the following day. Huge floodlights lit the work area and could be seen by every resident of the island. Spectators lined the dunes and watched in silence as work teams from multiple police agencies systematically excavated the site for evidence. In the background was the unspoken expectation that more bodies were yet to be discovered.

The island community, which had been slow to comprehend the meaning of missing teens, now reacted in quick defense. A house-to-house canvass was begun to gather information and leads. Police, meanwhile, set up a blockade on the one bridge leading to or from the island, preventing anyone from leaving. That night a thousand families went to bed with the knowledge and certain dread that a killer was in their midst, and, like themselves, he could not get off the island.

By Wednesday, the investigation began to pick up steam. Navy jets surveyed the island with infrared sensors in an effort to find more graves and decomposing bodies. Meanwhile, the composite sketch of a mustached assailant was widely distributed. Police on the island began to question several good suspects that had been reported to them by fearful, albeit well-meaning, neighbors. Their efforts were aided immeasurably by a critical detail they had chosen to withold from the public, an identification so singular it would make positive identification virtually infallible.

Finally, in North Charleston the victim of an attack that had occurred almost a year earlier noticed the composite drawing. Again, she approached naval authorities, but this time she was shown photographs of personnel stationed at the base. A suspect was identified, and the matter was referred to the Charleston County Police.

So informed county police officers went to the home of Richard Valenti, a six-year navy veteran and radar operations specialist on the submarine rescue vessel *Petrel*. The suspect was renting a house immediately across the street from the sandy grave of Mary Bunch. Neighbors would subsequently recall that the night after the three girls were found Richard Valenti had shaved his mustache and beard. But betrayed by the mark of Cain, Valenti also had a birthmark on his ankle—the unpublicized telltale detail.

To their astonishment, police realized that they had known the suspect all along. In fact, he had been one of the spectators who had lined the dunes watching the excavation; as his neighbor Robert Fennessy remembered, "He was watching the whole operation all day long."[6] Even more eerily, he had opened his home to investigators, allowing them to use his phone and offering them drinks as they worked. After Miss Bunch's body was found, he consoled his neighbors, as one said, "He told me, Don't worry, everything's going to be all right."[7]

Valenti was taken into custody at 4:10 P.M., Wednesday, and was brought to the Charleston County Police station for questioning. Interrogation began at 6:40 P.M. and quickly filled in the missing details of the case. The progress was recorded in the taped log:[8]

6:52 P.M.	He admitted assaulting the Mount Pleasant woman whose identification led to his arrest.
6:53 P.M.	The assault of the three Summerville girls was admitted.
7:14 P.M.	Valenti described the kidnapping of Mary Bunch.
7:41 P.M.	The deaths of Sherri Clark and Alexis Latimer were recounted.

At 8:50 P.M. Valenti led the police back to Folly Beach to a spot in the dunes just above the beach and excavation site.

In this area where spectators, including Valenti, had stood and watched, police now dug for the remains of the other two teenagers. The confessed killer then took the police to the place of their death, an outdoor shower room beneath his nearby house. Police searched Valenti's apartment and removed evidence, including what to on-lookers appeared to be a gun. Finally, Valenti was taken to the Charleston County jail but not before he was allowed to return home and pick up two Bibles.

When the realization sunk in that the killer was not a stranger but one of "us," the arrest left the island community shocked and bewildered. Suddenly aware of having been betrayed by a lethal traitor in their midst, the residents were forced to mentally replay the preceding months, to examine their contact with the accused, and to analyze his behavior as if searching for some sign that should have been evident and should have given him away.

Neighbors remembered the family as "quiet people who seemed so good." A strong theme of Christian faith was present in most recollections. Valenti was described as a "straight dude," a "Jesus Freak" who often went to the beach to meditate.[9] Shipmates characterized Valenti as a person who kept to himself and frequently read the Bible. In the words of one neighbor, "He seemed to be a super-Christian. This is a total surprise to me. The time I visited their home, they were singing Christian songs and talking about the bible."[10]

Even more dismayed and incredulous were the killer's parents. Contacted at home in Massachusetts, Valenti's mother was quoted as saying, "We had no inkling of anything like this until now. It's so unbelievable."[11] As if trying to deny all evidence to the contrary, she said, "He is a wonderful son, a wonderful father and the gentlest person in the world."[12] Then as if seeking understanding or absolution, she rendered the final epitaph, "The boy is sick."[13]

Richard Raymond Valenti, age 31, was arraigned by the Charleston County Grand Jury on May 27, 1974, almost a year to the day after he killed Sherri Clark and Alexis Latimer. Charged with three counts of murder, four counts of assault and battery with intent to kill, and one count of assault and battery with intent to ravish, Valenti was held without bail to stand trial the following month.

The trial that began in General Sessions Court on June 24 was a straight-forward affair. The prosecution chose to proceed with two murder counts, holding the murder of Mary Bunch in reserve. The only issues in contention were whether or not the defendant's taped confession and written statement and the testimony of the Mount Pleasant woman, which the defense maintained was "too prejudicial," would be allowed into evidence. The testimony was not allowed, but the confession was admitted. Thus the trial with a preordained conclusion became a grim public catharsis, a crucial judicial ritual intended to allay community anxiety and put closure on the grieving of the families.

The defense called Valenti's wife to testify in her husband's behalf. In tears for most of her testimony, Mrs. Valenti recalled how she became aware of her husband's fetish in 1969 when she found magazines with photographs of bound women. According to the witness, this unsharable knowledge had even led her to attempt suicide once. At times she allowed her husband to tie her up in a vain effort to satisfy his desires. In the end the strategy failed, she said, because she did not know how to act. When the couple moved to Charleston and became Christians, she thought the nightmare had ended. But then in the spring of 1973 she began to suspect something was wrong. Despite her misgivings, she took no action.

Dr. Gerald Donovan, a psychiatrist at the medical university in Charleston, testified that Valenti had been reared in a severely dysfunctional home by a mother who had tried to dominate him. His fetish, in the doctor's interpretation, was a means of reversing the domination and gaining total control over women. In the doctor's view, the two girls died as a direct result of this need to dominate. Dr. Donovan also testified that Valenti experienced fantasies and that he had trouble separating his fantasy life from reality. However, the doctor was forced to admit under cross-examination that Valenti was not psychotic, was able to distinguish right from wrong, and therefore was legally sane.

Without question, the climax of the trial was the replaying of Valenti's taped confession and the gruesome details it added to the story. Valenti told how he first encountered the girls while walking on the beach and got the urge to tie them up. He returned to his apartment, got a toy gun, and went back to the beach. Sensing what would come next, he voiced his misgivings, "I kind of hoped they wouldn't be there."[14] He approached the girls, drew his gun, and told them to follow him or he would shoot.

He took the girls to his house and forced them into an outdoor shower room. There he tied their hands and feet, partially undressed them, and made them pose in various positions. Valenti then made the girls stand on chairs while he tied nooses around their necks and secured them to an overhead waterpipe. He fondled them, and in their attempts to avoid his grasp the girls fell from their platforms and slowly hanged. Transfixed, Valenti looked on and masturbated. He described his fugue-like state: "Part of me wanted to help them, but I couldn't. I wanted to move, I wanted to get them down, but I just couldn't move."[15]

On the fourth day of the trial, the jury of eight women and four men heard final arguments and began their deliberations. Fifty-five minutes after starting, the jury returned a verdict of guilty on the two murder counts. Richard Valenti was given two life sentences to be served consecutively.

FOLLY BEACH REDUX

The preceding account is a synopsis of events surrounding one serial murder case as it was reported in the local newspapers at the time. As we review the facts, a crucial question is: how unique were the events that took place in Charleston in 1973 and 1974? Do they have anything in common with other serial killings that happen elsewhere? As for the murderer, is Richard Valenti a singular aberrant personality, or do his fantasies and actions represent a general class of thoughts and behavior that can be expected of other serial killers? We could, of course, ask the same sort of questions about individual reactions and the community response to the killings. How unique were they? Can we recognize any categories of reaction that other people or communities threatened by a serial killer share? Are the reactions predictable?

Popular and academic interest in serial murder centers largely around the first set of questions: who the killer is and why he kills. Less frequently considered is the impact of the killer on social life—specifically, how and why the community reacts when presented with the threat of a serial killer in its midst. As a start in this direction, this book identifies and describes typical ways communities and individuals respond when confronting the fear and danger created by the serial killer, reactions that are common across incidents separated by geography and time.

Looking back on the Valenti case, we can point to a number of landmarks in the way the community reacted to the tragedy. The initial response was one of denial, during which the authorities refused to believe the missing girls had come to harm despite the protests of their parents. The disappearances were dismissed, no investigation was undertaken, and the unusual events did not even warrant a mention in the local papers. The embittered parents, lacking official assistance, subsequently began their own search for the missing girls. They printed and circulated leaflets, and they placed missing persons ads in the paper. Finally, in desperation, one family consulted a psychic hoping his extrasensory powers would break the case.

When several kidnapped and bound girls were discovered, the connections became obvious, and it was no longer possible to ignore what had happened to the other missing teens. The residents' lingering doubts and unspoken suspicions crystallized around the now all too apparent and awful reality. Seemingly minor events of the past year, strange but benign in a previous context, were remembered and reinterpreted in light of the new information. Once the bodies were discovered, the community began a rapid transformation. The normal bonds of social life were broken in the face of the newly apparent threat to public safety. Personal integration into the larger whole was replaced by isolation. Neighbor avoided neighbor. Contact was held to a minimum. Newcomers to the island became a source of suspicion and were reported to the police.

By this time, the press had taken to the story with a vengeance. What once had gone unnoticed now became front-page news. Mass murder, serial killings, and the wanton destruction of innocent children were no longer events that happened at a safe distance, in large, impersonal cities—they happened in Charleston. Day after day, every detail of the investigation, arrest, and trial filled the papers.

An air of stunned disbelief followed in the wake of the arrest. The island residents had lived next to Valenti for years; they knew him and yet he was not what they thought him to be. The image of a god-fearing, responsible family man was nothing more than an elaborate façade erected to hide his true personality, a grotesque hoax perpetrated on his unsuspecting friends. His actions during the investigation were no less cynical. With his neighbors, Valenti watched as bodies were exhumed; he tried to calm their anxieties and even helped investigators. Throughout the ordeal he acted like a concerned, caring neighbor, and when the lie was exposed, the residents felt betrayed: the bedrock of their beliefs had been shaken.

The wonderment of it all was how they had not seen the truth before. Everyone scoured their recollections of the accused, looking for the flaws in his actions that should have given him away. More than anyone else, his wife should have suspected what he was capable of doing as she indulged his bondage fantasies. But like the others, she could not or would not recognize the killer beside her. The burden of responsibility and collective guilt emanated directly from the failure of those involved to comprehend the situation and stop the killer. Although the trial provided an opportunity to expose the pathetically perverted killer and bare his deeds in ghastly detail, it was not totally sufficient to absolve the community of its unwitting complicity.

Comparing these events and reactions with other serial murder cases, we find a striking similarity in structure, despite differences in the details. Not surprisingly, fear, anxiety, and sometimes even panic are the primary emotional responses to serial murder. Of course, fear is a normal and appropriate reaction to a perceived threat. But the truly unique character of serial murder causes the public to react excessively relative to the actual aleatory risk of physical harm. Disproportionate response is a byproduct of a special kind of attack on individual beliefs, values, and more generally on social order.

Fear is pervasive, and preoccupation with the crimes permeates all aspects of social life, giving rise to two types of behavior. First, both citizens and public officials use characteristic strategies to manage the ambient fear, keep it within functional limits, and make sense out of what is happening. In the Valenti case, the initial denial of the crimes and the parents' appeal to a psychic are two often repeated manifestations of more general strategies of fear management and the search for understanding.

A second category of response stems from the insidious effect of chronic fear on the community's collective cohesion and social health. Serial murderers betray the common trust and in so doing weaken the bonds that hold the community together. They tear the fabric of collective life and quite literally kill the community from within. As the killings continue without an arrest, the community's disintegration deepens as evidenced in the Folly Beach experience when human traffic and social intercourse notably declined and mistrust and suspicion grew. Media attention and the failure to recognize and stop the killer exacerbate and speed up the process of social dissolution.

Thus, the various forms of public response are dictated by the serial murderer's unique capacity to create inordinate fear among the populace. Community reaction, in turn, falls into two broad categories: strategies to understand the events and deal with resultant fear; and symptoms and processes of social dissolution. The next chapter explores these topics further, especially why serial murder produces such a strong reaction, how fear is managed, and its impact on social life.

Subsequent chapters analyze other serial murder cases, with particular attention to the strategy or process for which it is an especially good example.

The method used to illustrate these commonalities is identical to that used in this introductory chapter. Using public documents as indicators of thoughts, feelings, and mood, we will recap the facts of the case and then describe the community reaction to the murders.

Serial Murder: Public Reactions

"For those who fall prey to these offenders, their plight is a deplorable one indeed, but the odds of becoming a victim are minuscule when compared with the population as a whole."

—Eric W. Hickey
Serial Murderers and Their Victims

Homicide is a fixture in contemporary American life. Every year more than 20,000 individuals die at the hands of their fellow citizens, and of these, two-thirds will be killed by a family member or someone they know. Yet, over time the public has become inured to this staggering figure. So many violent deaths provoke no outrage or embarrassment. They cause no outward expressions of fear, and little is done to modify the conduct of everyday life in response.

By comparison, serial murder is a truly rare phenomenon. Although estimates vary widely, perhaps only 10 serial murderers are active in the United States every year, and they may account for just 100 murders annually, or less than 1 percent of the total homicide count. A person in the United States is as likely to be struck and killed by lightning as to die at the hands of a serial killer. Whether by a serial murderer or an act of God, the odds of death for the average American are below one in two million.

Despite its scarcity, serial murder receives inordinate attention in the media, having been the subject of innumerable movies, books, television plots, and news reports. Serial murder fascinates. It is so premeditated, methodical, vicious, and uncommon that we cannot escape its allure, its capacity to astonish and horrify, its power to instill fear. But beyond fascination, serial murder touches a more basic, primal level. It intrudes on the most protected and inviolable areas of experience and beliefs, expectations about life that are so fundamental they seem to have been genetically imprinted from birth. As such, serial murder has the ability to instill fear far in excess of the true risk it represents.

Serial murder strikes foremost at expectations that one is safe and free from personal harm. Victims selected by chance vividly illustrate an inherent vulnerability to personal violence. Serial murder conjures up images not only of painful destruction but, what is worse, also of death at the hands of a stranger with whom one could not expect to reason and from whom one could expect no mercy. In this regard, reactions to serial murder are similar to public perceptions of crime generally. Without question, the crimes that people fear most, such as murder and rape, happen the least often. Moreover, death and injury from crime are secondary to the fact that it is associated with strangers, mysterious and threatening individuals whose motives are unknown and hence whose attacks are unpredictable and indiscriminate. Thus, reactions to serial murder emanate from the same sources as fear of other crimes—personal vulnerability, defenselessness, risk of death and injury, and most of all, fear and mistrust of strangers.

While reactions to serial murder and other forms of personal violence have much in common, serial murder is indeed unique. It has the capacity to activate fears and keep them alive like no other crime can. A single homicide, though tragic, has an element of finality to it. The deed is done, the killer has been caught, and the threat is over. The event is quick and isolated, and the risk to others does not extend beyond the victim. With serial murder, the risk is wider, the threat continues, and fear is ubiquitous and increases with time.

The number of deaths and the length of time involved act as accelerators to the buildup of fear. Elapsed time permits the body count to grow, emphasizes the futility of police efforts, and generally contributes to feelings of personal helplessness and collective risk. The sense of vulnerability increases with each new body discovered, while anticipation of the next murder becomes as much a source of dread as the discovery itself. As a result, public passions intensify the longer a killer is free, causing fear to grow exponentially.

An interesting corollary to this state of mind occurs in those instances where the killer is never caught. For some unknown reason, as inexplicably as their starting, the murders cease, leaving the public to speculate that the killer has left the area, died, or been incarcerated for an unrelated crime. Of utmost importance is the fact that it is not immediately obvious that the string is finished; it could be that another body will be found any day. The investigation continues, winding down slowly over time, and gradually just stops. Meanwhile, the public is cheated out of the closure an arrest provides. There is no clear demarcation that allows the fear to end and the healing to begin.

Perhaps the best example of this type of situation is the Green River

Killer. So named because of the site where his first victims were found, the Green River Killer used as many as three dumping places in and around the Seattle–Tacoma area. From 1982 to 1984, the killer was responsible for the stabbing and strangulation deaths of at least 48 prostitutes. Although the killings stopped, the investigation has continued since, as reported in *Time* in 1987: "another prospect concerns investigators: that the Green River Killer may emerge from his hibernation and provide fresh clues in the form of fresh victims."[1]

At the core of the fear caused by serial murder is the incomprehensibility of what is happening. The killer's motivations and actions are beyond the experience of daily life and impossible to understand. In this way, serial murder differs fundamentally from the everyday violence that is tolerated with such sangfroid; as one specialist on serial murder noted:

Homicidal crimes of passion, though reprehensible, can at least be understood and dealt with rationally. Thus, given the cultural context of this society, most adults can "understand" that volatile interpersonal relations sometimes end in a homicidal act. Even in felony homicides and "classical" murder, it is possible in a grim sort of fashion to make sense of the homicide in terms of patterns of relations, between the killer and victim. But this cannot be said of serial killings, where an innocent person is slain, sometimes after inhuman torture and degradation by a stranger.[2]

The killer's motives are unknown, and the unknown is feared most of all.

Often serial murders can display a considerable degree of planning and thoughtful execution. It is especially difficult to appreciate how such irrational behavior can be committed so rationally. The fact that the killer is within the community only compounds the sense of unreality. How is it possible that a killer can function sanely, rationally, and normally on most occasions but visciously attack on other occasions? How can people live beside them as Sharon Valenti and the residents of Folly Beach did, and not see that Mr. Hyde lurks within Dr. Jekyll?

Characteristics of the victims can also affect a community's reaction to a serial killer. The safety of some members of society is viewed as sacrosanct, especially children, the elderly, and to a lesser degree women. When these groups are targeted and slain, the public outcry is pronounced. Serial murder, which is unfathomable to begin with, is made more incomprehensible when innocents are slaughtered. In addition, the balance of force between the killer and killed is so asymmetric that there is no hope the victims can defend themselves. Other groups are responsible for their protection and safety, and therefore, when it cannot be ensured the reaction is strongest. The irony is that when innocents are killed, the public is put in the place of the police, charged with maintaining security for loved ones, impotent to do so, and stricken with guilt as a consequence.

The collective conscience is let off the hook, so to speak, when the killer selects adults, males, or victims targeted for their lifestyle. Adults and men are perceived to have the capacity to defend themselves, even if their ability to do so proves illusory in practice. By comparison, those who are selected because of their lifestyle, for example, prostitutes, drifters, and homosexuals, are viewed as having complicity in their own demise. There is a tendency to believe, if not voice it, that they had it coming. In a sense the public is relieved of collective responsibility and consequent guilt by denying the legitimacy of the victim; their death is due to the personal choices they made to live at the fringes of society.

Initially, then, a serial killer at large awakens a number of elemental fears, chief among them the fear of personal mortality and particularly a cruel, capricious, untimely, and meaningless death. It evokes dormant fears of strangers, both those who live outside the community and those who live within it but whose actions are beyond understanding. Because of its repetitiveness, serial murder creates a sense of anticipatory dread and feelings of helplessness that one cannot alter what fate dictates. Fear out of proportion to the threat is therefore the product of an inability to comprehend the repetitive slaughter of innocents by a member of the community whose disguise is the normalcy of everyday life.

PUBLIC REACTIONS

The Power of Reason

The initial response to the killer among us is to find refuge in the rational. An attempt is made to find reasons for events that lie within the domain of normal behavior. Consequently, even suspiciously abnormal occurrences are interpreted as representing the most likely, ordinary, and commonplace eventualities. When teenagers disappeared in the Valenti case, the first interpretation given was the most obvious: they ran away. This explanation was given rather than the highly unlikely one: they came to lethal harm.

In the early phases of an investigation, especially before bodies are discovered, explaining behavior in everyday terms is equivalent to denying that a crime has occurred. As such, it constitutes a collective defense mechanism against the awful potential of what might have happened. It serves a similar function for authorities, allowing them at once to deny the crime by denying the victims and hence providing a basis for inaction. At some point, however, bodies are discovered, and it is clear that the logic of everyday experience has been suspended. What one has come to know and expect no longer provides reference points to navigate in the unknown.

For the public the shared features of the murders and victims, the common denominators, provide the basis for a rational understanding of the crimes. Even inherently irrational actions are made comprehensible if they have an internally consistent order or pattern. The paradox of serial murder is that the characteristic that makes it most beyond our capacity to understand, repetition, at the same time provides the key to the public's ability to apprehend it. Thus, it is the repeated killing that cannot be grasped. Yet if the murders are connected in some fashion, they have a logic which, however abnormal, the public can discern and use to explain the crimes.

From the point of view of investigators, rationality translates into a reliance on logical, scientific means to catch the killer. When their own efforts fall short, police appeal to experts whose specialized knowledge and proprietary methods of discovery are expected to solve the case. All manner of specialists are consulted—psychiatrists, psychologists, criminologists, forensic pathologists, hypnotists, handwriting analysts, lie detector specialists, computer scientists, to name a few. There is an implicit respect for the authority of learned men and faith that they will outsmart the killer. The experts' special knowledge is expected to illuminate what appears on the surface to be irrational action and to decode the encrypted motives in the evidence left by the killer.

A closely related example of the quest for a rational explanation of events is the effort by scholars and law enforcement professionals to study serial murder and characterize it in scientific terms. The result of this endeavor is a body of accumulated knowledge that can be used to analyze criminal behavior and bring it within the reach of our understanding. Based on the research findings, it is now possible to describe serial murderers with a high degree of accuracy. A number of common patterns have emerged that, while they may not allow authorities to pick the killer out of a crowd of suspects, at least are valuable in ruling out large groups of individuals.

In many respects, the study of serial murder by academics is another type of collective defense mechanism. Seemingly irrational behavior is intellectualized, and in so doing is removed from a personal, emotional domain to an objective, dispassionate one. Furthermore, although the behavior studied may be abnormal, the methods used to study it are the most rational available. If experts cannot stop serial murder or predict when it will occur, at least the behavior can be seen as being consistent with a pattern of past serial murders. The behavior becomes "knowable" in the broadest sense even if there is no experiential basis for comprehending it.

The belief in the infallibility of the scientific method extends beyond simply trying to understand serial murderers or explaining why they behave as they do. Frequently, the faith is expressed that science is the way to salvation, the means by which the scourge of serial murder will be removed from society. It is assumed that even aberrant behavior must have a cause, and more importantly, the causes for which serial murder is simply the behavioral manifestation are within the reach of the scientific method. In this view, it should be possible to determine the causes, prevent them in the future, and eventually eliminate serial murder. In the quintessential expression of this belief, those who subscribe to a medical model see serial murder as a disease that can be diagnosed and cured.

Ultimately, experts, academic research, and scientific methods are almost never instrumental in apprehending a serial killer, or as one criminologist specializing in the study of serial murder noted, "A review of serial murders occurring over the last few years reveals that most serial murderers are caught by chance or coincidence and not by ratiocination or scientific investigation."[3] As time passes without a successful resolution to the case, faith in rational processes, experts, and the scientific method diminish. In its place, the police and public will turn to supernatural explanations for the crimes and superhuman methods of finding the killer.

Supernatural Appeals

Coexisting in the public's imagination with rational explanations of serial murder are a set of interconnected beliefs whose foundation is the assumed role of supernatural forces in daily occurrences. From the standpoint of collective reactions to serial murder, belief in the supernatural is expressed in three ways: (1) that the killer's behavior is caused by otherworldly, especially demonic or satanic, forces, (2) that the killer possesses superhuman powers, and (3) that the case will be solved by miraculous means. Hence, events are thought to be determined by extraordinary forces that are inherently mysterious, unknowable, or explainable only by faith.

Concepts such as evil, monsters, and demonic possession are ancient and culturally universal, forming something of an archetypical imprint on the collective psyche. As one expert on serial murder pointed out, "In the past, explanations for mass and serial murders were often derived from demonology or the belief that events were controlled by external forces or spirits. The notion that life on earth was primarily controlled by forces of good and evil has its origins in the belief in the existences of gods and devils."[4] While science has illuminated many of the unknowns that give rise to superstitions and phantasmagoric images, belief in supernatural causation remains widespread. Indeed, responses to serial killers demonstrate how thin the veneer of rationality is and how quickly people revert to atavistic ways of thinking.

The extreme inhumane actions of the killer often reinforce and substantiate belief in the supernatural. Excessively cruel torture or brutal slayings, what experts call "overkill," completely divorce serial murder from normal behavior and even from routine homicide. The killer clearly gains something more from the process than just the end result, the death of the victim. Concentration on the process of murdering, the fact that it is a source of enjoyment, entertainment, and satisfaction for the killer, is taken as proof of malevolence.

Other aspects of the murders lend further credence to the belief that serial killers are immanently evil. Killers who dismember corpses, cannibalize, drink blood, or have sex with the dead evoke antediluvian images of vampires and werewolves. Even the popular lexicon used to describe the killers as fiends, ghouls, and monsters and the names given to describe them such as Richard Chase "The Vampire Killer," Albert Fish "The Cannibalistic Killer," or Richard Ramirez "The Night Stalker" recall ancient myths and fears. The fact that many murders are committed in a ritualistic fashion, repeated over and over, and that some serial killers have dabbled in the occult, been involved in covens or satanistic cults, or leave satanic symbols at the crime site provide the final proof of supernatural influence, if any more were needed.

Added to the pantheistic notions of demons, witches, and vampires is the good-evil duality embedded in religious teachings. If God is the agent of creation and can perform miracles, then a devil destroyer exists who is equally powerful. And if divine presence can take human-saintly form, the devil must have disciples who are evil incarnate. The undercurrent of the supernatural, and particularly religious beliefs, in responses to serial murder also explains some seemingly anomalous behavior after the killer is caught. A presumption exists that no person, no matter how evil, is beyond redemption. Killers and the public alike can hold this view. As a consequence, it is not uncommon for convicted killers to embrace religion and repent their past sins, and they can do so with an obsessive fervor that once characterized their murders. Also not uncommon are attempts to convert or save the convicted killer.

Supernatural causes imply supernatural remedies and spiritual cures. At times the public may appeal for divine intervention and deliverance from the crime spree. Or they may see the hand of Providence in the fortuitous circumstances that lead to a killer's arrest. As an example, Tracy Edwards, who narrowly escaped death at the hand of Jeffrey Dahmer and subsequently led police to the killer's apartment, saw himself as an agent of God's will. He thought his life had a larger meaning as a result; in his own words, "God sent me there to take care of the situation."[5]

When the murders are committed in a single place, the site itself can assume an evil aura, forever tainted by what took place there. As in the case of John Wayne Gacy whose house was leveled and now is a vacant lot, the building may be razed; its eradication is viewed as a necessary step in the healing process. In Milwaukee, families of the victims initially performed an exorcism outside Jeffrey Dahmer's apartment to rid the building of evil spirits. Eventually, a community group bought the entire apartment complex for the sole purpose of destroying it.

Perhaps the most common appeal for supernatural assistance during a serial murder investigation involves the introduction and use of psychics. In virtually every serial murder case that goes unsolved for any length of time, at least one psychic will become a key player in the drama. Some well-known psychics such as Gerard Croiset, Jr., who was involved in the Valenti case, are consulted regularly. More high-profile psychics such as Peter Hurkos even make something of a part-time career out of assisting serial murder investigations.

The use of psychics, like other supernatural elements in the public's response to serial murderers, has deep historical and cultural roots. Myths and literature are filled with stories of heroes who consult oracles, seers, and soothsayers for a vision of the future and insight into how to achieve specific goals. Interestingly, predictions are often given in obscure and cryptic form such that a number of interpretations could be supported. Common among these legends is an appeal to a person or persons whose clairvoyance enables them to foresee the future and aid men who are not so gifted.

Psychics used in serial murder cases follow this paradigm precisely. They are assumed to have special powers of clairvoyance that are innate or gained by an accident of fate. Furthermore, while the insight psychics provide into past events can be stunningly accurate, descriptions of the likely killer are often couched in terms of characteristics that could apply to many individuals. The net result is enough valid information for the police and public to marvel at the psychic's power and maintain their faith in the supernatural but not enough concrete information to solve the case. Unfortunately, psychic powers are no better than scientific means of profiling in finding the killer.

Transference

If the police cannot catch the killer with their normal investigative methods and the superhuman powers of psychics are also ineffective, in the public's mind there must be another reason why the killer can continue to escape. The only remaining explanation is the killer himself. It must be something the killer does or some ability he possesses that enables him to murder at will. It is this logic train, arising after all rational and supernatural methods of investigation have failed, that begins the process of transference. The defining feature of this stage of public reaction is reached, therefore, when the qualities of omniscience and omnipotence that were once reserved for those pursuing the murderer are gradually ascribed to the killer.

Transference as a collective response bears many similarities to processes that occur on a psychological level. One of the paradoxical outcomes of hostage crises occurs when the captives begin to identify with the aggressors. This process, named the "Stockholm Syndrome" after an incident during which authorities were startled to see hostages embrace their captors after a long siege was broken, culminates when the captives transfer complete trust to the hostage-takers. On a personal level, transference represents a mechanism for captives to live with the constant fear that engulfs them in the situation and is a means to elicit empathy from captors who have complete power to decide their fate. The emotional bond formed under these situations can be intense and outlive the actual event.

The analogous situation on a community level occurs when a serial killer holds the collective conscious captive. The community has no respite from the killings, and they intrude on all aspects of social life. Chronic fear is the end product. Like the individual, one strategy the community uses to deal with the fear is to identify with the aggressor. Trust once felt for authorities and belief in their capabilities to catch the offender are transferred to the killer who takes on an image of invincibility in the public imagination.

Transference is expressed in a variety of ways. The killer can be seen as exceptionally intelligent, carefully planning the next crime. The fact that many serial killers, in fact, do have above-average intelligence and do dwell on and perfect their modus operandi lends credence to this belief. The killer might also be described as having special physical abilities; the hands of a watchmaker and the ability to scale the sides of buildings were skills attributed to the Boston Strangler. And of course, supernatural powers once thought vested in psychics are ultimately attributed to the killer; they can anticipate every move the police make, or they can spellbind their victims, ensuring they will be trusting and compliant before death. The cumulative effect of transference results in the killer taking on larger than life dimensions in the public mind.

Much of the official and community response to the serial killer is driven by his seemingly uncanny ability to evade the police. One aspect of the evasion is the killer's ability to abscond with a victim, sometimes in broad daylight and in public, without causing a commotion or tipping anyone off to what lies ahead. More than any other factor, the ability of serial killers to get victims to cooperate in their own capture gives rise to the belief in their superhuman powers. And yet, although appeals to the supernatural and transference form the basis for a large portion of the public reaction to serial murder, the reality is much more mundane. Far from being omnipotent, serial murderers are uncommonly ordinary, and their ability to evade the police is more a function of their anonymity and external social forces than their supernatural powers.

In every serial murder case then, a dynamic tension develops between the rational and supernatural. Both investigators and the public vacillate between the two. When dealing with events rationally, the police will appeal to experts to help solve the crimes, while the public will seek the inner logic of common denominators that connect the murders or the victims. When rational explanations and solutions are abandoned in favor of the supernatural, the killer is seen as immanently evil, a slave to demonic forces, while resolution of the terror is sought by appealing to those with otherworldly power. If the murderer remains at large long enough, the belief in superhuman power is transferred from those seeking to catch the killer to the killer himself. The killer assumes an aura of omniscience in the public consciousness and is thought to possess superhuman powers that help him avoid capture.

SOCIAL IMPACT

Ordinary Obscurity

One of the abiding mysteries of serial murder investigations is why it is so difficult to apprehend the killer. Despite the efforts of legions of police, special task forces, the services of experts, and the intervention of individuals with supernatural powers, killers routinely escape detection. If the killer is ever captured, it is usually not quickly and not often as a result of official activities.

It is even more puzzling that in many cases, the killer is a suspect and frequently one of the earliest to be picked up and questioned by investigators. For any one of a myriad of reasons, different for each case, the killer is released by the police and inadvertently allowed to continue killing. Perhaps the most well-known example occurred when police found a naked Asian youth, handcuffed and bleeding, staggering in the street. Unsuspecting, they turned him over to a man they thought was his homosexual lover, Jeffrey Dahmer, who killed him within hours.

If this example were an isolated incident, it could be attributed to the homophobia of the Milwaukee Police. But it is not; there are countless other examples. John Norman Collins was one of the first suspects questioned after a coed was found murdered, but he was ignored when his uncle, a State Police officer, vouched for him. Ironically, after six more murders, the same uncle would suspect correctly that not only had his nephew committed the murders, but at least one had also been committed in the basement of his house. Albert DeSalvo escaped the Boston dragnet because his sex offenses did not appear on his arrest record. A mistaken lab test deflected suspicion from Andrei Chitalinko, although he had been seen in the company of a murder victim, been identified from a composite drawing, and when searched was found with the murder weapons. As these few examples illustrate, the inability to recognize the killer as such is one of the endemic problems of a serial murder investigation.

A number of reasons may account for these fatal oversights, one of which is what experts call "linkage blindness"—that is, the inability to see that crimes are related and the tendency to treat them as separate unconnected incidents due to the inability or unwillingness of investigative agencies to share information and coordinate their activities.

The problem is exacerbated by our federalist form of government. There are more than 25,000 law enforcement jurisdictions within the United States, and frequently, as in the case of state, county, and city police, they may have overlapping authority. Many different police departments can be involved in an investigation. In the Richard Valenti case, for instance, the Folly Beach and James Island Police, the Charleston County Sheriff's Department, the State Police, and U.S. Navy officials were all involved at some point.

In the best of cases, when the various agencies are cooperating, there can be enormous difficulties in coordination. The expertise levels of the groups can differ widely; the accumulation, storage, and dissemination of information and leads may not be standardized; and there may be no formal channels of communication. Consequently, even when the police have the same objective and want to work together, there may be insurmountable barriers to overcome.

In the worst cases, there is little willingness to cooperate. Police departments come under enormous pressure to solve the crimes, and their resolution can be a major coup for the successful organization. Professional jealousy and competition can and often do undermine the best intentions.

Even if linkage blindness did not exist and only one police department investigated the crime, it is still likely that the police would fail to recognize a serial killer when confronting one. One reason is the level of training and expertise resident in each police department. The case may be a once in a lifetime experience and so vastly outside normal practice that the police cannot separate the important from the incidental. Therefore, the simple rarity of serial murder may prevent it from being solved.

Not only do police have little opportunity to investigate serial murders, but their method of operation and function in the judicial system almost preclude their ability to identify a serial murderer when presented with one. Simply put, police do not often solve crimes. Usually, the perpetrator is caught in the act or, in the case of homicide, is someone known to the victim and easy to locate. Police activities are directed primarily toward amassing evidence that will convict an offender who is already in custody. An investigation is a process of building a case, not solving one, and if an offender can escape the crime scene and is unknown to the victim, the odds of apprehension are low.

Even when police are proactively trying to find a criminal, the barriers to an arrest are daunting. The problem is not a paucity of good leads. Quite the contrary, there are too many, and every bit of investigative work just adds to the total. In the typical serial murder investigation, the police are inundated with leads, tips, evidence, and good suspects. The logistical difficulty in managing so much information can create insuperable problems. For example, in the Yorkshire Ripper investigation "the paper records at one point weighed 24 tons, requiring a move within the building in which they were housed because of concerns over the building's structural integrity."[6]

The police strategy used to deal with this ocean of information and sea of suspects is both natural and effective. They proceed by a process of exclusion rather than inclusion. As a consequence, the police attempt to find reasons to eliminate a person as a suspect rather than to continue to keep that person under suspicion. The goal is to whittle down the list of suspects, and to this end reasons are found to rule them out, not in. So in the end, one contrary piece of evidence can invalidate and supersede all indications of guilt.

Even when the killer comes face-to-face with authorities, sometimes with bodies in tow, the killer is allowed to escape. Police, like all humans, tend to explain events in terms of experiences that they encounter daily. When ruling out suspects, then, they are most apt to find a normal, everyday reason for suspicious behavior, and hence they ignore what may seem obvious in retrospect. It was more natural to think Jeffrey Dahmer was a homosexual having a domestic quarrel with his lover than it was to suspect him of being a serial killer and sometime cannibal.

The killer, in turn, does nothing to make investigators wary or suspicious. Unencumbered by the guilt and remorse most murderers feel, they fall back on a disarmingly genial manner and easily talk their way out of trouble. Hidden by a false mask of sanity, then, their behavior seems to be too normal to be that of a person capable of atrocities.

Finding a serial killer is, on balance, then an extraordinarily difficult endeavor. The obstacles to apprehension are encountered at every turn—in the structure of the political system, in the competition between police forces, in the accumulation and management of mountains of investigative data, in the psychology of the investigators, and in the behavior of the killers. It is not surprising that a man like John Wayne Gacy can stay in place and kill for years. With all the advantages on their side, the truly remarkable fact is not that killers evade arrest so easily but that they are ever apprehended at all.

Media Circus

Any channel of information that makes the public aware of the murders or sustains interest in them will increase public response. At times, the public's insatiable desire for news, the media's commercial interests in providing it, and the killer's need to publicize his invincibility can create a synergistic situation that spirals out of control. Even in less extreme cases, the media can play an enabling and perpetuating role in community reaction.

Of course, the public is not an innocent bystander in the process. Just the opposite: people have a limitless desire, even need, for information, and the more outrageous and abhorrent the crimes, the greater the public fascination. Something tantamount to a self-fueling engine of public opinion is created. Fear, uncertainty, and morbid curiosity lead to a demand for more news, delivery of which generates a higher level of anxiety and interest. The intensity of public feeling is ratcheted ever upward.

Competition between news agencies only exacerbates the potentiating impact of the media. Simply having multiple sources provide the same information increases the amount of exposure given the crimes, and therefore increases the likelihood that a person will learn about or be reminded of the murders. In addition, professional and financial rewards accrue to the reporters and services that can provide fresh and ever more detailed information. Not surprisingly, the more lurid the details provided, the greater the public interest and acclaim for investigative reporting.

Everyone it seems who is remotely involved with the murders becomes a celebrity, and reporters are no less immune to publicity's siren-song than others. Anne Schwartz, the *Milwaukee Journal* reporter who broke the Dahmer story, provides a vivid description of what it was like to be a reporter covering the case.

As the news spread, the paper received calls from around the country. We found our stories all over the world, and they ran in the *Los Angeles Times*, the *New York Times*, and the *International Herald Tribune*. We saw our bylines in French, Spanish and German. Reporters from out-of-town papers called the newsroom and spoke to whoever picked up the phone, as if he or she were an expert on the case. If you worked for the *Journal* you must know something about Jeffrey Dahmer.

Who wants to do "Larry King"? a secretary yelled out. Reporters lunged for their phones. We got calls from *People* magazine, a producer from "Geraldo," a Canadian radio talk show, and a publishing company looking for someone to write a book in a month.

We were celebrities. We were dizzy with it.[7]

Having access to information about the case, or for that matter proximity to information, became a saleable commodity. Reporters became the story, and the media became the news.

Just the process of reporting the news can shape and change it. Witnesses to the Dahmer tragedy continually modified and embellished their stories under the glare of media attention. Tracy Edwards, whose escape led directly to Dahmer's arrest, became an instant celebrity and the darling of the talk show circuit. On the night of Dahmer's capture, Edwards was a humble near-victim who was thankful for police support. On the talk shows he became a self-styled Houdini who brought Dahmer to justice. Predictably, he eventually sued the police for their alleged lack of assistance on the fateful night.

The media have even been implicated in a more insidious form of influence, encouraging others to commit murder. Evidence for this presumed effect are the frequent occurrence of copy-cat murders and the hysteria surrounding product-tampering cases. Indeed, during the Boston panic, police were convinced that several murders were disguised to appear as if they had been committed by the Strangler, while in Milwaukee, one man was heard to say he was "going to do a Dahmer thing" just before he bit off his lover's lip during a violent argument.

The killer, equally, can be caught up in the media vortex and influenced by it. But unlike reporters and witnesses who are passive observers of events, the killer can determine them. In fact, the psychology of some serial killers is such that media attention is inextricably bound up with their pathology. For them media attention becomes a means through which they can extract greater psychic gratification from the murders. News stories are not only watched carefully, savored, and even kept as souvenirs, but in some cases the press is manipulated, becoming at times almost a public relations agent for the murderer.

The apotheosis of media involvement comes when the media become directly involved with the killer. The killer leaves notes at the scene and eventually begins to communicate directly with prominent media figures. Editorial writers address their columns to the killer, speculate on his motives, and write impassioned pleas for the killer to surrender to them personally. A self-serving reciprocity is established between the killer's need for attention and the media's need for a story. In the interest of both the killer and the press, public emotions are whipped into a frenzy.

In summary then, the media have a multidimensional impact on a serial murder case. Media reports make the population aware of the murders and help maintain their preoccupation with the killings. Those involved with the case and even those who report it become instant celebrities in constant demand by a news-hungry public. Notoriety, in turn, influences the actions and interpretations of those involved in the case so that in the end media attention can shape and potentially make news. For a particular type of serial killer, news reports can be a source of extended gratification and can help propel the murderer to further killings. For those killers who have a special perspicacity into the workings and impact of the media, it can be a means to dominate and control the popular imagination.

Community Dissolution

Fear experienced on a personal level is manifest in individual actions. Typically, people act in accordance with their expectations, even if the expectations do not accurately reflect reality. When presented with a real or perceived threat, personal behavior is modified accordingly. Taken on a collective basis, changes in countless numbers of social contacts and interactions, no matter how brief or seemingly inconsequential, have enormous impact on social cohesion and grave consequences for community solidarity.

This is never more evident than when a murderer lives within a community and emerges periodically to destroy others. Repeated killings underscore the continuing threat, the fact that the killer is still present and dangerous. At the same time, the killer's behavior, normal by most standards, deflects attention. The killer uses the very elements that promote social cohesion to maintain anonymity and continue killing. As one observer in Milwaukee stated, "If someone as nondescript as Dahmer could be so dangerous, what about the others around us? What do we really know about other people?"[8] Since the killer is able to hide among the body populace, blending with the crowd, it follows that anyone could be the killer or, equivalently, everyone is suspect.

Not only does the murderer force everyone to be vigilant when dealing with others, but also a level of suspicion is created that destroys social bonds. Neighbor is turned against neighbor, family members begin to suspect one another, and one may, as I did on Folly Beach, even doubt oneself. Suspicion, in turn, breeds isolation. All forms of social contact are avoided, including those with neighbors, friends, and family. People restrict their movements, go out less often, and are unwilling to venture into areas that are unfamiliar or places where strangers may be encountered. In the end, social solidarity is as much a causality of the serial killer as the unfortunate victims.

With the breakdown in social cohesion comes a breakdown in social control and, most importantly, in the informal mechanisms of crime prevention, which, as one criminologist points out, are "probably more effective in preventing crime than formal methods of social control such as the police."[9] Fear of crime restricts contact and social interaction, one of the primary deterrents of crime. One of the deleterious aspects of fear of crime is that it feeds on itself. In some respects, the serial murderer inadvertently helps himself by engendering mass fear in the populace.

Ultimately, the feeling of suspicion generalizes to social institutions. Faith in public officials and law enforcement agencies diminishes rapidly and finally evaporates entirely. The outcry is particularly pronounced after the killer is captured, often by chance alone, and it is learned that numerous opportunities were missed to stop the killings earlier.

Fear of the serial killer also magnifies the divisions that exist within the community. Since the killer is viewed as an outsider and a stranger, all those who are different are categorized as a threat. Intolerance, bigotry, and scapegoating increase, as does the use of racial and ethnic stereotypes. A common byproduct of a serial murderer at large is an upswing in anti-Semitism, racial conflict, and gay bashing.

Identifying the offender with another social group contains the threat. It allows people to distance themselves from personal risk by simply avoiding contact with the outsiders. In so doing, a sense of psychological comfort is produced that enables people to continue to work and function in the regions in which they feel secure. Not coincidentally, it enables them to react more strongly, express outrage more openly, and demand retribution more vehemently than would be possible if the killer were viewed as a member of their own social group.

A reciprocal process can occur among minority groups. They may react defensively to the anger directed at them from the wider community. More often, the killer selects victims from their ranks. This fact at once gives foundation to the majority belief that the killer is a member of the group. The minority group is doubly maligned, first to be the focal point of community rage while at the same time being the most at risk. In response, the minority group may question how willing and able the community is to protect them. The police and city officials, as representatives of the majority population, are most apt to take the brunt of minority reaction.

The net result of the cycle of mutual distrust is a reinforcement of traditional boundaries and stereotypes. Old wounds are opened, and long-simmering disputes and affronts come to the surface. The murders polarize the community along social, ethnic, and lifestyle lines and exacerbate extant political tensions. The resultant social damage long outlives the killer's murderous career.

On a community level, the killer among us isolates individuals and causes them to question those in authority. These symptoms of community dissolution take on a more active, virulent form when emotional release is directed at minority segments of the society. The killer may be seen as being part of a particular social group, the group may be blamed for allowing the killer to go undetected, or they may be just a convenient scapegoat for the fear and guilt that are more generally felt. For any of a number of reasons then, specific social groups may become the outlet for the tension of the general population.

The social consequences of a killer at large within the community can be seen then as a three-part process. First, the causative factor, chronic fear, originates in the constant threat posed by the killer and the failure of the investigation to remove the threat, the reasons for which are found in the composition of human consciousness and collective behavior. Second, operating according to their own economic demands, the media constantly remind the public of the threat, intensify popular sentiments, and may inadvertently add to the gratification the killer receives from the crimes. Third, the end result is a breakdown in collective solidarity and social order due to defensive changes in patterns of behavior by numberless individuals, disintegration of social structure, and self-defeating conflict along political, ethnic, economic, and lifestyle lines.

CASES

In the chapters that follow, each type of reaction and form of social impact is illustrated with the case history of one serial murder. While every case combines elements of all of the strategies and processes, in each one particular expression of public response dominates. Which method of adaptation or social consequence comes to the foreground is often determined by the individual character of the city in which the killings take place, its history, economic base, ethnic composition, and social structure.

The image of Boston, Massachusetts, and the outlook of its residents is influenced by the number and prominence of the universities and institutions of higher learning in the metropolitan area. Thus, when single women, old and young, were strangled at the rate of almost one per month over an eighteen-month period during 1962–1964, it was natural that public officials and citizens alike would strive to find a logical way to connect the homicides. The investigation similarly was typified by the use of scientific methods and tools to solve the crimes and understand the criminal. This search, official and unofficial, for a rational explanation of events is documented in Chapter 3.

For two years in the late 1960s, John Norman Collins almost singlehandedly created the murder rate in Washtenaw County, Michigan. But, as shown in Chapter 4, his impact on the twin university cities of Ann Arbor and Ypsilanti was due not just to the area's unfamiliarity with homicide but also to the disappearance of the victims despite heroic measures instituted for their protection. The climax of the mystery was reached when the last victim, in front of witnesses, appeared to go knowingly and willingly to her death. What began as a series of ever more baffling disappearances ended as a struggle between the killer's challenging disposal of corpses and the extrasensory powers of a psychic.

The complex interplay between the killer, the public, and the press is described in Chapter 5. David Berkowitz, the Son of Sam, not only had the pathological need to manipulate the press and the intelligence to do so, but also launched his attacks within the most intense media environment in the country. The symbiotic contribution of the media to the development of his reputation and persona can be grasped easily by imagining how differently he would be remembered had he killed in Detroit or Denver.

Chapter 6 details the systematic predation of young children that took place in Atlanta, Georgia from 1979 to 1981. Passions were inflamed by the murders and the violation of so many cherished values and beliefs they represented. The city "too busy to hate" with a history of leadership in the civil rights movement became a cauldron of mistrust, conspiracy theories, and scapegoating. Two decades of progress in race relations were nearly destroyed and ultimately may only have been preserved when the killer, Wayne Williams, was found to belong to the same race as the dead boys.

Chapter 7 relates the disastrous consequences that followed the discovery of a killer who could have been but was not stopped. Despite increasingly overt and outrageous behavior, no one who knew Jeffrey Dahmer could conceive that such a passive and ordinary man was butchering young men at an escalating rate. When he was finally captured, a self-righteous and politically correct community wreaked fearful vengeance on anyone who had come in contact with him, the police being only the first and most obvious target.

The last case considered, in Chapter 8, is that of arguably the most famous of all serial murderers, Jack the Ripper. All the elements of reaction and impact evident in the preceding case studies were present in nineteenth-century England. Thus, the experience of London a century ago demonstrates that patterns of response are neither modern nor exclusively American but rather originate in human consciousness and the organization of social life.

The Common Denominator

ALBERT HENRY DESALVO: THE BOSTON STRANGLER
Boston, Massachusetts (1962–1964)

"We have to assume that one man might have committed three of the murders because of their similarity. On the other hand, we have not been able to find a single common denominator among the victims."
—Lt. John Donovan, Boston Police Department
Boston Globe, August 26, 1962

After ten hours of research in the clipping archives of the *Boston Herald*, I emerged covered with newsprint and the accumulated dust of the past thirty years. Not nearly finished, I needed to make arrangements to come in again the following day. So I walked down the hall to speak with my benefactor, *Herald* Librarian John Cronin. When I entered the room, John looked up and said, "Well, did you solve the case yet? Did DeSalvo do it?"

This lighthearted poke at my efforts quite succinctly sums up everything I had learned or was to learn about the Boston Strangler case. To this day, more than three decades after the killings stopped, and despite a detailed confession, there is no unanimity of opinion that Albert DeSalvo was in fact the Boston Strangler. But why should this be so?

More than anything else it is a pattern that defines serial murder—a set of common characteristics of the victim or means of death that leads to the inference that a single individual or, less frequently, a small team are committing murder over an extended period of time. Thus, long brown hair parted in the middle connected Ted Bundy's victims, while a singular style of attack led Carlton Gary to be dubbed the "Stocking Strangler." These "common denominators" determine which murders are related and which should not be included in the string. They indicate when the series began and when it ended.

The pattern is crucial for police work because it provides insight into the character and motivation of the killer. From these conclusions, a fairly detailed profile of the likely killer can be deduced, including age, race, employment history, living situation, and psychological makeup. Strategies for investigation and interrogation can also be derived from the profile and hence, ultimately, the pattern. Pattern recognition is so integral to serial murder investigations that failure to detect the pattern early on and to relate seemingly isolated killings, so-called linkage blindness, is considered one of the most serious barriers to effective police work.

The pattern or recognition of common denominators is just as crucial to understanding how the public reacts to serial murder and especially why it provokes such a disproportionate amount of fear and panic relative to the quite small risk that any individual will fall victim to the killer. Pattern recognition is fundamental to human psychology. We can understand something and make sense of it when it fits into the framework of our experience. We have come to depend on a pattern of causes and effects in the most profound sense.

More than anything else, the serial killer challenges our expectations about human motivation. Even murder is somehow understandable if it is an impulsive act committed in the heat of passion or is done for clear economic gain. What is not fathomable is how a person can systematically stalk other human beings and destroy them, sometimes in the most grotesque and horrible manner, for no obvious or apparent reason, or certainly for no reason most of us share or can understand. Killing is an anathema to social order, and to kill in the same fashion repeatedly, often with careful planning, compounds the affront to our beliefs.

A pattern is also comforting in a way. At least we know who is vulnerable to the killer, and hence the risk is confined to a small portion of the populace. The killer's behavior becomes in its own way predictable, and it is possible to create a new framework to explain his actions, no matter how abnormal the rationale might be. The pattern defines the potential targets and limits of risk, and thereby makes the fear more manageable.

The pattern becomes in many respects a rational explanation of the crimes. People hold the implicit view that there is a hidden rationality to the seemingly irrational acts, which finds expression as the common denominators of the crimes and victims. These few signature characteristics that all the murders or victims share provide an immanent "why" for the killings. They offer a rationale whereby the murders can be understood by the man in the street. Failure to discern a clear pattern in the killings therefore tends to damage the collective psyche. When events occur that do not fit our framework of understanding, we are filled with unease at the most basic level, as if the very foundations of existence were being challenged. The psychic discomfort can only be removed by reestablishing the pattern and making things fit again. Losing the pattern can be so threatening that at times we will go to great lengths to mold events to fit our framework or if necessary to modify it to encompass all the facts.

The Boston Strangler case is the story of one city's attempt to find a rational explanation for the series of killings that were committed between June 1962 and January 1964. It is characterized initially by the attempts of those involved to find the pattern in the crimes, their common denominators. Every time the pattern was thought to be uncovered, however, a new killing would seemingly violate one or more of the signature traits and threaten the validity of the pattern. This would then set off sometimes frantic attempts to reestablish the pattern and again make the facts and the victims connect in some logical manner.

It is also a story colored by the character of the city in which it occurred. Bostonians, living in the most learned of all American cities, seemed to have a special need to explain the killings in a rational, logical, and even scientific manner. There was almost a naive faith in the power of reason to solve the crimes. As a result, experts were called in from every conceivably relevant discipline. As one of the consultants, Dr. Kenefick, the assistant director of the Boston University Law and Medicine Research Institute, said at the time, "I guess you'd call it police work on a Ph.D. level."[1]

Faith in the power of science to rid society of the scourge of serial murder never flagged, even after Albert DeSalvo confessed. Key players sought to make the experience redemptory by claiming it had promoted a larger understanding of human deviance. They argued that DeSalvo represented a rare opportunity for research and that, like a prize laboratory specimen, he should be sent to a state hospital rather than prison so he could be studied by qualified scientists. The befuddled killer, unable to comprehend his own motives, expressed the same desire.

THE BOSTON STRANGLINGS

The killings began on June 14, 1962. Within ten weeks, by the end of August, six women had been found murdered, half the entire count that would eventually be attributed to the Boston Strangler. Perhaps even more frightening than simply the number of murders was the near-drumbeat regularity with which the bodies were discovered. The first four bodies were found over a twenty-seven-day period from June 14 to July 11. There followed a six-week respite. Then in quick succession two more victims were found, one on August 21 and the second on August 30.

The second wave of killings began three months after the first in December 1962 and continued for the next year. The spacing of the strangulations showed less of the pent-up fury that was typified by the first six weeks, however. Two women were found dead in December 1962, another was discovered in September 1963, then one in November, and the last victim on January 4, 1964. The second string of killings was differentiated from the first not only by time but also by the fact that the first six to die were elderly, whereas the next five were much younger. This circumstance goes to the heart of why it was so difficult to find a unifying pattern as well as the belief that there was no single strangler.

Table 3.1 was printed in the *Boston Traveler* on January 6, 1964 just after the murder of Mary Sullivan, the strangler's last victim. The table presents the scorecard of the murders as they were known to the public at the time. Updated after each successive strangling, the table became a morbid box score of the strangler's handiwork. The running tally was also instrumental in maintaining the public's preoccupation with the crimes and periodically fueled the search for common characteristics among the dead.

The list in the table is not identical to the one ultimately attributed to the Boston Strangler. For example, when he confessed, Albert DeSalvo did not include Margaret Davis among his victims. Conversely, he did confess to killing Mary Mullin, 85 years old, on June 28, 1962, Mary Brown, 69 years old, on March 9, 1963, and Beverly Samans, 23 years old, on August 6, 1963. Which list is correct therefore depends on whether or not one believes that Albert DeSalvo was indeed the Boston Strangler. For our purpose, we are interested in how the public reacted to the crimes, and in this regard Table 3.1 provides the best summary of what the community believed were the murders while they were taking place. It was quite simply the raw data from which they tried to discern the pattern.

The first woman to die was Anna Slesers, a 55-year-old seamstress, and her death was in many ways typical of the others. The murder took place in the victim's apartment at 77 Gainesborough Street in the Back Bay section of the city. A long-time divorcee, she lived there alone and, in fact, had moved into the apartment only two weeks earlier on June 1. Her new apartment was a short walk from Symphony Hall and thus afforded her a ready outlet for her one abiding love—classical music.

Anna Slesers' body was discovered by her 25-year-old son, Juris. He had come to take his mother to a church party at 7:00 P.M. When she did not answer his knock he waited on the front steps and, finally becoming concerned, broke into the apartment at 7:45 P.M. He found her lying on her back, her blue bathrobe open so that from the shoulders down she was completely naked. Beyond simple nudity, the corpse seemed to have been arranged so as to display the obscenity. Her legs were spread wide apart and one leg was bent at the knee to increase genital exposure. A later autopsy revealed that she had sustained head injuries either in an attack or subsequent fall and had died by strangulation.

Further inspection of the victim and the apartment revealed the three trademarks that would become the signature of the strangler. First, the victim had been strangled by her own bathrobe belt, which was found knotted tightly around her neck. More importantly, the belt had been tied in an exaggerated bow under her chin as if to decorate the corpse. Second, the motive was clearly sexual. Although there was no evidence of rape, the body had definitely been sexually assaulted. Moreover, there was no indication that anything of value had been taken, eliminating robbery as a motive. Finally, the apartment and victim's personal effects had been subjected to a calm, systematic, and thorough search. Again, since robbery did not appear to be the reason, the killer seemed to be prying into the victim's life. This crime profile would become the calling card of the Boston Strangler: strangulation with characteristic bow decoration, rape or sexual assault, and the postmortem ritual search.

Of course, other similarities between Anna Slesers and the women who followed would be noted; the most obvious common threads were that she lived alone, was older, and loved music. These commonalities became the focal points in the effort to find the common denominators that would tie the dead together and provide a rational explanation for the crimes.

CITY IN PANIC

By Labor Day 1962 six elderly women had been killed in the Greater Boston area in a short ten-week period. The female residents of the city, especially those living alone, were held hostage by their own fear and dread. They lived under siege, blockaded behind locked doors and bolted windows, prisoners of the terror they could not control. One woman quite literally died of fright when she mistook an encyclopedia salesman for the strangler.

With the benefit of thirty years' perspective, it is difficult for us to fully appreciate just how paralyzing the shared sense of impending doom was. Nonetheless, a flavor of the prevailing mood is given in a September 2, 1962 newspaper article. Printed under the headline "A Frightened Woman Calls," it read:

A Back Bay woman called the Sunday Advertiser yesterday. In a voice taut with strain, she spoke for all her elderly "sisters"—the forgotten women of the city who live in loneliness and now in terror.

"No one knows fear as we know it. Nobody knows what a woman alone feels.

Everyday is an eternity. I don't go to bed until I'm exhausted and even then I can't sleep. I don't dare close my eyes. Every noise in the night has me in a panic.

I'm so nervous, I have come home from work and cried. I can't eat. I'm losing weight. I am close to a breakdown.

That these good women should come to such a death and such abuse . . . is a terrible pity. It's heartbreaking. And it's petrifying.

I can't excuse this killer, insane or not. I hate him for what he has done, and what he is doing to the rest of us.

I live with the frightening question, who will be next?"[2]

By January 1964, the number of known killings had climbed to eleven, but now young as well as older women were victims. As a result, the fear

Table 3.1
The Stranglings

Date	Victim	Status	Scene	Weapon	Notes
June 14, '62; 5:30 p.m.	Mrs. Anna E. Slesers of 77 Gainesborough St., Back Bay Age - 55	Seamstress and divorcee, living alone	Kitchen floor of 3rd floor apartment	Cord from own housecoat	No forced entry Apartment ransacked
June 30, '62; 5:30 p.m.	Mrs. Nina G. Nichols of 1940 Commonwealth Ave., Brighton Age - 68	Semi-retired physiotherapist, living alone	Bedroom of 4th floor apartment	Her own nylon stocking	No forced entry Apartment ransacked
June 30, '62; but not found until July 2	Miss Helen E. Blake of 73 Newhall St., Lynn Age - 65	Registered nurse, living alone	Bedroom of 2nd floor apartment	Her bra and nylon stocking	No forced entry Apartment ransacked
July 11, '62	Mrs. Margaret Davis of 139 Blue Hill Ave., Age - 60	Widow, living alone	South End hotel room	Bare hands	No forced entry
Aug. 19 '62; but not found until Aug. 21	Mrs. Ida Irga of 7 Grove St., Beacon Hill Age - 75	Widow, living alone	Chair in 5th floor apartment	Pillow case	No forced entry

Date	Victim	Status	Location Found	Ligature	Entry
Aug. 20 '62 (approx.), but not found until Aug. 30	Miss Jane Sullivan of 435 Columbia Rd., Dorchester Age - 67	Practical nurse, living alone	Bathtub, 1st floor apartment	Unknown	No forced entry Apartment ransacked
Dec. 5, '62	Miss Sophie Clark of 315 Huntington Ave., Age - 21	Student, living with two co-students	Apartment living room	Stocking and petticoat	No forced entry
Dec. 31, '62	Miss Patricia Bissette, of 515 Park Ave. Age - 24	Secretary, living alone	Apartment bedroom	Stockings and blouse	No forced entry
Sept. 8, '63	Mrs. Evelyn Corbin, of 224 Lafayette St., Salem Age - 50	Divorcee, living alone	Bedroom of First floor apartment	Two stockings	No forced entry
Nov. 23, '63	Miss Jo Ann M. Graff of 54 Essex St., Lawrence Age - 22	Single, Pattern designer, living alone	Apartment bedroom	Two stockings; leotard	No forced entry
Jan. 4, '64	Miss Mary E. Sullivan of 44A Charles St., Boston Age - 19	Single, Finance firm worker, living with two girls	Apartment bedroom	Two nylon scarves, one stocking	No forced entry

was undiminished and more widespread. In an article entitled "Women Write of Dread" published in the *Boston Record* on January 13, 1964,[3] many of the same symptoms of fear voiced by the anonymous caller fifteen months earlier were still evident; excerpts from the letters read: "I live alone and am terrified." "I couldn't go to sleep last night after hearing the news." "I know I won't sleep until he is caught," and from as far away as Providence, Rhode Island, "This letter is written by a frightened mother." One letter expressed a final benediction on all those involved: "God have mercy and God help us soon."

Throughout the strangler's reign, warnings were issued to the community, which probably protected no one but certainly added to the ambient terror. Police Commissioner McNamara warned all Boston residents, especially older women, to keep their doors locked, call the special police number if they suspected anyone, and not admit any gas, electric, or telephone employees until first checking with their supervisor.

Needless to say, the effect on occupations that required door-to-door contact was immediate. The Water Department noted that 50 percent of all calls had to await verification, and even those with photobadges were denied entry. Residents frequently shouted through the door to have estimated bills sent in the mail. Police had difficulty pursuing the investigation because it was rumored that the strangler dressed as a policeman. The strangler singlehandedly ended the Fuller Brush trade in Boston and with it the livelihoods of forty salesmen.

But while one section of the economy suffered, others experienced a windfall. When an article appeared noting that locks in the victims apartments were defective or easy to pick, sales of new locks skyrocketed, increasing by as much as 400 percent. Some merchants were not above taking advantage of the situation, as pointed out in the *Boston Traveler*, "Hundreds of women are heeding a sign in the windows of one Cambridge shop. It reads, 'Keep the Strangler out'."[4] Locksmiths even backed a bill to make it more difficult for consumers to obtain tools that could be used to break locks. Of course, the tools could also be used to install locks, but this mercantile motive was lost in the altruism of the moment.

Official warnings were accompanied by admonitions from the press. Two reporters for the *Boston Record American*, Loretta McLaughlin and Jean Cole, who became self-styled advocates for the female population of the city, offered suggestions for self-defense in an article entitled "Girl Reporters Cite Do's & Don'ts to Foil Strangler." They noted that it had become a necessity to be physically fit to ward off the strangler's attacks and that women should become diet and exercise conscious. As for weapons, the reporters suggested hat pins, brass knuckles, whistles, pepper, and chamberpots. Finally, as if addressing a troop of girl scouts, they added this summation: "Be alert . . . be suspicious, be cautious and be prepared. Plan your protection as well as the strangler plans his crimes."[5]

By this time, of course, the female population needed little counseling self-defense. Adoptions of dogs at animal shelters increased by 500 percent with many shelters being cleaned out of dogs by noon each day. Big dogs were the first to go. Women also began to arm themselves. Typically, the Boston Police would issue ten permits per year for women to own guns; during the strangler terror, permits were issued at the rate of twenty-five per month.

The best self-defense in the end was for women to become less vulnerable by modifying their behavior. Waitresses traveled in groups. Babysitters were reluctant to take jobs in isolated areas and demanded to be escorted home when they did. In the working-class sections of Dorchester, South Boston, Charlestown, and the South End where stoop sitting was taken as an inalienable right, the streets were empty. Even as venerable an institution as Boston politics was not immune. Canvassing South Boston door-to-door in the best Irish ward tradition, candidate Billy Bulger recalled: "One elderly woman said through her closed door, 'I'm going to vote for you Billy, but I'm not going to open the door'."[6]

Rumors about how the killer gained entry to the victims' homes were rampant. He was variously said to dress as a policeman, pose as a doctor, masquerade as a nun. Everyone seemed to have his own theory on who the strangler was and how best to catch him. He was a medical student, an OSS ranger commando, a house detective, or dressed as a woman. One man in offering his ideas for solving the crimes noted that he was "something of a rocking-chair criminologist";[7] he was not alone. People suggested using ESP, contacting Scotland Yard, checking absenteeism records, and looking at old murders as ways to solve the crime.

The police meanwhile gave the public an opportunity to aid the investigation and established a lead hotline. Once published, the number became a lightning rod for pent-up suspicion and in some cases even revenge. Strangers were identified by the dozens, neighbors turned in other neighbors, and wives reported wayward husbands to keep them at home. No one could or would be trusted. The cohesive bonds of public trust weakened, and the city began to disintegrate from an organic body into a atomized state of isolated individuals.

The mistrust went deeper until individuals began to question themselves. A thirty-four-year-old janitor, army veteran, and father of two confessed to the crimes after suffering blackouts and noting that whenever he came to there was another strangling. Drunks also turned themselves in believing they killed while experiencing alcohol-induced amnesia. Gerold Frank in his book *The Boston Strangler* notes a similar effect on the special police investigative team after they received their first training session with the FBI.

The fifty detectives emerged from the lecture room shaken, but with one certainty: never trust appearances, never overlook the kindly old man living next door; anyone,

anyone—including yourself—could be the one. The evil lay in every man. God help him in whom it got out of control. One detective, father of a teenage daughter and himself a Catholic, walked from the lecture thinking wildly, *we are all suspect; the day the Pope left Rome, he became a suspect.*[8]

Naturally, a city in fear and panic brought out the seamier side of some of its residents. Women received threatening phone calls from heavy breathers telling them they would be next. A letter received by the *Boston Record* read: "I'm not making any visits to lonely women at present,"[9] and was signed "The Strangler." The limit of this cruel and sadistic behavior was reached when packages were mailed to some women containing dolls that looked as if they had been strangled.

COMMON DENOMINATOR—THE UNOFFICIAL SEARCH

A partial explanation for the near-hysterical reaction of Boston residents to the killings is accessible if we project ourselves into that time and try to appreciate the unfamiliarity of the general public with violence. The Boston Strangler case preceded the urban riots that tore cities apart in the middle 1960s. It antedated the Vietnam War and the nightly diet of combat footage shown on the evening news. Drugs and their associated violence were not yet serious public concerns. Americans thirty years ago, quite simply, were used to a greater level of personal safety. Our gradual acceptance of escalating violence is one aspect of the innocence we have lost since then.

Even within the United States at that time, the Northeast generally and Boston specifically had relatively low crime rates. For example, in 1961, the year before the first murder, the total number of murders in the Boston Standard Metropolitan Statistical Area (SMSA), comprising four counties and two other major urban centers (Lowell and Lawrence), was 52. The murder rate was 1.7 per 100,000 residents, nearly ten times lower than Atlanta's 10.8 rate for that year.

In the city of Boston itself, the Department of Health recorded twenty-four homicides in 1961, of which thirteen were women. With this statistic to set the context, we can see why the strangler had such an exaggerated impact. Seven women were killed by the strangler in 1962. Thus, one man accounted for 30 percent of all the murders that had occurred in the previous year and more than half of all those that had been committed against women. The fact that all of these murders took place in the last half of 1962 only exacerbated the situation, making 30 percent appear like 60 and seemingly doubling the female homicide incidence.

Without question then, the level of violence introduced by the strangler was unexpected and unusual, but was it enough to explain the panic reaction of the citizenry? Probably not, since after all the actual risk for any single individual was still quite small. Also contributing was the complete irrationality of the acts, an insanity that virtually screamed out for an explanation. The unbelievable nature of the crimes was only fueled by their sexual nature and the fact that the first victims were elderly and not generally viewed as attractive targets.

The first six victims, who were killed in the summer of 1962, were older, having an average age of 65. Almost immediately, the public noticed other similarities. They all lived alone, were fastidious, methodical, neat housekeepers, had been widowed or divorced, wore glasses, and rode the MTA. There was even a striking physical similarity among several of the women. The likeness was so pronounced, in fact, that the son of one victim, 77-year-old Ida Irga, on seeing the photograph of another, 68-year-old Jane Sullivan, commented: "When I saw Miss Sullivan's picture, I thought it was my mother."[10] So it seemed the pattern had been set.

As police labored to find the killer and withheld facts to further the investigation, the news media stepped in to satisfy the public's craving for information. In particular, if the authorities could not find the common denominator that linked the victims, maybe reporters could. What emerged was a young female reporting team, Loretta McLaughlin and Jean Cole, known ever after as the "Girl Reporters," who developed their own theories on the common denominator linking the victims and used their paper, the *Boston Record American*, to promulgate their views.

The Girl Reporters became crusaders for the female population of Boston, convinced they could lift the siege that held them prisoner. The key to deliverance, they believed, was to uncover the pattern that tied the women together and explain why each, out of all the women possible, had been chosen to die. Loretta McLaughlin would later characterize her motivation as follows: "The obscurity of the women fascinated me. Had they not been strangled, the world would never have noted them. Why them [*sic*] were these 'Nobodies' singled out for a similar, violent, criminal death."[11]

More importantly, once the skein of logic that tied the victims together was discovered, it would lead back to the killer who would be uniquely identified by the insanity of his drive to kill only certain women. This faith was enunciated in the article introducing the series of reports that detailed the Girl Reporters' investigative efforts. "What they discovered is set forth in the hope that a pattern may emerge, one that will lift the burden of fear from women and lead to the capture of the man who makes them his victims."[12]

The pattern was therefore paramount, and the Girl Reporters put all their efforts into finding it. In this regard, the first murder took on added importance because it established the pattern. McLaughlin and Cole found special significance in the fact that Anna Slesers had moved into her apartment only two weeks before her death:

Why did all these stranglings take place? Why did they begin in June? Why was Anna Slesers the first victim? She met new people . . . did new things . . . looked for a new beauty parlor where she could get her hair done. Truly her pattern of life had changed. . . . And . . . just as the pattern of life for Anna Slesers underwent change . . . so did the pattern for the killer change. Hiding his desires no longer, he went on to kill . . . and kill . . . and kill.[13]

Her attempt to establish a new pattern in her life had provided the opportunity for a more sinister pattern to begin, according to the reporters.

The victim's son, Juris, took a somewhat less symbolic and more realistic view of his mother's death and her relationship with the killer. "I feel it was the meeting of two strangers. By that I mean, her killer was a stranger to her although he may have watched her."[14]

If the changes in one victim's life set off the killer, it was the regularity in the others' lives that kept him going. Illustrating this point with the behavior of Helen Blake, the Girl Reporters first postulated that the killer had carefully planned her death. Because she would not let anyone into her apartment, they reasoned, he had to learn her habits, know when she was alone, before he struck. The fact that Helen was immaculate in appearance and meticulous in manner attracted the killer. Her personality fit the crime and the need for careful planning in its commission. Thus, the predictable pattern of behavior in the dead woman's life made the crime possible.

The pinnacle of the search was reached when the team revealed what they felt were the common denominators. The theory was outlined in an article entitled "Girl Reporters Find 'Links' to Strangle Victims" that appeared in the *Boston Record American* on January 24, 1963:

> How do the paths trod daily by unsuspecting Boston women cross the evil tracks of a sex driven strangler?
> This is the question that lurks constantly in the shadows of our minds as we piece together endless bits of information on all of the victims.
> In addition to finding out—for the first time by anyone but the police—the entire story of their gruesome deaths, we have checked and checked again all of the little, inconspicuous things about the lives of these women hoping to find a clue that would give us the one, or even two, links that bind them together in a chain of death.
> After tedious sifting and searching, we feel we know what those two links are.
> The first explains how the paths of the victims and their killer cross. A person of science would perhaps call it the "M and M Syndrome." Very simply, it is this:
> The double M's stand for medicine and music.[15]

Thus, the dead were united in their love for classical music and their involvement in medical-related occupations.

The M and M Syndrome seemed to catch fire in the public mind, providing, as it did, a perfectly plausible connection among the victims. One reader from Glastonbury, Connecticut, who wrote to the Girl Reporters, endorsed the theory, adding her own embellishments:

After reading your articles, my husband and I feel convinced MUSIC is the clue to solving these murders. These ladies, all having a love of music in common, could have been in the habit of calling a radio station and requesting a play of their favorite records. Often such callers are asked for personal information as part of the program. Isn't it possible the killer could have gotten his leads this way?[16]

But other observers of the scene were less sanguine, and the notoriety gained by the Girl Reporters engendered considerable professional jealousy. George Frazier of the *Boston Herald* wrote a particularly vitriolic attack, calling the Girl Reporters the "sob sisters" and blaming them and the Hearst papers for the rebirth of yellow journalism in Boston. Frazier then turned his poison pen on the victims, in effect blaming them for their demise. "All of the 11 women who died of strangulation were not images of innocence."[17] He concluded by commending the Boston Police for their patience when confronted by "amateur imaginings to indict the performance of professionals."

Nevertheless, the M and M Syndrome was firmly established in the public imagination, and little could be done to dislodge it. But then the pattern changed. After a three-month hiatus, on December 5, 1962, the strangler struck again, and this time the victim was young. Not only was the dead woman, Sophie Clark, only 21 years old, but she lived with two other women and was black. From that point on, the murdered women, known to the public, were much younger, averaging under 28 years of age. As noted in the *Boston Herald*, the growth in fear was commensurate with the female population put at risk. "We find the fear is greater now than it was in the fall. Then the victims were in a limited category, elderly alone."[18] Now it appeared that a second pattern had been established, but did that imply there was a single killer or two? And what about the cherished pattern; would it remain valid?

It became increasingly difficult to maintain the music and medicine connection, and when twenty-four-year-old Patricia Bissette was murdered on the last day of 1962, the dual connection was nearly lost for good. Ms. Bissette was a secretary and had absolutely no link to hospitals either at the time of her death or before. Undeterred, the public found the pattern again when it was learned that her apartment had been occupied by several nurses before she took it over. Her death did after all fit the pattern.

The Bissette link and those of subsequent victims might stretch credulity, but it was worth it. The public needed an explanation, and music and medicine was it. These common denominators were the only things that allowed the killings to make sense, and they had to be defended no matter how tenuous they became. The dead women had to be connected to understand the killer's motivation, to make sense of the crimes, and ultimately to manage the fear until he was caught.

COMMON DENOMINATOR—THE OFFICIAL SEARCH

Probably no murder investigation before and few since have taken on the size and scope of the pursuit of the Boston Strangler. Some 2,350 police would eventually become involved, and their efforts were Herculean. A total of 36,000 people were interviewed, nearly 5 percent of the population of the city. At some point, 3,500 men were suspects. Hundreds were fingerprinted; forty were given lie detector tests, six of whom flunked so badly that they volunteered to take "truth serum" to clear themselves.

Draconian measures were the order of the day. A special tactical squad of thirty officers patrolled the Back Bay section of the city. When it was thought that two broaches were missing from Anna Slesers' apartment, pawnshops within a fifty-mile radius were checked. Every known sex offender was tracked down and interviewed. Believing the victims might be linked by their work at hospitals, police checked into the backgrounds of 3,500 hospital aides. Patient leaves from mental institutions were carefully correlated with the known time of the murders. The workload and pressure were staggering; some police cracked under the stress, and two asked to be relieved because of nerves.

As the strangler terror continued, police set up a special task force of handpicked officers, among them marksmen and karate experts. They were the best the police had to offer and were assigned full-time to the case. Because the stranglings were outside the realm of normal police experience, the officers were given special training. To assist, the FBI gave a special seminar on fifty varieties of sexual perversion, sex crimes, and the personality of sex offenders. Fifteen officers later participated in a more extensive two-week training session.

Police were never at a loss for suspects; in fact, they had too many, and what a bizarre collection they were. In the apartment building where Anna Slesers was murdered lived a man who answered Lonely Hearts ads in the paper. With promises of marriage, he enticed women to the city, involved them in a whirlwind courtship, which presumably included prenuptial sex, and subsequently sent them packing. Another man posed as a cardiac physician, called women at random, and made appointments to check their hearts. When finally captured in the strangler dragnet, he confessed to having had intercourse with over 100 women, but all had been willing and he had killed no one. This was quite a remarkable double life for a man who worked as a pickle salesman.

One suspect was especially interesting and surprisingly quite dead. After Jane Sullivan had been found strangled, a suicide was found several blocks away. Of particular interest to the police was the way the man, George

Stubbs, died: he strangled himself with a pair of women's nylons tied around his neck and knotted in a bow. Further investigation revealed that the man had a deviant sexual history, but most curious of all, after his death the profile of the murdered women changed from elderly to young.

To make sense of it all, police recognized early on that they would need outside help. In September 1962 a panel of legal and medical experts was convened with the following stated purpose: "The experts in legal medicine will try to find a common denominator in the slayings."[19] Every discipline that might be remotely relevant was included: medical examiners, representatives from the state police laboratory, psychiatrists, psychologists, clinical anthropologists, graphologists, and hypnotists. Many famous crime solvers acted as consultants, most notably Dr. James Brussell, who had developed a stunningly accurate personality profile of New York's Mad Bomber.

When the panel of experts was established, Dr. Richard Ford, Suffolk County medical examiner, stated its goal: "The objective is to find some common denominator, perhaps how and when these women met their deaths, perhaps something relating to the mode of living of the women. We just don't know what it might be."[20] Unfortunately, they never would know what it might be. But the task before them was daunting. After DeSalvo confessed, it was easy to see which crimes were related. At the time it was not. For example, on the day Nina Nichols' body was found, July 2, 1962, two other women were murdered; one was 17, the other 75. Should they be included among the strangler's victims? Other murder victims raised the same perplexing question.

Modiste Freeman—a Negro woman ambushed and mutilated in an alley

Daniela Saunders—also mugged in an alleyway and strangled

Margaret Davis—strangled with bare hands in a hotel room

As noted earlier, the crimes which the public believed the strangler had committed (Table 3.1) did not exactly coincide with those eventually claimed by DeSalvo.

Try as they might, the panel was never able to find the elusive common denominator and hence was never able to determine which of the murders belonged in the string and which did not. Furthermore, they never reached unanimity of opinion on whether one man or several had committed the murders. Only Dr. Brussell steadfastly maintained that there was a single killer. While the search for a common denominator focused on the lives and habits of the victims, he felt there was no need to relate the dead women. He summed up his position as follows:

Forget everything else. Forget age, size, complexion, locale and so on.
Concentrate on the modus operandi of the killer, his method of operation.

It is always the same. It has three essential elements: the garrote, the appearance of sexual assault and a search.[21]

Nevertheless, the situation was so confusing that as late as March 1963 Police Commissioner McNamara would deny a strong connection among the victims; "only three or four of these strangulation cases have a similarity,"[22] he said. But the public thought otherwise.

By March 1963 the victim tally had grown to eight, and it seemed that the best efforts of the police and experts were getting nowhere. Attorney General Edward Brooke declared that a state of emergency existed in the Commonwealth. Governor Peabody seconded this declaration, noting: "A state of terror exists and grows with each story of a new slaying. There is a pressing need for information to lead to a solution."[23] But in fact, a paucity of information was not the problem. Quite the contrary, police were drowning in the product of their efforts. The number of suspects exceeded 10,000, and the investigation had generated 800,000 pieces of paper. More to the point, then, police needed a way to consolidate the existing information, coordinate all the disparate sources of information housed in multiple jurisdictions, and evaluate the mountain of facts.

Enter the computer. Donated by a Concord company, the computer was to be the electronic brain that would finally crack the case. With unshakable faith that a common denominator must exist, the computer would find the connection among victims that had somehow eluded investigators to this point. The computer became simply another tool that would be used to find the pattern in the crimes and provide the elusive rational explanation for them. In a development that would foreshadow Boston's place of prominence in the coming technological revolution, police pointed with pride to the fact that this was the first time a computer had been used to solve a criminal case.

But, of course, it was easier to acquire the computer than to use it. The mountains of data had to be entered before they could be systematically searched for commonalities, and this was nothing short of a monumental effort. So it was not until the summer of 1964, six months after the last murder, that the computer began processing the data in earnest.

Initially intending to investigate the "hospital connection" among the victims, the search picked up another unusual similarity in the lives of the victims. As Chief Investigator Robert Bottomly said at the end of July 1964, "Information being fed into an electronic computer has turned up 'new common denominators in the lives and habit patterns of the victims'."[24] It seemed that five of the first six murdered women had a previously unknown connection through their friends and acquaintances, who, in turn, were linked by their lifestyles. Attorney General Brooke elaborated on the new-found theory: "Some of their interests were unusual to say the least and brought them in varying degrees into contact with unstable individuals in the homosexual community of our society."[25] From this Brooke concluded that the strangler had, in fact, only killed the first five victims, while the remaining women were killed by imitators who made their crimes resemble what they had seen on television or heard on the radio.

But by then no one had been strangled for seven months, and in another seven months, Albert DeSalvo would give a detailed confession. The homosexual link was quickly forgotten, and the computer that would illuminate the investigation only added to the bewilderment by leading investigators to see a pattern that did not exist.

By early 1964 after a year and a half of trying, traditional police methods, the computer, and the collective brain power of the panel of experts had made little headway. Completely frustrated, Attorney General Brooke took the unusual step of bringing psychics into the investigation to help solve the case. The quintessential pragmatic politician, and under mounting pressure to do something, Brooke noted that the city had everything to gain and nothing to lose by using the services of those who possessed supernatural powers.

Realizing that this unprecedented move smacked of superstition, magic, and conjuring, Brooke went to some lengths to define it in objective and quasiscientific terms. Brooke described them not as psychics at all, but as practitioners in the field of psychometry for which, thankfully, he provided the following definition: "Divination of facts concerning an object or its owner through contact or proximity with the object."[26] As "psychometrists," the psychics were presumably more palatable to skeptics since the name implied they could empirically quantify and measure psychic phenomena.

To lessen the blow for the law enforcement professionals and credentialed authorities on the case, Brooke hastened to add, "The use of a psychometrist is just one of several methods now being employed in an effort to bring this coordinated investigation to a successful conclusion."[27] Apparently, this attempt at appeasement failed. Relations between Brooke and the Boston Police Department, strained to begin with, became destructively hostile and pointedly uncooperative thereafter.

One of the two psychics involved in the case was none other than Gerard Croiset, Jr., the Dutch grocer whom Mrs. Latimer would consult a decade later to help explain the disappearance of her daughter, Sherrie Jan, on Folly Beach, South Carolina. But the more prominent and controversial of the two was Peter Hurkos, the man who became involved in the investigation at Brooke's invitation. Like Croiset, Hurkos had a habit of popping up at high-profile serial murder investigations in the 1960s and 1970s.

Hurkos was always somewhat larger than life, and his implausible personal story did little to dispel the nagging feeling that after all he might be nothing but a charlatan. A house painter by trade, he had fallen from a ladder, broken his skull, and lapsed into a coma. Upon awakening after three days, he was clairvoyant and possessed the ability to describe past or future events by coming into contact with people or objects related to them. He quickly parlayed this newfound talent into a nightclub act and became the other-worldly companion of several Hollywood celebrities including Glenn Ford.

Despite Brooke's invitation, Hurkos's involvement was strictly ex officio, with his fee and expenses paid by an anonymous Boston businessman. Furthermore, his entry into the case did little to enhance his credibility or endear him to the local law enforcement officials. To start, he was spirited into town with a personal bodyguard in tow and secreted in a motel in Lexington, a suburb some ten miles outside Boston, where he was held incommunicado. While there, he made several pronouncements about two unrelated murders, one a housewife in nearby Lincoln and one the killing of a fourteen-year-old babysitter in southern New Hampshire.

But what he lacked in tact or initial goodwill, Hurkos quickly made up for with his prodigious psychic powers. Presented with sealed envelopes containing pictures of the crime scenes, Hurkos provided detailed and flawless descriptions of the content of each. He even correctly identified the one bogus envelope containing pictures of an unrelated murder police included as a test. The accuracy of the descriptions was unnerving and left even the most hardened policemen shaken.

Almost immediately, Hurkos developed a psychic image of the killer. He described the killer as a smallish man between 5'7" and 5'8" and weighing between 130 and 140 pounds with a sharp nose, scar on his left arm, and something wrong with his thumb. Hurkos also claimed the killer loved shoes and lived in the nearby suburb of Newton. Then, while driving through Back Bay, the psychic made investigators stop in front of an apartment building while he told of terrible things that had happened inside. Unbeknownst to him, the building had been the home of Nina Nichols. Finally, in the most bizarre phase of his involvement, Hurkos fell asleep and seemed to carry on a two-way conversation between one of the victims and the killer. Some of the dialogue was in Portuguese, a language unfamiliar to Hurkos but the native tongue of Sophie Clark's father.

Armed with Hurkos's insights, investigators reculled the suspect lists. Almost too good to be true, they quickly found a man who matched Hurkos's description in nearly every detail. He was 5'7½", weighed 130 pounds, had a very sharp nose, had scars on his left arm, and had a deformed thumb. Sometimes employed as a door-to-door salesman of women's shoes, the suspect had also attended St. John's Seminary in Newton. Add to this a history of mental illness, and it appeared that the police may have had their man at last.

Brooke moved quickly and invoked an obscure law permitting the arrest and imprisonment of the suspect for a ten-day observation period. This, in turn, set off a backlash of protest by the ACLU, which tried to have the man freed. But despite the efforts of civil libertarians, the man's family agreed to extend the observation period for another forty-five days. In the end it all came to naught; the suspect clearly had no knowledge of the crimes, and so another promising lead quietly died away. Hurkos, meanwhile, was long gone, having left the city on February 6, 1964, only one week after he arrived.

What started as high drama now ended in low farce. The FBI arrested Hurkos for impersonating an officer. The charge seemed largely manufactured in an effort to embarrass Brooke, and Hurkos was released soon after the arrest. Those who suspected ulterior political motives pointed to the convenient coincidence that Boston Police Commissioner Edward McNamara had formerly been an FBI agent.

The final twist in the search for the common denominator was provided by the confessed killer himself. Describing his behavior immediately before a murder, DeSalvo said,

See, when this certain time comes upon me, it's a very immediate thing. When I get up in the morning and I get this feeling and . . . instead of going to work, I might make an excuse to my boss and start driving, and I'd start in my mind building this image up and that's why I found myself not knowing where I was going.[28]

In the end, therefore, the ultimate irony was that there was no pattern: the victims had been chosen at random. No common denominator ever existed, and there had never been a way to predict future killings.

But if the crimes could not be predicted or the class of victims identified in advance, then the commonality must be within the killer. Perhaps he shared something with other serial killers that could be used to prevent crimes of this sort in the future, or as it was voiced in the *Boston Record* on September 8, 1966:

All authorities it seems to us, should strive very hard, without further delays, toward a single objective—the use of this whole experience to produce some answers which will enable the elected and delegated protectors of society to recognize and incarcerate seemingly harmless citizens who, in fact, are prepared to kill, kill and kill until they are finally stopped or, as in this instance, apparently, until they stop on their own accord.

It is bad enough that these women were strangled, but the ultimate tragedy would be to let their deaths serve no purpose at all. If Mr. S (DeSalvo) is the Strangler, then he is unquestionably the greatest living, breathing laboratory that medical-legal science has ever had the opportunity to study.[29]

The authorities' final attempt to find a rational explanation for the experience came as a result of their efforts to study DeSalvo, to uncover what made him tick. DeSalvo apparently was willing to participate, according to a psychiatrist quoted by the paper. "He has said, as we understand it, that he is willing to turn himself over completely for studies of any kind that may answer why he did what he says he did, something he himself doesn't understand."[30]

Whatever attempt may have been made to study DeSalvo ended when he was sent to Walpole Prison in 1968. Five years later no less an authority than Dr. James Brussell lamented the missed opportunity: "I urged over and over that guys like Albert should be gathered by the National Institute of Health and studied. I appealed that it was possible they might find something in the genes that could eventually lead to a serum that could be used to inoculate for the removal of apparent criminal streaks."[31] Thus to the end he held fast to the idea that there must be a reason for the crimes and that science could uncover it.

THE BOSTON STRANGLER

Perhaps no serial killer was ever better trained in callous violence or more practiced in his method than Albert DeSalvo. Growing up in an excessively abusive family, Albert watched his alcoholic father, Frank, routinely beat his mother senseless. In one particularly notorious and gruesome incident, Albert was present when his father first knocked out his mother's teeth and then one-by-one bent her fingers back until all were broken.

Frank DeSalvo's violent rages were typically unconstrained. Albert and his brothers and sisters were also the targets of his father's violent temper and physical abuse. Desperate for money, Frank once even sold Albert and two sisters into slavery to a Maine farmer. The price—nine dollars. With such a role model, it is hardly surprising that Albert as a child also became abusive of weaker living things. He was known to hurt animals and once killed a sleeping cat with a nail tied to the end of an arrow.

In addition, DeSalvo's early experiences were virtually certain to preclude any normal sexual activity. His father frequently brought prostitutes home and made his children watch as he had sex with them, a behavior that was pointedly demeaning to women generally and his mother in particular. For his part, Albert claimed to have had his first sexual episode at the age of six or seven. Thereafter, sex became a regular part of his life with other children and the homosexuals who paid him for sex. Throughout his life, DeSalvo possessed an insatiable sexual appetite and would often have sex several times a day.

As if to round out his apprenticeship in deviance, Albert was taught to steal. Again, the architect of instruction was Frank DeSalvo. In this instance, his father took him to a store and showed him how to shoplift; Albert was five years old at the time. At twelve he was sent to a correctional home for stealing jewelry. Thus by the time he reached his teens, Albert DeSalvo was an accomplished thief, a skill he would use throughout his life.

When it came to schooling a future serial killer, Frank DeSalvo was the perfect teacher. However, as the years passed, he became less of a fixture in the DeSalvo home until finally he completely abandoned the family in 1939 when Albert was eight. By that time, however, the damage had been done.

With the influence of Frank DeSalvo diminishing, Albert started to succeed and even excel in certain areas. In 1948 he joined the Army and adapted easily to the routine and discipline. He was made Colonel's Orderly numerous times, took up boxing, and became the middleweight champion of the Army in Europe. But he always retained a rebellious streak, and, of course, his sexual philandering was unceasing. In 1950 he was court martialed for disobeying an order, got into scrapes for bedding officers' wives, and was accused of sexually molesting a nine-year-old girl, a charge that was eventually dropped. Despite this mixed record, Albert was honorably discharged in 1956.

His Army career was significant for a second reason. While stationed in Germany, Albert was married. After leaving the Army, he and his wife Irmgard returned to Boston and settled in the working-class suburb of Malden. DeSalvo worked sporadically at a series of laborer and maintenance jobs and supplemented his income with an occasional burglary. In fact, he was twice arrested and convicted for breaking and entering in 1958 but was given a suspended sentence in both cases. One of the great ironies of the Boston Strangler case is that DeSalvo was able to escape detection in one of the largest manhunts ever undertaken in which all known sex offenders and literally thousands of other suspects were questioned. The reason was quite simple. DeSalvo was known to the police as a B & E man, and they were unaware of his sex offenses.

Two children were born to Irmgard and Albert, first a boy, Michael, and subsequently a girl, Judy. The girl is an especially tragic figure for the part she was to play in the unfolding drama. Born with a hip deformity, Judy required braces and constant physical therapy administered by the parents. More importantly, her birth coincided with Irmgard's sexual rejection of Albert. Denied sex by his wife, Albert began his career first as the "Measuring Man," then the "Green Man," and ultimately the Boston Strangler. It has even been hypothesized that on a psychological level, when killing, Albert was symbolically strangling Judy to regain the love and sexual attention of his wife. In this regard, it has often been noted that the bows used to decorate the strangler victims were nearly identical to those Albert tied to his daughter's leg braces to cheer her up.

For his part, DeSalvo claimed that the killings began with Irmgard's rejection and stopped when she took him back. Irmgard, in turn, expressed the usual shock and disbelief when Albert confessed. She was quoted as saying: "I can't understand how my husband could be like that—he was so gentle with me."[32]

The road to becoming the Boston Strangler brought together all of DeSalvo's talents for survival—his charm and facile manner, the cool audacity of a burglar, a job that allowed him to roam the city freely without supervision, and, of course, his insatiable sexual desire. Missing initially was the extreme violence that would characterize the strangulation killings.

The first manifestation of his predation of Boston females became known as the Measuring Man. Adopting an idea he had seen on the Bob Cummings television show, DeSalvo posed as a photographer's agent. He would talk his way into apartments, compliment the occupant profusely, and ask to take her measurements in preparation for the visit of a professional photographer who would come at a later time. Using this strategy, DeSalvo measured, and occasionally bedded, hundreds of women in Boston and Cambridge.

DeSalvo was arrested in Cambridge, Massachusetts in 1961 while masquerading as the Measuring Man. He was charged with attempted breaking and entering and lewd and lascivious behavior. Subsequently, he was convicted and spent eleven months in prison.

The Measuring Man metamorphosed into the next expression of perversion, the Green Man who terrorized women along the New England seacoast from Massachusetts into Connecticut. So-called because DeSalvo wore green coveralls, he posed as a workman and gained entry into the victim's apartment. Once inside, he raped and humiliated the occupants at knife point. It was a short trip from Green Man to Boston Strangler.

DeSalvo's career as the Green Man ended when one of his victims was shown police files and was able to identify his Measuring Man mugshots. He was arrested for the Green Man crimes on November 4, 1964 and was sent to Bridgewater State Hospital for observation. Following preliminary assessment at Bridgewater, DeSalvo was returned to the Cambridge jail, where he displayed bizarre behavior and was suspected of being suicidal. Hence, he was once again sent to Bridgewater State Hospital.

In February 1965 DeSalvo approached another inmate at Bridgewater, George Nassar, and intimated that he was actually the Boston Strangler. Presumably convinced that DeSalvo was indeed the Strangler or possibly inspired by a desire to collect the over $100,000 of reward money, Nassar contacted his attorney, F. Lee Bailey, with the case-breaking news. The fact that Nassar was incarcerated at Bridgewater for the particularly vicious murder of a woman immediately inspired conspiracy theorists to conclude that Nassar was himself the Boston Strangler, that he had convinced the attention-seeking DeSalvo to confess to the crimes, and that he had coached him in the minutiae of the murders.

Whatever Nassar's role in the killings, Bailey interviewed DeSalvo and became convinced that he was authentic. Bailey's next step was to convey the information of the Boston Strangler's discovery to the proper authorities. He did so, and DeSalvo was next interviewed at length on multiple occasions by Assistant Attorney General John Bottomly. The interrogations, amounting to an extended confession by DeSalvo, contained numerous bits of information known only to the police or verifiable statements of fact.

DeSalvo's recounting of the crimes was nearly flawless, and authorities were convinced the Boston Strangler had finally been captured.

The prosecution of DeSalvo was a convoluted affair. Defense attorney Bailey wanted DeSalvo committed to a mental institution, where he would be treated and studied by psychiatrists. Not coincidentally, if DeSalvo were sent to a mental hospital he would escape the electric chair. The State, meanwhile, had no hard evidence, fingerprints, or eyewitnesses on which to build a case and had to rely exclusively on DeSalvo's confession. Initially, the State was willing to let DeSalvo plead insanity in exchange for the use of his confession in court, but, eventually, positions hardened and the quid pro quo arrangement fell apart.

To resolve the situation, Bailey brokered a deal that would have DeSalvo stand trial for the Green Man crimes rather than the Boston Strangler murders. The defense strategy hinged on the idea that DeSalvo would be found legally insane during the Green Man trial. Then he would be committed to a mental institution for those crimes and would not have to stand trial for the Boston Strangler murders. Both parties would get what they wanted: the defense would keep DeSalvo alive and secure treatment for him, while the prosecution would have the Boston Strangler incarcerated for life.

The positions of the adversaries were succinctly stated in their summations to the jury. For the defense, Bailey argued, "If the science of psychiatry were a little more precise . . . you might as citizens hope and expect that there would be some way to remove people like this from the world before they can do great harm and injury and even death."[33] In case any juror doubted how this could be done, Bailey completed the rationalist's syllogism calling DeSalvo a "phenomenon." He stated, "We've never had such a specimen in captivity. He should be the subject of a research grant from the Ford Foundation or a similar institution."[34] Most importantly, this was a once in a lifetime opportunity that should not be denied by desires for retribution. Bailey explained, "What I'm stating here is not a defense, it is a sociological imperative. Aside from the moral, religious, ethical, or other objections to capital punishment, to execute DeSalvo is just as wasteful, barbaric, and ignorant an act as burning the witches of Salem."[35] The search for a logical and scientific explanation for the crimes became the murderer's last line of defense.

In response, the prosecuting attorney, Donald Conn, was equally impassioned. He admonished the jury not to be fooled by a man pretending to be mentally ill and hoping to be sent to a mental institution, to be "conned out of their shoes" in his words. Instead, it was their responsibility as citizens to see through the stratagem and convict DeSalvo:

You have a duty . . . to the commonwealth. I am the vehicle of the commonwealth and I am only one small person. It is a duty to every citizen of this commonwealth of ours, to your wife, to my wife, to everyone who could conceivably be the subject of an attack of this type. You . . . are the mirror whose duty it is to reflect the truth from the evidence presented to you.[36]

The jury proved to be the societal reflection of truth the prosecution had hoped for, and it found DeSalvo both sane and guilty.

Albert DeSalvo was convicted of the Green Man charges of indecent assault and armed robbery on January 18, 1967. He was sentenced to life imprisonment and remanded to Bridgewater State Hospital to await final disposition to a maximum security prison. Before reassignment, however, he and two other inmates escaped. After 38 hours on the run, Albert called his attorney and voluntarily surrendered.

He was then sent to Walpole Prison where he spent the rest of his life. In prison he delighted in making jewelry, particularly necklaces which he dubbed "chokers," noting the name was a good gimmick. On November 25, 1973, DeSalvo was found murdered in his cell, stabbed sixteen times in the chest, supposedly in a dispute with other prisoners over food or drugs. His killers were never found. At the time of his death, Albert Henry DeSalvo was 42 years old.

EPILOGUE

To return to the question posed at the outset of this chapter: Was Albert DeSalvo the Boston Strangler? Believers cite his nearly flawless recall of crime scenes, especially unpublished details, as evidence that he was indeed the strangler. Doubters, in opposition, point out that DeSalvo was never tried or convicted of the crimes, was never identified by an eyewitness, including the only woman known to have fought off and survived a strangler attack, and ultimately recanted his confession.

As late as 1988, Dr. Ames Robey, one of the many medical experts on the case, maintained that DeSalvo never killed anyone, while Jack Barry of the Boston Police Department noted he simply had too much knowledge of the crimes not to be the strangler. As these two opinions indicate, there may never be total agreement. However, as pointed out in the *Boston Herald* on the twenty-fifth anniversary of Anna Slesers' murder: "This much was certain: When Albert DeSalvo went behind bars, the rape-strangulations stopped and women began to feel safe again in Boston."[37] With Albert DeSalvo in prison, the pattern of killings ended.

In the final analysis, acceptance of Albert DeSalvo as the Boston Strangler or even whether or not there was a single individual who committed all the killings rests on the belief in the pattern that connects the crimes. For those who believe the pattern exists and are able to see the similarities in the deaths of all thirteen women, there is only one killer, and it is Albert DeSalvo by virtue of his detailed knowledge of the crimes. For those who see the differences in the crimes and victims, the case remains unsolved.[38]

The Coed Killer and Clairvoyant

JOHN NORMAN COLLINS
Ypsilanti, Michigan (1967–1969)

*"He knows I'm coming. I'm after him and he's after me. But I am not afraid.
I come thousands of miles to find him and I won't give up."*
—Peter Hurkos
Detroit Free Press, July 22, 1969

In October 1968 a rumor spread across the campus of Eastern Michigan University to the effect that a string of murders would start within days. According to one version bruited about, fifty coeds at four Michigan colleges would be killed over a ten-day period by a man posing as a woman. Another account had it that forty women belonging to a sorority starting with the letter "D" would be hatcheted to death by the female impersonator. Throughout the state, terrified coeds went home for the weekend.

The source of the rumor was reputed to be a prediction made by the renowned seer Jeanne Dixon. In an attempt to determine the veracity of the report, the university newspaper, the *Eastern Echo,* contacted Miss Dixon at her home in Washington, D.C. When asked whether she had anything to tell the women on campus, Miss Dixon replied, "Yes, tell all the girls I never made any such prediction and all this is nothing but unfounded rumors. Tell them there is nothing to worry about and they can feel safe."[1] In retrospect, it may have been the least prescient denial of a prediction in history since by that time the coed killer had already killed twice, both Eastern students, and over the next eight months would claim five more victims.

Jeanne Dixon was only the first of many psychics, famous or otherwise, to be associated with the coed killer case. And psychics, in turn, were just one manifestation of the process of epistemological transformation involving the police and public as they tried to adapt to the exigencies thrust on them. The coed killer case is one instance in which the serial nature of the murders was recognized early and the terror extended long enough for the community and its law enforcement agents to traverse all the stages of public reaction in their effort to explain the slaughter and manage the concomitant fear.

There was as always a strong element of rationality in the reactions as the police tried to solve the crimes and the public tried to understand them. Common denominators were sought and found, even though none seemed to apply universally to the victims. With their own prodigious efforts going nowhere, police looked outside their ranks for help. First they appealed to the public for missing information that would break the case. When there was none to be had, they sought extra resources and expert assistance, technical, human and animal. Inevitably, the case would be solved by nothing more cerebral than perseverance and plodding police work.

With the crisis deepening and the police seemingly powerless, a subtle shift took place in the public mind. The community began to interpret events in supernatural terms and to seek unearthly remedies. The populace, with the begrudging acquiescence of the police, called in the most famous clairvoyant of the era, Peter Hurkos, to solve the crime by extraordinary means. In a broader context, Hurkos' involvement was only the most prominent of a number of appeals to a higher power to find the killer. Also evident was a strong belief in divine intervention for the deliverance of the beleaguered masses. This belief was so pervasive that even the death of the victims was thought to have a sacrificial purpose and spiritual significance.

Belief in beneficent forces implies the existence of the antithesis, the power of evil. The metamorphosis of public thought and response reached its consummation with transference, a change from faith that supernatural forces could solve the crimes to the presumption that they had supernatural causes. This transformation in collective psychology was embedded in the victim–killer relationship and was abetted by the actions of the killer. With each successive murder, his arrogance and sense of invulnerability seemed to grow, as did his mocking challenges to the police and Hurkos. In the end, the investigation became an epic struggle between good and evil, with Hurkos playing the knight-errant and the killer the prince of darkness.

The coed killer case is also a story influenced by the time and locale in which it took place. As shown in the headlines of the period, the residents of Washtenaw County, like people everywhere, were experiencing the curse of living in interesting times. War, urban riots, international conflicts, moon walks, drugs and freaks, the Prague spring, the *Pueblo* incident, Woodstock, the passing of heroes of another age symbolized by Eisenhower's death—events were occurring at a mind-boggling pace. Reflecting on New Year's Eve, one student summed up the tenor of the times:

The kaleidoscopic panorama of 1967 unfolded in my mind. The year gone by was like a wild roller-coaster ride through tragedy and comedy, beauty and pathos, collapse and renewal. The things I had witnessed in the previous twelve months took on a surrealistic quality that seemed hardly believable. Certain scenes remained ineradicably etched in my mind. The hit song "Light My Fire" had blared from the radio as I watched the city of Detroit burn. San Francisco became a mecca for the young and disenchanted as the Beatles changed their refrain from "I Want to Hold Your Hand" to "I'd love to turn you on." Twice in Detroit and Washington, I had seen the United States Army in action against their fellow Americans. The pungent odor of marijuana became ubiquitous, spreading from the big cities to suburbia, and in Ypsilanti, the price of Zig-Zag cigarette papers doubled.[2]

It was an era in which the foundations of society and the structure of beliefs seemed ready to crumble.

THE COED KILLINGS

The murders began, for the public, in August 1967 when the first body was discovered, and they ended two years later with the arrest of John Norman Collins. It is generally accepted that over that period Collins killed seven young women ranging in age from 13 to 23. The perception was cemented in the community's consciousness by a vulturine press that printed a detailed, tabular summary of the crimes updated after each murder. Table 4.1 presents the last of these morbid spreadsheets published in the *Detroit Free Press* under the headline "A Pattern of Death: An Anatomy of 7 Brutal Murders" on July 28, 1969, marking the discovery of the last body.[3]

Again, public perception and reality do not necessarily coincide. Collins was implicated, at least superficially, in fifteen murders. He almost certainly was responsible for the death of a young woman, Roxie Phillips, in Salinas, California in June 1969 and very likely killed thirteen-year-old Eileen Adams, who was abducted in Toledo, Ohio in December 1967 and found raped, strangled, and stuffed in a gunny sack, south of Ypsilanti in January 1968. Conversely, there is some doubt that Jane Mixer, the third presumed victim, was actually slain by Collins. Unlike the other six murders, her body was dumped on the east side of Ypsilanti, in a densely populated area; there was no evidence of rape or sexual assault, no brutish beating or mutilation, and the corpse was fully clothed. Nevertheless, there were similarities, a ligature around the neck and missing shoes, among them.

Barring a confession from Collins, which in twenty-five years he has been unwilling to give, we will never know the exact number of coed murders. Nonetheless, the actual total and the specific murders that belong to Collins is irrelevant to the "Coed Killings" as a social phenomenon: those that were unknown did not influence the public, whereas those that may in truth have been committed by someone else were nonetheless attributed to the killer. From the perspective of public reactions, perception is reality, and Table 4.1

Table 4.1
A Pattern of Death: An Anatomy of 7 Brutal Murders

Victim	Last Seen	Where Found	How Killed
Mary Fleszar, 19, of Willis	Went out for a walk about 8:30 p.m. July 9, 1967, near Eastern Michigan University (EMU) campus.	Near Geddes and Le Forge Roads between Ann Arbor and Ypsilanti Aug. 7, 1967.	Stabbed several times in chest.
Joan Schell, 20, of Plymouth	Hitchhiking in front of EMU Student Union about 10:30 p.m. June 30, 1968.	Near Glacier Way and Earhart Road on outskirts of Ann Arbor a week later.	Stabbed five times, throat slashed.
Jane Mixer, 23, of Muskegon	In apartment on University of Michigan campus 30 minutes before she was supposed to meet a "David Johnson" for a ride to Muskegon March 20, 1969.	In a cemetery in Denton Township just inside Wayne County the next day.	Shot twice in head with .22 caliber gun.
Maralynn Skelton, 16, of Romulus	Hitchhiking in front of Arborland Shopping Center between Ann Arbor and Ypsilanti March 24, 1969.	Near Glacier Way and Earhart on outskirts of Ann Arbor the next day.	Massive skull fracture; skull cracked in three places.
Dawn Basom, 13, of Ypsilanti	Hurrying home about a half-mile from house near EMU campus April 15, 1969.	Near Gale and Vreeland Roads the next day.	Strangled with black electrical wire.
Alice Kalom, 23, of Portage	Dancing at a party at the Depot House in Ann Arbor June 7, 1969.	Near North Territorial Road and U.S. 23, close to an abandoned barn.	Shot once in head.
Karen Sue Beineman, 18, of Grand Rapids	Buying a wig in a shop in Ypsilanti, July 23, 1969.	In a ravine off Riverside Dr. near Huron River Dr. in Ann Arbor Twp.	Strangled.

Table 4.1 (Continued)

Other Injuries	How Body Was Found	Identity	Clues
Fingers and feet cut off, forearm and some fingers missing. Probably raped.	Killed elsewhere. Clothes piled neatly beside body.	EMU coed working as a secretary; an accounting major.	None. Body too decomposed to yield any clues.
Sexually molested.	Killed elsewhere. Clothes were removed and blue miniskirt twisted around her neck. Body was believed kept by killer in a cool place, probably a basement.	EMU art major.	Believed she got into late-model red and white car with three youths.
None.	Killed elsewhere. Body fully clothed except for shoes placed neatly next to the body. Stocking (not hers) twisted around neck.	Freshman law student at University of Michigan.	Man using alias of "David Johnson" was scheduled to give her a ride home. Red burlap purse missing.
Whipped with a belt, sadistically sexually molested.	Killed elsewhere. Clothes next to body, shoes placed neatly near her feet, handkerchief stuffed in mouth; garter belt (not hers) wrapped around her neck. Earrings and cheap engagement ring missing.	High school dropout; drug user; ran with hippies.	Wooden club used to kill her found; reported to have accepted ride in blue panel truck.
Slashed across breasts and buttocks.	Wearing only blouse and bra; handkerchief stuffed in mouth; blue stretch pants missing. Killed elsewhere.	Eighth-grade student at West Junior High School.	Believed killed in deserted farm house where sweater and remainder of electrical wire was found.
Stabbed twice in chest, slashed in neck and raped.	Clothes ripped off and scattered around. Killed elsewhere. Shoes she was carrying missing.	U-M graduate in fine arts; enrolled as a graduate student.	Seen dancing with long-haired youth at Depot House party.
Face battered beyond recognition.	Killed elsewhere. Body nude.	EMU freshman attending summer classes.	Seen driving off with a young man on a motorcycle.

Source: "A Pattern of Death: An Anatomy of 7 Brutal Murders," *Detroit Free Press*, July 28, 1969. Reprinted with permission of the Detroit Free Press.

provides the most concise description of the crimes, the basic information all members of the community shared.

Common denominators among the victims were readily apparent, and the public spent hours analyzing the patterns. Most of the girls had pierced ears and long brown hair. Often bodies were found semi- or completely nude. Although clothing was frequently left at the site, when it was inventoried certain articles, especially shoes, were missing. Perhaps symbolically, the bodies were dumped in areas known as lovers lanes, which when combined with the missing clothes created problems for investigators. As Washtenaw County Prosecutor William Delhey pointed out, "I never realized how much clothing is lying around Washtenaw County. There is enough in those lovers' lanes to fill a lingerie store."[4]

The geographic commonalities in the crimes were also striking. Several of the victims lived or disappeared within blocks of each other. Six were found in the rural area separating Ann Arbor and Ypsilanti, and five were found in a tight circle. As shown by a map of the area with the discover sites superimposed (see Figure 4.1), only one instance did not seem to fit the geographic tendency, and as with most other common denominators it was the murder of Jane Mixer.[5]

While there were always some puzzling discrepancies among the victim characteristics, the modus operandi of the murderer was more uniform, and it was these similarities that caused speculation about the death of Eileen Adams. The Adams murder was never officially tied to the coed killer, but it exhibited all of the characteristics that would come to be recognized as his method.

First, the girl had been strangled with an electrical cord like one used in a subsequent killing. And like a later, similarly aged victim, Dawn Basom, her bra was twisted around her neck. She had been tortured, cruelly beaten with a hammer as if the killer had been in a frenzy, and, as a final indignity, a 3–inch nail had been driven into her skull. Her stockings were neatly arranged on the body, but her shoes were missing. There was evidence of sexual assault, and as always, the body was put in plain sight, where it was certain to be found. Finally, as *Ypsilanti Press* crime reporter John Cobb noted, "Also tying the Adams death in with the other five are indications that she may have left with her killer willingly."[6]

These then would be the characteristics of death at the hands of the coed killer: strangulation or ligature around the neck, depersonalization by savage beating around the head and face, articles of clothing missing, nude or semi-nude body, sexual assault or rape, disposal to ensure discovery of the remains, and—the source of transference—disappearance without struggle, at times perhaps even cooperation with the killer.

Far more important than the common denominators connecting the murders, from the standpoint of explaining community response, were the trends underlying them. In this regard, three features of the murders were critical:

Figure 4.1
Death Map Expands

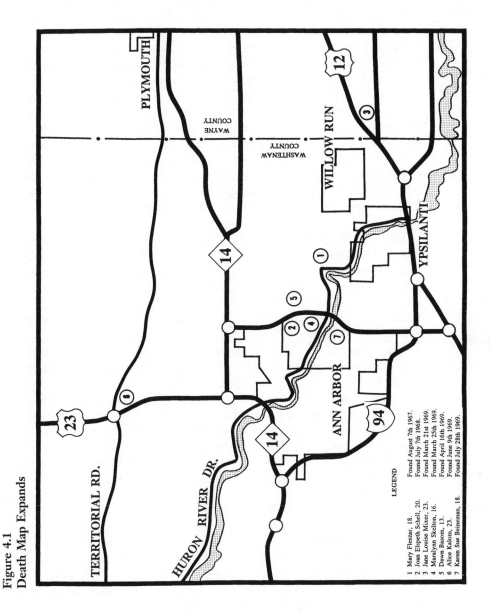

LEGEND

1 Mary Fleszar, 18.   Found August 7th 1967.
2 Joan Elspeth Schell, 20.   Found July 7th 1968.
3 Jane Louise Mixer, 23.   Found March 21st 1969.
4 Maralynn Skelton, 16.   Found March 25th 1969.
5 Dawn Basom, 13.   Found April 16th 1969.
6 Alice Kalom, 23.   Found June 9th 1969.
7 Karen Sue Beineman, 18.   Found July 28th 1969.

the number and length of time between murders, the disposal and discovery of bodies, and the circumstances surrounding the disappearance of each woman. Each of these characteristics changed over time as if an emboldened killer were calculating what would have maximal effect on the community psyche.

Murder was a relatively rare event in Washtenaw County; then suddenly murders occurred with increasing speed as if building to a crescendo. The first murders were separated by almost a year; nine months later two more murders were committed back-to-back only three days apart. Beginning in mid-April 1969, murders occurred at intervals of roughly one every six weeks. Police efforts to catch the killer and public anxiety over police failure grew proportionately. To recapture the sense of dread that the number and rapidity of murders engendered, we need only note that when, by sheer happenstance, the body of Joan Schell was found 100 feet inside Ann Arbor city limits and came, as a consequence, under the jurisdiction of the city's Police Department, it was their first murder investigation in eighteen months.

The second significant feature of the murders was the way the bodies were disposed of. The corpse of the first victim, Mary Fleszar, was dumped 150 feet from the nearest road and was hidden in some bushes; the killer returned at least three times to adjust the position of the body, and most importantly, cut off the hands and feet in a futile attempt to prevent identification. The killer made only a half-hearted attempt to conceal the body of the next victim, Joan Schell. The corpse was dumped in a clump of trees just 12 feet from the road and was covered with a thin blanket of grass that did little to disguise its whereabouts. Thereafter no effort was made to hide the bodies; just the opposite, they were left in plain sight, grotesquely displayed, where they were sure to be found. Washtenaw County Sheriff Harvey commented on this trend as it applied to the placement of Dawn Basom's body, "These Superior Township roads have scores of brushfilled places where a body might be concealed for months. He picked a spot which was exposed to cars north and southbound on Gale, at the bottom of a hill where vehicles would normally be slowing down, within sight of two houses. He wanted her found."[7]

As disposal became more blatant, the elapsed time between disappearance and discovery narrowed. Mary Fleszar's body was found a month after her murder, Joan Schell's a week, and the last victims within hours. It was clear the killer was growing bolder, less worried about being caught in the act. His confidence was building. It would become finally an arrogant belief in his own omnipotence expressed as an open challenge to the police.

The deadly game of catch-me-if-you-can was reinforced by the way the killer selected and acquired victims. Progressively, the method moved from abduction to unwitting complicity to enticement. Two of the earliest victims, Mary Fleszar and Maralynn Skelton, simply dropped from sight, while two others, Jane Mixer and Joan Schell, sought rides by hitchhiking or ride sharing. The last three victims disappeared mysteriously, without a struggle, and there was strong evidence that the last two went willingly with their assailant and the final one even as if she knew what lay ahead. In the public mind, therefore, there was a perception that increasingly over time victims went more readily with the killer until at last they became active participants in their own capture.

IN LOCO PARENTIS

At first glance, reactions to the coed murders were not dissimilar to those seen anywhere else. There were, as always, the protective measures hastily put in place, the steps taken for self-defense, and the impact on the economic life of the community. Beyond these, in Washtenaw County community response was exaggerated and made more pervasive by two indigenous conditions: the unusual makeup of the population and the attitudes of the populace at the time.

One factor that magnified the impact of the killings was the skewed demographics of the county, caused by the presence of two large universities in an otherwise quite rural setting. Roughly 50,000 students were enrolled in the University of Michigan and Eastern Michigan University in the late 1960s, 35,000 and 15,000 respectively, of which about half were female. As a consequence, a huge number of people and, more importantly, a disproportionately large segment of the population, one in eight, felt directly threatened by the killer.

In addition, relatively few of the coeds were from the immediate vicinity. Rather, Eastern Michigan students came from all over the state, and even the governor had a daughter enrolled there. The more prestigious University of Michigan had an even wider constituency, drawing students from around the nation. As many as 10,000 out-of-state students attended the two schools. Although the students may have been fairly stoic in the face of the threat, their parents were not. Each killing sent a ripple of fear coursing through households around the state and across the nation.

It was, moreover, an era in which young women, even in college, were assumed to be not sufficiently worldly or mature enough to take care of themselves. Parents exercised far greater control over their children's lives than at anytime since and fully expected to make most of their significant decisions for them. In the absence of parents, school administrators were to act in their stead. College was an extension of the family chrysalis in which coeds were to remain safe and chaste (or at least not pregnant) until a suitable marriage partner could be found.

Boyfriends also were expected to take care of their dates, keep them from harm, and bring them back to the dorms on time. The guardian mentality was generalized to all males and people in authority. Bartenders, as an example, would not let male patrons buy drinks for women who were not their dates. It was, quite simply, an era and an area in which there was a broader sense of responsibility for the welfare of one's fellow person. Everyone was expected to look out for others, especially women, and the vast majority of people did.

Within the prevailing ethos of the age and locale, the two universities responded in fundamentally different ways. The larger, more liberal University of Michigan with its eclectic student body tended to view coeds as adults who were capable of managing their own affairs. By contrast, Eastern reflected the conservative, midwestern, working-class attitudes of the families from which its students were drawn. Administrators at the University of Michigan were quick to realize the futility of university-imposed measures, whereas Eastern administrators acted like frightened parents, trying desperately to guard the women.

At the University of Michigan, President Robben Flemming chose not to impose restrictions on students, even after two murders in late March, since in his view the violence was not tied directly to the university. Two months later, he paid the price for the decision when University of Michigan coed Alice Kalom was the next woman killed. Called to identify the body of his daughter, an anguished Joseph Kalom stormed,

I'm not going to claim her body. I'm going to tell them (people) not to send them to this university—it's too big. They don't give a damn about anything but money and politics. I'm not going to bury her. Let them bury her on the president's lawn.

I've worked too damn hard to raise her, to send her here. I don't want her dead. She gave them enough. I gave them enough. I don't want her body. I want her alive.[8]

Even twenty-five years later it is difficult to read his words. At the time an abashed Flemming could only say, "I don't know what you can do to protect people. We can't go around taking everyone by the hand wherever they go."[9] He was right, of course, but gained little sympathy for his coldly realistic stance. A letter to the editor of the *Michigan Daily* two days later noted that the university was able to find $250,000 to put new turf in the football stadium but dragged its feet when it came to expenditures that would improve safety for students, while a second letter criticized the paper for "preserving the fiction that Ann Arbor is a safe place to live."[10]

With 25,000 female students afraid to venture out, the consequent impact on commerce in the county, particularly in Ann Arbor which had little industry other than the university, was devastating. Bars were emptied by 7:00 P.M. because women, even those with dates, wanted to be off the streets before dark. Theater traffic dropped, and girls never went to the movies alone. Stores that once thrived on nighttime business such as laundromats and pharmacies were empty. Realtors refused to talk to the media because the bad press was depressing home sales. Quantifying the magnitude of the effect, one merchant said, "I don't like to admit it, but my business is down 25 percent from last summer and summer business is always slow."[11]

Students, not unaware of their contribution to the local economy, expected the city fathers to provide services in return, or as one letter to the editor of the *Ann Arbor News* expressed it, "The vast majority of students are decent, hard-working, law-abiding and to be crass, bring money into Ann Arbor; surely they deserve more attention to their welfare than only from the police, only after murder has occurred."[12] Students felt, in this regard, that they had to unnecessarily expose themselves to danger by hitchhiking because the city was unwilling for financial reasons to provide bus services. Expounding on this theme, two University of Michigan coeds, in a second letter to the *Ann Arbor News*, wrote: "Monetary concerns have been given priority over the concern for lives, both by university and city officials."[13] In Ann Arbor and at the University of Michigan, therefore, reactions to the threat tended to be viewed in financial terms, as a quid pro quo, student business for safety expenditures.

Eastern Michigan University provided a much more sheltered environment for its students. Most importantly, school administrators viewed it as their obligation to parents to do so. Dorm curfews were commonplace to, as one dean of women put it, "provide some guidance for freshman in adjusting to college life and the responsibility of college."

But it was also an era of rapid change when students chafed under the strictures imposed from outside. Boycotts for open housing were only the most visible expressions of a more profound struggle over who had the right to control the students' lives. An indication of the extent and speed of change sweeping the campus is evidenced by the history of housing rules at Eastern:

1961   Room cleanliness checks for women

1964   Dorm key privileges for women over 21

1965   Nightly bed checks for women stopped

1966   Key privileges for juniors

1967   Key privileges for sophomores

At the time of the murders, the university was considering providing dorm keys to freshmen but only with their parents' permission since as the head advisor of one student dorm said, "I don't think as a whole, freshman can handle everything at once."[14] The university was, as always, reluctant to relinquish control.

Understandably then, the Eastern Michigan administration took a more forceful hand in security precautions. The campus police force was beefed up, extra squad cars were added, and unmarked cars patrolled the campus. Mercury vapor lights were installed, bus service was added, and the university took control of the informal ride-sharing system. Warnings were incorporated in freshman orientation, and for upperclassmen regular meetings were held in residence halls and off-campus apartments. A strict sign-in, sign-out procedure was implemented in the dorms, with coeds required to state where they were going and when they would return. Students were warned not to hitchhike, walk alone or off campus, or associate with unknown persons; they were urged to avoid dangerous places and especially to guard against an "it can't happen to me" attitude.

EMU President Harold Sponberg reminded his charges of their obligation to be concerned about their fellow students and to report absenteeism and students checking out without telling anyone where they were going. Students by and large responded to the call. Fraternities provided coed escort services. Students in ROTC or ex-servicemen were pressed into service to patrol the campus, while those with no military training were assigned to watch parking lots and remove unauthorized visitors from women's dorms. The campus paper, the *Eastern Echo*, established a tip line and offered a $5,000 reward for information leading to the arrest of the killer.

Despite the administration's best efforts to keep the students safe, it proved an impossible task. When Karen Sue Beineman, a freshman, disappeared, the crisis in confidence was complete. University enrollment suffered as a result. Although few women who were then students withdrew, in July 1969 applications to Eastern for the fall term were down 23 percent, from 5,130 to 4,175.

At the most basic level, reaction to the danger was a private matter, and for some people the most effective way to deal with the omnipresent menace was to repress thoughts about it. A grandmother wrote the *Ypsilanti Press*, objecting to the reprinting of the dead girls' pictures. The *Detroit Free Press* was taken to task by one letter writer for printing the "Anatomy of Murder" chart because, she felt, the "hideous details need not be repeated and repeated."[15] A student in Karen Sue Beinemen's residence hall described the reaction of many coeds: "A number of girls in the dorm, myself included, were unable to sleep that night and congregated in lounges on the third and fourth floors. We speculated concerning her disappearance and deliberately changed the subject."[16]

Ultimately, protection too was a matter of self-defense. Routine behavior was modified to minimize exposure to danger. Students locked their doors when they went out to empty the trash, rode bikes rather than walked, refused blind dates, and went home on weekends. Weapons were the order of the day. Women carried everything from tear gas to switch blades. As one coed said, "I always carry an ink pen to the library at night—and not just to write."[17] Hairspray and long, sharp hat pins were among the most popular items sold in drugstores, as were devices to call attention to oneself if attacked, such as whistles and flashlights.

Effective defense also meant fighting back if necessary. Newly offered classes in karate and judo were swamped with hundreds of applicants within days of opening. Knowing the limits of their own ability to protect tens of thousands of students, law enforcement officials encouraged the trend. In June 1969, as if preparing a class for a multiple-choice test, Ann Arbor Police Chief Walter Krasny recommended, "If you are accosted, scream, run, kick, all of the above."[18] By this time, all coeds realized the correct answer was D—all of the above.

KEYSTONE KOPS

Like the Boston Strangler case, the search for the coed killer was a demonstration in the limitations and frustrations of proactive police work. Try as they might and with all their might, the police could not readily find a killer who could strike at will, dispose of remains with little fear of being detected, and easily meld into the tens of thousands of students who populated the area. After each murder there would be a brief flurry of activity, but within days all leads would be exhausted and the trail grow cold again until the next murder.

If manpower and hard work were all that was required to catch the killer, he would have been apprehended early on. In all, six law enforcement agencies were drawn into the investigation, including the Ann Arbor and Ypsilanti Police, the Washtenaw County Sheriff's Department, campus police at Eastern Michigan University, and the University of Michigan and the Michigan State Police. All eighteen detectives of the seventy-man Sheriff's Department were assigned to the case. The State Police chipped in forty-five officers, and the EMU police twelve more. Investigators worked twenty-hour days; leaves and vacations were canceled for the duration.

At times it seemed as if the law enforcement agencies were trying to catch the killer by brute force. Police went door-to-door in the vicinity of several disappearances, in the process interviewing the killer without knowing it. Thousands of leads were checked, hundreds of suspects questioned, scores of lie detector tests administered. Computer databases were searched, and in perhaps the first use of the data superhighway, which then was little more than a footpath, crime prevention police installed a teletype system to keep in touch with other agencies. At the height of the crisis in July 1969, sixty police officers, including fifteen on horseback, patrolled the five-mile radius circle in which all but one of the bodies were found.

Police diligently ran to earth every viable lead they had. Jane Mixer was last seen in the company of a David Johnson. After her murder, the seventeen David Johnsons listed in the Ann Arbor area were interviewed and eliminated as suspects. Of the 200 people who attended the party at Depot House where Alice Kalom was last seen, 100 were found and questioned. After Karen Sue Beineman rode off with a stranger on a motorcycle identified as a Honda 450, police systematically checked records on the nearly 7,000 Hondas registered in the state and the 60 registered to EMU students.

And when Joan Schell was last seen entering a late-model black and red Pontiac, police stopped every similar car in sight, including one driven by an Ann Arbor city councilman who complimented the officers on the thoroughness of their investigation.

One of the disheartening aspects of the investigation was the endemic pattern of violence against women it illuminated. It was the investigators' dreary job to separate the incidents that were related to the murders from ones that were not. Police from around the nation descended with a host of similar unsolved murders, including two in New Jersey, one of which was a nineteen-year-old stabbed repeatedly and covered with leaves, a coed killed near the University of Wisconsin, Senator Charles Percy's daughter murdered near Chicago, and three murders in California, one of which probably was committed by the same killer.

Within Michigan, there were three murders in Benton Harbor, a woman raped and stabbed in Midland, a thirteen-year-old missing from Toledo and found strangled and dumped south of Ypsilanti (again probably a true connection), a thirty-three-year-old secretary whose partially nude and stabbed body was found in a grassy field near Grand Rapids, and the murder of a University of Michigan coed who was conducting research on the case for a study of violence at the Institute of Social Research. Short of murder, an attempted abduction of a coed by two men at the University of Michigan, a motiveless stabbing in a laundromat in Milan, and the kidnapping and torture of an eight-year-old in Fowlerville all had to be checked. The depressing litany went on and on.

And, of course, the case brought out its share of braggarts and compulsive confessors. The usual assortment of drunks and mentally ill volunteered their guilt. A factory worker bragged about killing the girls, as did an ex-convict in Flint and a former EMU groundskeeper who wanted to impress his girlfriend. As always, husbands and boyfriends were turned in by suspicious partners; so too was an unfortunate laborer who showed up at work with scratches on his arms. As one detective said, "Everybody has got a suspect. And everybody's a cop."[19]

The police command post was flooded with tips after each murder. Some were live, some ludicrous, all laborious. A few of the typical tips included: a coed, presumed missing, who liked to hitchhike; a peeping Tom incident that occurred ten years earlier; and a person who asked directions to the cemetery where Dawn Basom was buried. Following Miss Basom's murder alone, over 800 individual tips sheets were filled out and tracked down by police. Karen Sue Beineman was spotted on the back of motorcycles in a dozen towns from Bay City to Toledo to Windsor, Ontario. In the final days of the investigation, with public hysteria reaching its peak, calls were received at the rate of thirty per hour, a truly phenomenal outpouring in a county with only 200,000 residents.

If this sounded like the Boston Strangler investigation all over again, the most remarkable parallels were yet to come. Shortly after the third murder, the front page of the *Ann Arbor News* ran a story detailing a rent strike against owners of off-campus housing. A leader of the protestors, prominently pictured on page one, was none other than one of the principal suspects in the Boston Strangler case. A graduate student at the University of Michigan, he was known to be brilliant, with an IQ in the 155–170 range, but also to have a history of mental illness. He had been a patient in Bridgewater State Hospital, where DeSalvo was briefly held and examined, and had been diagnosed as "acutely psychotic" and a woman hater.

His picture was noticed by another player in the Strangler drama, Dr. Ames Robey. Then director of the State Center for Forensic Psychiatry at Ypsilanti State Hospital, Robey formerly had been director of Bridgewater State Hospital. In that capacity he had the opportunity to observe both DeSalvo and the new suspect, known in Gerold Frank's Book, *The Boston Strangler*, as David Parker. Robey had come to the conclusion that DeSalvo was not the Strangler but strongly suspected that Parker was. To substantiate his belief, he noted that the killings of Jane Mixer and Maralynn Skelton bore the "earmarks" of the Boston murders, specifically the stocking tied around their necks. He also recalled that once, while being examined, Parker unconsciously tied his shoes with an extra-looped half-hitch that characterized the Strangler's garrote.

Robey contacted the police immediately with his suspicions. However, after looking into the matter, police found no extra loops in the choking garments left on either of the corpses. In addition, Parker, it was determined, had not been in the area when the first murder was committed and therefore, if the murders were connected, could not be the killer. But then it occurred to the investigators that Robey knew a great deal about both sets of crimes and had moved to the area before Mary Fleszar was murdered. By discharging his civic duties, Robey made himself a prime suspect for a time.

With their own efforts proceeding slowly and without result, investigators began a series of appeals for outside help. Initially, they called on the public to provide information. Particularly galling for investigators was the fact that Joan Schell was seen entering a car with three men, only one of whom was thought to be the killer. Police could not understand why the other two would not cooperate and promised immunity and anonymity to entice the accomplices to come forward.

Sheriff Harvey asked for even broader assistance, saying: "If ever there was a time for people to get involved, now is it."[20] And get involved they did. CB radio operators set up an informal warning and observation system. The civil air patrol joined helicopters, squad cars, and a mounted posse in surveillance of likely dump sites in rural areas. After Karen Sue Beineman was last seen riding with a mystery cyclist, a local motorcycle club offered to work with witnesses to identify the type of bike.

The *Detroit News* got into the act establishing a Secret Witness program complete with rewards, a special phone number, and instructions on how to contact the paper without revealing one's identity. Secret witness tips led police to dive in the Huron River in an unsuccessful attempt to recover a murder weapon reported to have been dropped there. A news broadcast was modified, in accordance with an anonymous letter writer's instructions, in a vain attempt to communicate with the tipster who claimed the murderer had not been caught because he was "above suspicion." Total rewards offered eventually reached $43,500, a princely sum in a year when the median household income in the county was just over $12,000.

Police were not above taking help from any proven crime solver, even if the expert was something other than human and whose skills were olfactory identification. In April 1969 authorities announced that a "new crime-finding device" was entering the investigation. The "secret weapon" turned out to be two German Shepherds brought in from Philadelphia by their handler who had volunteered their services. For the dubious, the police proudly pointed to the fact that the dogs had apprehended no fewer than eight murderers in the past, and one even bore the scars from bullet wounds received in the line of duty when catching another desperado. Possibly because of the heavy rains that always seemed to accompany the murders, the dogs could not pick up a scent at the crime scenes, and so another brief, bright hope was dashed.

By June, investigators were prepared to try more traditional, albeit less colorful, experts. Chief Krasny summed up the thinking of police: "It's apparent we need a new, fresh look at the crimes. It's possible that a trained, competent criminologist can, through his expertise and training give us a new approach. I'm certainly willing to try."[21] Police found their "top-flight criminologist" in the person of Dr. Richard Ford, professor of Forensic Medicine at Harvard University and another Strangler veteran. Apparently forgotten was the fact that no expert had been instrumental in bringing the Strangler to justice.

Meanwhile, Michigan Governor William Milliken was losing faith in local enforcement efforts and attempted to involve the nation's preeminent authorities on crime, the Federal Bureau of Investigation. He appealed directly to then Attorney General John Mitchell, constructing an elaborate legal argument to show that the murders were, in fact, federal crimes. Cited as justification was evidence that at least one woman had been kidnapped and that the others undoubtedly were put in fear for their safety and were held against their will in violation of the Civil Rights Act. If this reasoning failed to sway Mitchell, Milliken offered a third rationale. He stated that the girls disappeared in the southern part of the state, close to two state borders, and hence there was ample reason to believe the killer had crossed state lines. Mitchell, unmoved, refused to assign FBI agents to the cause, offering instead to put its full analytic expertise and crime laboratory facilities at the state's disposal.

As if their standing with the community were not in enough jeopardy, the Washtenaw County Sheriff's Department, at the height of the coed killer crisis, managed to become embroiled in one of the ever-present political demonstrations of the day. On this occasion, it was a thoroughly pointless standoff with a group of rampaging teens who chose a warm, early summer night to proclaim South University, a street bordering the University of Michigan campus, "free" and express their desire to convert the area into a "people's park."

At first, University of Michigan President Robben Fleming tried to defuse the situation, but he was shouted down with obscenities and told to "shut up" not by the demonstrators but by Sheriff Harvey. The tone was set, the call to action given. Perhaps the Sheriff's Deputies were releasing the pent-up frustration of the unproductive murder investigation, or maybe they felt it was high time to reinstitute law and order on the liberal campus. Whatever the reason, what followed was a police riot akin to that in Chicago during the 1968 Democratic National Convention. The deputies simply ran amok wading into the unarmed teens, at times marching and countermarching through their own tear gas, clubbing anyone within reach—demonstrators, innocent motorists dragged from their cars, or hapless students returning from the library.

The community's reaction was swift, harsh, and double-edged. Sheriff Harvey was the lightning rod in the storm of controversy. The *Detroit Free Press*, in an editorial titled "One Dumb Cop," criticized Harvey's handling of the situation and the overreaction of the deputies. A recall petition was circulated in an effort to get the 15,000 signatures needed to remove Harvey from office; over 1,000 county residents signed on the first day. A demonstration, attended by over 100 students, against Sheriff Harvey's management of the murder investigation was held on the main diagonal of the University of Michigan campus. Just when it was most needed, the Sheriff's Department was dangerously close to losing public trust.

But there were as many supporters as detractors. Shortly after the incident "Sock it to 'em, Doug" bumper stickers began to appear. An article in the *Ann Arbor News* noted that protestors had instigated the fracas by taunting the deputies, and letters to the editor of the paper ran heavily in favor of the police. A letter to the editor of the *Ypsilanti Press* stated categorically that law and order had to prevail, while one in the *Michigan Daily* denigrated Ann Arbor radicals who, in an era of antiwar and draft protests, could find no better cause than the liberation of a thoroughfare. More to the point, an editorial in the *Ann Arbor News* chastened the demonstrators, noting, "Such diversions of police manpower obviously are not helpful to an all-out effort to end the series of tragic slayings in Washtenaw County."[22]

Then came an incident that used up the sheriff's remaining goodwill. Dr. Conrad Mason, a University of Michigan astronomy professor, happened upon Karen Sue Beineman's body as he went to pick up his morning mail.

The profoundly shaken scientist immediately called the Sheriff's Department, which, in turn, threw up an impenetrable security cordon around the site. For the next twelve hours, Sheriff Harvey kept the discovery quiet, not even notifying his colleagues and fellow investigators from the Ann Arbor Police Department. Several days later he would try to justify his actions by stating that identification of the remains was delayed because Miss Beineman's face had been so badly beaten.

In truth, the sheriff was trying to capitalize on the fact that the murderer may have revisited several dumping sites after the original disposal of remains. In a plot right out of a television police drama, the body was removed and in its place was put a nude mannequin borrowed from the store window of a nearby J.C. Penney's. Police then surrounded the area and waited for the killer's return. Almost according to script, later that night a man did walk directly to the spot, stop within touching distance of the decoy, and stand looking at it. He then bolted into the surrounding woods, with deputies hard on his heels, and simply vanished.

When word of the bungled trap leaked out, the sheriff's humiliation was complete. Not only had he violated the trust of fellow officers, but an entire troop of deputies let an unwary, surrounded suspect slip through their fingers, thereby snatching defeat from the jaws of victory. The public and the press were furious. The *Detroit Free Press* railed against Sheriff Harvey and his stewardship of the investigation in an editorial titled "Keystone Kops."

The governor had had enough. On July 30 he invoked, for the first time, a 1935 law putting the investigation under state control. Michigan State Police Director Colonel Frederick Davids took over the next day. Unbeknownst to the governor, however, an EMU police officer had already identified the killer, and sheriff's deputies were quietly building a case against him. When John Norman Collins was taken into custody one day later, on August 1, it was the governor's turn to be embarrassed. As Prosecutor Delhey said, "I regret the governor did not contact me because I could have advised him of this fact (the impending arrest). We had him (Collins) in the palm of our hands. All we needed was the crime scene."[23] Milliken had not bothered to find out what progress had been made and so to most observers looked like a man out-of-touch who had overreacted.

A GREATER FORCE

The desperation of the community seemed to bring out anyone who thought they had a special, perhaps God-given, ability to solve the crimes. As an exasperated Sheriff Harvey said, "I'm getting everything from mind readers to vision people. They're sincere but far out."[24] And indeed they were.

Letters from self-appointed psychics and soothsayers arrived from across the nation. But the police did not need to go so far afield to find extrasensory assistance, for there were plenty of volunteer clairvoyants in the county. One woman professed to have "psychic vibrations" each time a person was slain, while another said the murders were faithfully reenacted in her dreams. Ann Arbor Police Captain Walter Hawkins received a tip that Karen Sue Beineman could be found tied to a tree. Arriving at the designated spot, Hawkins instead found two teenagers wandering in a wooded area searching with a flashlight where their "psychic talents" told them to look for the body. The two psychic samaritans admitted to having made the call to police in the first place.

A Chicago postal worker and part-time astrologer was certain there was a celestial pattern waiting to be uncovered in the crimes. In a letter to the *Ann Arbor News* he observed that he had assiduously studied "various astrological combinations that might influence the killer at birth." Guided by the stars, the seer was able to zero in on several birth dates with the greatest potential to have spawned a serial killer. In a slightly more earthbound moment, he was forced to confess: "Logic compels me to admit the odds are against the real killer being in the group."

Like the weird coincidences that have been postulated to mystically join the Kennedy and Lincoln assassinations, people saw cryptic connections between the murders, which were often tenuous at best. In this regard, it was pointed out that Karen Sue Beineman lived in Downing Hall and that Jane Mixer's body had been placed at the base of a headstone that read "Downing, William C. 1882–1943." This seems like grasping at straws now, but then, in the mystery of the moment, it appeared to have deep relevance.

At the same time half a continent away, two mass murders were committed in quick succession, complete with apocalyptic messages written in blood. With the local murders coming in rapid order, the Tate–LaBianca murders seemed to provide further evidence that evil was "going to and fro in the earth and walking up and down on it." So when Peter Hurkos suggested that the coed murders might be the sadistic initiation rite of a "blood cult," the idea tapped a wellspring of fear in the supernatural and seemed to resonate in the popular imagination.

And if the devil might be behind the murders after all, it only stood to reason that deliverance would come from divine intervention. Following the Kalom killing in June, proselytizing letters to the editor began to appear that catalogued the virtues and power of prayer. In one letter to the *Ann Arbor News*,[25] the writer took as a point of departure the headline from a news article, entitled "Murder Probe Begins to Stall"; the author asked rhetorically, "What could the re-action of a Christian be to these words?" Leaving nothing to chance, he answered for the reader, "All agree that in an extremity we are to seek God's guidance and help. There probably are not only one or two, but hundreds upon hundreds or even thousands upon thousands of Christians here in Ann Arbor who would be willing to make this a matter of prayer." If so, the author promised, "It may be that such prayer on our part, 'pray for your enemies,' converts him that he sees the evil of his ways and comes to true repentance, and confesses and is willing to accept his just temporal rewards for his deeds. It could also be that God trips him up so that he is brought to justice and has time for repentance. Thus his soul might be saved." Then like a spiritual salesman, the writer ticked off other product benefits of prayer, pointing out that anyone who prayed would have "less fear of the evil-doer" and that collective appeals to the most high would lend moral support to the police.

Another writer, Baptist minister S. L. Roberson, preferred intensive rather than extensive prayer.[26] He suggested that everyone begin praying at noon, noting, "If we can get people to really pray—men, women, and even children—it will be a mighty force." Of course, it would not do just to go through the motions; the altruistic appeal had to spring from true belief: "If the Christians in our community would go into sincere prayer for the apprehension of this individual, it might bring this man to justice."

With such spiritual undercurrents in the collective psyche rising to the surface, when it came time to establish a unified command post to direct the multi-agency investigation, known colloquially as "murder central," it was not surprising that the site chosen was the Holy Ghost Seminary. As Reverend Roberson put it, "This has come to the point where we have to ask a greater force for help."

In the last manifestation of the appeal to a higher authority for meaning and salvation, the senseless slaughter of innocent children was seen as having a larger purpose. Marjorie Beineman, living every parent's unspeakable nightmare, was convinced her daughter had been "sent" to her fate to save others: "God must have sent Karen to find the killer. That could be the only reason."[27] The only solace a grieving mother could find was refuge in the belief that her daughter's sacrifice was according to God's plan, a divine purpose that would spare others.

THE PSYCHIC DETECTIVE

Prayers, amateur astrologers, homegrown psychics, cosmic connections— nothing worked. But, of course, nothing yet tried had the proven powers of Peter Hurkos, the psychic detective. There was talk of bringing Hurkos in to help find the killer as early as June 1968, following the murder of Joan Schell. When the next two murders occurred within days of each other in March of the following year, the calls for Hurkos' intervention were unceasing.

Much of the demand for Hurkos' involvement in the case stemmed from his presumed role in the Boston Strangler investigation. As related in the preceding chapter, Hurkos developed a stunningly detailed profile of the strangler, and police were amazed when they determined that they had a suspect who fit the description exactly. But after DeSalvo's dramatic confession, Hurkos's suspect was quickly forgotten, and his credibility as a crime solver was badly damaged. Nevertheless, throughout the remainder of his life Hurkos steadfastly insisted that he had identified the right man and that DeSalvo was not the Strangler.

Although any number of Boston authorities would agree with his conclusion regarding DeSalvo, they were much less charitable about Hurkos' role in the hunt for the Strangler. When he learned that Hurkos might come to Ann Arbor, Massachusetts Assistant Attorney General John Bottomly offered a scathing critique of his contribution. Interestingly, however, his comments also contained a large measure of ambivalence that typified most assessments of Hurkos's capabilities.

He was no help in the Boston Strangler case, that's for sure. He's unreliable and won't keep his word; you can't depend on him. And some of the things reported in the Boston Strangler book that have to do with him just aren't true.

But some of them are, and I have seen myself him do things that I can't explain by what we now know about extrasensory perception. The man is unusual. I'm sure of that, and he's something different from the rest of us.[28]

Despite such negative appraisals, the popular perception was that Hurkos had been instrumental in solving the case and, by implication, he could do it again in Ann Arbor.

But if Hurkos truly did have psychic powers, it should have been possible to demonstrate them under controlled conditions. Hurkos claimed that he had, in fact, done just that in a hospital in Maine. However, when given the opportunity to be tested at the well-respected Parapsychology Institute at Duke University, he refused. He did agree to a test on the West Coast under the auspices of a parapsychology research group headed by faculty members from Stanford and the University of California at Davis. Stanford Humanities professor Dr. Jeffrey Smith summarized the results of the test, again with characteristic ambivalence:

Mr. Hurkos' abilities were not statistically demonstrated during our rigid, impersonal laboratory examinations. This was very disappointing to us because I am extremely impressed with his extra-sensory abilities. There is no question to me that he has very great psychic abilities, indeed.

Of course he is an excellent showman and he is a shrewd psychologist who uses all manner of verbal devices to elicit information from his subjects. But over and above this, after I discount the showman and entertainer, I am left with too many graphic demonstrations of knowledge he has had to acquire psychically.[29]

Like the citizens of Washtenaw County, Dr. Smith wanted to believe.

For their part the police were not terribly enthusiastic about the prospect of Hurkos joining the investigation, but they were in no position to refuse help from any quarter, especially one that enjoyed such popular support.

Consequently, they assumed a neutral posture, as this excerpt from an interview with Ann Arbor Police Chief Krasny and Deputy Chief Olson printed in the *Ann Arbor News* on March 27, 1969 indicates:

Q: At one time during the initial stages of the Schell investigation, there was talk of bringing in Peter Hurkos, the man who reportedly helped police locate the so-called "Boston Strangler." Could Hurkos' powers of concentration through which he supposedly is able to tell people about obscure items in their personal lives help in this case? Would you accept his help?

A: This of course is a police investigation but we certainly would not refuse help— if it's genuine help—from any source. There's no real way of knowing if a man of Hurkos' talents could be used in this type of thing. We certainly are willing to talk with anyone.[30]

County Prosecutor Delhey, who was not yet on the hook to convict the killer, was a bit more caustic in his appraisal of Hurkos' potential role in the investigation. "I, myself, don't believe in fortune tellers, soothsayers or clairvoyants. If I were paying his fee you'd have change for a nickel,"[31] he said. When it was clear that Hurkos would in fact join the effort to find the killer, he added, "Let's just say we're not rolling out any red carpet for him."[32]

Bringing Hurkos to Ann Arbor turned out to be something of a conjuring trick in its own right. He was originally approached by a "citizen's committee" led by a local real estate salesman, Archie Allen. The committee consisted of "hippies, radicals and young Ann Arborites" attached to a local group known as the Psychedelic Rangers (it was the 60's after all). At the outset of negotiations for his services, Hurkos requested a fee of $2,500 plus $600 for traveling expenses. While some thought the amount exorbitant, Allen saw the situation differently: "For this type of service you can't put a price on it."[33]

The Psychedelic Rangers then went about the task of raising the necessary funds. After a public appeal for donations, however, they received only two contributions, each for $5. On hearing the news, Hurkos canceled his plans to come to the city. Two days later an anonymous source pledged $1,000. In the interim, not wanting to miss such a high-profile murder case and perhaps wanting to recoup some lost prestige after the Boston Strangler experience, Hurkos too had a change of heart. He agreed to come and would do so at no cost, asking only to be reimbursed for expenses.

Hurkos arrived at Detroit Metropolitan airport on July 21, 1969 with psychic vita in hand. Among his purported accomplishments, Hurkos listed the solution of twenty-seven murders in seventeen countries. To further establish his credentials, he passed out a bibliography to the attending media containing eighteen citations in which his feats were discussed. Thoroughly smitten, the media trumpeted the good news: the "wizard" had come to expose the killer.

As was his usual method, Hurkos began by reviewing pictures of the murder scenes in closed envelopes and recreating the murders. His reconstructions were so faithful that, again as usual, he began to make converts of a skeptical police force, for example:

Lt. Fuller, EMU Police: "He made observations that I don't think he could have made except for having some kind of special power."[34]

Lt. Mulholland, Washtenaw Country Sheriff: "He's making me a believer."[35]

Chief Krasny, Ann Arbor Police: "The guy has got something. You can't run away from it."[36]

Others remained doubtful, noting that many of the facts Hurkos provided were already in the public domain, having appeared in the press.

As the investigation continued, Hurkos increased his posturing, providing frequent updates on his progress through his sometime bodyguard, spokesman, and publicity agent Ed Silver. Always conscious to manicure the mystique, Silver told a breathless public that Hurkos was so totally caught up in his work that he had gone all day without eating and slept only fitfully. A break in the case was promised daily. Silver announced, "We feel we can tie up the Basom case today or tomorrow," but as tomorrow passed was forced to recant. Once Silver proclaimed Hurkos had made "remarkable progress" and had given the police the name of the killer, and he said the officers were "amazed." Sounding anything but, Chief Krasny retorted, "Hurkos did give us a name which we will treat no differently from five or six names we receive in the mail every day."[37]

Right from the start, Hurkos positioned his involvement as a titanic struggle between good and evil, brain power versus psychic power, intelligence pitted against his gift. Almost immediately he described the killer as a "genius," one who was running the police in circles. "He's playing with the police, just playing with them. He thinks he's smarter than anyone else."[38] But, Hurkos assured the frightened public, the killer would make a mistake that would lead to his capture and, of course, only he—Peter Hurkos—would be perceptive enough to see it when it happened. Not only would this be a battle between two gifted adversaries, but also it would be a fight to the death. Hurkos aggrandized his involvement by suggesting that he too might be at risk of personal harm. "After I explain what he looks like, he may go after me. I am not afraid. I will stay here until I find the key. I am certain I will find it."[39]

Interestingly, the killer seems to have taken up the challenge. Two days after arriving, Hurkos received a call telling him to get out of town before he was responsible for another murder. There is evidence also that John

Norman Collins went to Hurkos' hotel and tried to obtain a table near Hurkos so he could eavesdrop on his conversations. Friends recalled that Collins joked derisively about Hurkos, calling him a fraud.

Within a week of his arrival, a tall young man in a turquoise shirt handed the desk clerk in Hurkos' hotel a note telling Hurkos to investigate a cabin on Weed Road where he would find "something interesting." The site was near where bodies had been discovered, and when he examined the message Hurkos said he had a "feeling" about it. With hopes up, police sped to the spot but were unable to locate a cabin. Hurkos meanwhile backpedaled, saying he did not see a body but might see one later. Peter Hurkos was being taunted too.

Immediately after the Weed Road incident, Hurkos raised the stakes by publicly challenging the murderer. In a television interview on July 27, Hurkos said he was beginning to visualize the killer and predicted an arrest would come soon. Then personalizing the battle even more, Hurkos said he hoped the killer was listening. But at nearly the same time as the broadcast, the coed killer picked up his next and last victim.

The bizarre disappearance of Karen Sue Beineman was interpreted in many quarters as a personal challenge to Hurkos. Chief Krasny, moreover, suggested that the Beineman kidnapping would be the real test of Hurkos' power since nothing had yet been printed about it, and it was not immediately known if she was dead. When given a picture of Miss Beineman, however, Hurkos admitted lamely that it provided no vibrations. He did say he felt strongly that Miss Beineman had met foul play—but, by this time the city did not need a psychic detective to tell them the likely implications of her disappearance.

Hurkos did predict that Miss Beineman's body would be found by a roadway named Riverview or River Drive. Several days later it was found in a ditch running alongside Huron River Drive. It had been flung like a gauntlet within one mile of both "murder central" and Peter Hurkos' hotel. Upon learning that the body had been discovered, Hurkos began striking himself in the face with a clenched fist shouting, "Her face was beat, beat, beat. It was wrinkled, like a monkey face,"[40] and then he described the disposal site perfectly.

Hurkos left Ann Arbor the next day, returning to his home in Los Angeles where he continued to maintain that he was close to solving the case and would return soon to wrap it up. He planned to return to the city in the first week of August, but his visit was upstaged by the killer's arrest. His involvement ended as it began, in a whirlwind of boasts, descriptions, and predictions. It had been a lot of sound and fury—but had it signified nothing?

In the aftermath of the arrest, the citizens of Washtenaw County, like the people of Boston before them, tried to figure out what to make of Hurkos.

Two weeks after John Norman Collins was taken into custody, the *Detroit Free Press* printed a summation that could apply to both cases equally well:

In assessing Peter Hurkos' role in the Washtenaw County murders, it would be unfair to the police to say that he provided possible solutions to them. But it would be equally unfair to Hurkos to say he was a liability either. His part in the investigation—like his strange ability itself—is impossible to explain.[41]

At one time or another throughout his stay, Hurkos described the killer as: a genius who had not had much formal education, a sick homosexual, a man who dressed as a woman, one who wore a bra, someone who played with dolls and stuffed animals, a member of a blood cult consisting of three to five hippies and drug addicts, a daytime salesman, a person who had held a variety of jobs, and someone who hung around garbage dumps and picked up articles. As for physical features, he said the killer was 5'6" or 5'7", 136–146 lbs., 25–26 years old, blond, and baby-faced. He predicated further that the murder count would reach 19 and that a Negro or Spanish woman would be killed west of Ann Arbor. In all, Hurkos made 60 descriptive statements, some of which proved true, some false, and the vast majority unprovable either way.

As events unfolded, observers typically remembered only the predictions that fit the facts, thereby confirming their faith. After the case was successfully resolved, they also tended to interpret Hurkos' prognostications so they would conform to the facts. Hurkos once said that a body had been left by a bridge; authorities noted there was a culvert nearby. He predicted that another body lay beside a short ladder; believers pointed out that it was discovered in a ruined farm house, the cellar stairs of which were broken in half. It was hard not to be right when given such a wide tolerance for error. Thus, one's assessment of Hurkos' ability ultimately rested on faith—you either had it or you didn't.

If, decades later, we try to assess the contribution of Peter Hurkos in the two cases, it is clear that his predictions of future events were most often wildly inaccurate. Conversely, his description of past events when he came in contact with evidence from them could be insightful and precise. Over the years he impressed too many analytical, skeptical, and sober witnesses for one to write off his talents as purely showmanship. But he also provided no substantive help in the solution of either the Boston Strangler or Coed Killer cases. With respect to the latter, the only clairvoyant turned out to be Sheriff Harvey, who concluded, "I think these murders will be solved with good old-fashioned policework."[42]

TWO FOOLISH THINGS

With the investigation grinding on without success and Peter Hurkos equally powerless to find the killer, investigators and the public inevitably turned their attention to the victim–killer relationship. How had the killer enticed his victims? Why had they gone with him? Ann Arbor Police Chief Krasny summed up the puzzlement of the police: "One of the things that bothers us the most is how the killer is making contact and getting these girls into his car."[43] The climate of bewilderment was compounded by the fact that the killer seemed to take new victims to demonstrate his prowess and dispose of them to illustrate his invincibility.

The first killings created little cognitive dissonance for the community. Mary Fleszar disappeared before the threat was known, Jane Mixer and Joan Schell advertised for rides, and Maralynn Skelton "ran with fast company." But by April 1969 the danger was established beyond question, the investigation was in full swing, and protective measures and warnings were ubiquitous. And still, the killer was able to pick women off the streets with ease. The community simply could not understand how it could continue. A sample of quotes about the last three victims tells the story best,

Basom: Neighbors wondered how Miss Basom's killer was able to lure or overpower her. They spoke of her as a strong young girl and as an obedient one. "I don't think Dawn would have gotten into the car with any older person. She was well disciplined by her mother."[44]

Kalom: Why would a girl leave her apartment—to go anywhere—without her purse. Even on a trip to the corner store the purse would be taken. But we found no sign of a struggle.[45]

Beineman: Detectives still are puzzling about Miss Beineman's actions in accepting a ride on a motorcycle from a young man she apparently knew only slightly.[46]

Initially, the reasons given for the victims' strange acquiescence were built on a plausible foundation. People hypothesized that the victims knew the killer, that he used a pistol, drew a knife, or was disguised as a policeman. Great significance was read into the fact that heavy rains often accompanied a disappearance or the discovery of a body. It was suggested that women might be more willing to accept rides then, or that the bad weather depressed the killer who then sought out females, or on a more utilitarian level, that rain washed away clues. The killer was thought to have an accomplice; it could be two men, a man with a woman acting as a decoy or, for that matter, two women. One person suggested that a sadistic couple was at fault because it would take more than one person to hold the victim while they were being tortured, because a girl was more likely to enter a car with a couple than a single man, and, finding importance in the fact that several victims were molested but not raped, "because her murder served to arouse sexual excitement in a couple and not satisfy it in a madman."[47]

It was the Karen Sue Beineman murder that put these speculations to rest for good and moved the discussion to a different plane, one on which the killer became all powerful. When the facts were known, it could never be argued that Karen Beineman was unaware of the ambient risks or that she had gone unwillingly with her kidnapper after a struggle.

Karen Beineman knew full well the potential danger she was exposing herself to by coming to Ypsilanti, and she took steps to minimize it. Her parents tried to talk her out of attending Eastern Michigan because of the murders, but she chose the school over Central Michigan when she received a scholarship. Taking no chances, she sent her tuition in early to be assured of a room on the second floor of the dorm. During freshman orientation, which she had just finished, entering coeds were routinely warned about the killings and told how to protect themselves. Signs in her dormitory admonished the residents, "Don't Go Out Alone." She joked with friends that because of her diminutive size, 5'1" and 96 lbs., she would have a football player escort her around campus. She once advised a friend not to go on a blind date because the man could be the killer. When an article about the murders was published in the campus newspaper, the *Eastern Echo*, Karen sent a clipping of it to her parents with a note that read "Don't Worry, I'm Careful."

By all accounts, Karen was not the kind of person who would be easily duped or take unnecessary or frivolous chances. Her boyfriend referred to her as "a cautious, smart, good girl," while others described her as "shrewd, mature, sensible, not scatterbrained." She was a serious student who volunteered to work in a Head Start program and intended to major in special education. Always dependable, she never missed curfew. Friends said Karen was realistic when it came to others, that she could tell if someone was real or put on. But they also said she could be gullible and too trusting, and as things turned out, perhaps fatally so.

All of these facts, actions, and personality traits suggested Karen Sue Beineman would be the last person in the world one would think could be vulnerable to the coed killer. For precisely these reasons then, her behavior on the last day of her life is so incongruous. The last time she was seen alive she had just alit from the back of a motorcycle driven by a tall, handsome young man wearing a green EMU T-shirt and entered a store, "Wigs by Joan," on the main street in downtown Ypsilanti. Her male companion waited outside on the bike.

Inside the store she purchased a wiglet or fall. She told the shopkeeper she intended to wear it at a friend's wedding the next weekend. Karen was in an ebullient mood and before leaving said to the proprietress, Joan Goshe, "I'm the bravest customer you've had today. I've only done two foolish things in my life: buy a wig and accept a ride on a motorcycle from a stranger."[48] But if Karen did not perceive the threat, Miss Goshe did. She tried to persuade Karen against accompanying the man. When that failed, she left her store, went to the street, and watched the pair ride off. In her mind's eye, Joan Goshe took down a detailed description of the rider and his machine.

To this day, Karen Sue Beineman's motives are impenetrable, as incomprehensible now as they were then. But now her actions are a curiosity, an anomaly to be studied; at the time, they represented a real and indefensible threat. If someone as aware of her surroundings and as level-headed and dependable as Karen Sue Beineman would go willingly with the killer, then no one was safe. The darkest suspicions of the community were confirmed: the killer could indeed strike with ease and impunity. The community had to defend itself against this starkly demonstrated reality. There had to be a reason for what had happened.

In most of the cases reviewed here, the reactions of the community can be discerned only from what survives in the public record. Having lived through this experience, I can personally attest that what was published in the local papers, though accurately indicative of the public mood, was only the smallest fraction of the popular sentiment. After Karen Sue Beineman went seemingly in league with her killer, preoccupation with the murders was total, they were never far from our thoughts, and they crept into nearly every conversation.

Everyone had a theory of who the killer was and how he or they evaded the police. Slowly, but inexorably, the explanations began to center on the killer. People were baffled by the killer's uncanny ability to seduce his victims; he simply had to have special powers. I can recall quite vividly, as an example, a conversation with an acquaintance who speculated that the mystery cyclist could hypnotize women on the spot and make them come quietly with him to their demise. The longer the killings went on, the wilder the speculation became, and the greater the killer's omnipotence became in the eyes of the townspeople.

Even the professional argot that reporters adopted to refer to the killer began to use superhuman terms. In an article printed in the *Detroit News* on July 28, 1969, under the headline "7th Co-ed Slaying Mocks Police," the killer was described as "fiendishly clever," "the slender cyclist" who "vanished like a phantom."[49] Inexplicable events and the failure to stop the crimes by rational or superhuman means cried out for an explanation. The only remaining place to find it was in the extraordinary capabilities of the killer.

Transference reached its logical culmination in a special article in the *Detroit News* on July 31, 1969, written by Al Blanchard and titled "Washtenaw Slayer's Secret."[50] The author began with the question that was on everyone's mind, "Why in light of the cautions raised by the nature of the previous crimes, is the killer so able to win a new victim?" Searching for an answer, Blanchard then succinctly outlined the operative mechanism of transference: "apparently, something in the make-up of the killer . . . despite what reservations might exist within them . . . causes these young victims to accompany him trustingly to their deaths."

In this regard, Blanchard noted that the actions of the Boston Strangler, the most celebrated serial murder case to that time, paled by comparison with the coed killer. The Strangler sought out victims, finding them in the privacy and presumed security of their homes. The Boston women had no complicity in their deaths. "But here we have something else. In each case, it would seem that the victim willingly joined her murderer." The Washtenaw County killer was therefore all the more powerful.

But what was the source of his allure? Blanchard had the answer: "The crime always is done in the open, so to speak. Somehow, this murderer has an attraction that entices his victims to accompany him." Having articulated the last stage of the emotional transformation of public opinion, the search for meaning, Blanchard underscored the point with another in the cascade of questions, "Who is this man, who is so attractive that young women will go with him, seemingly a stranger who approaches in the midst of a rash of murders?" Miasmal magnetism, lethal charisma, fatal charm, however it was labeled, it was an immanent quality of the killer.

Where these ruminations might then have led we will never know because John Norman Collins was arrested the next day.

MANNERS GALORE

John Norman Chapman was born on June 17, 1947 in Windsor, Ontario. His parents were divorced when he was a child, and subsequently he and his mother moved to Center Line, Michigan, a suburb of Detroit. His mother Loretta remarried several years later, and John, who had a good relationship with his stepfather, took his last name, Collins. Such details, on the surface not important, would have significance thirty-five years later.

Nearly all references to Collins were prefaced with the adjective "All-American Boy," and he did seem to have come from central casting. In Center Line, John attended St. Clemens High School and by all indications was a big man on campus. As an honor student, his caption in the school yearbook referred to his thoughtful bent: "Inquisitive, intellect explores the unknown, seeks logical solutions." Collins was also an all-round athlete. He lettered all four years in three sports, was a star pitcher for the baseball team and a tri-captain of the football team where he was known as a "real fighter on the field," and was president of the C-Club for lettermen.

Socially, Collins was equally adept. He dated regularly and was noted for his "eye-catching dancing ability." After his arrest, those who knew Collins described him as "nice," "polite," "normal," a person who "always showed respect," who had "manners galore" and always opened doors for women and elders. Good looks, athletic ability, intelligence, and impeccable manners turned out to be a killer combination.

His career at Eastern Michigan was more of the same. Collins transferred to the university in 1966, ten months before Mary Fleszar disappeared, because of its reputation as a teachers college. After graduation, he planned to teach upper elementary grades in public school. At Eastern Collins was considered a good student, was vice president of the university ski club, played intramural sports, and was a member of Theta Chi fraternity. As in high school, he was socially active and dated several women, one of whom once told him that he looked like the composite drawing of the killer.

But there was also a darker side. In high school he was described as a person with unusual tastes, who dressed with a flair so as to stand out in a crowd. He was known to be moody, and a high school girlfriend remembered that, though not vicious, he was "mad most of the time." Once angered, she recalled, he stayed mad and refused to talk. At Eastern Collins was considered a loner and a person who liked riding motorcycles more than he liked girls. In retrospect, several of the coeds who went out with him remembered Collins as sexually aggressive. He also left the fraternity under a cloud, ostensibly because he did not pay his dues, but in reality because other members suspected him to be the person responsible for a string of petty thefts that plagued the house.

Collins' identification as the coed killer and apprehension were the result of dogged police fieldwork that was nearly undone at the last moment by his disarming All-American Boy demeanor. The first step involved an EMU security guard, Larry Mathewson, who noted the resemblance between Collins and the composite drawing of the killer. This in its own right was not necessarily significant, for as Colonel Davids once said, "We found some who look like they posed for that picture."[51] Mathewson, however, remembered that Collins also owned a motorcycle.

As a matter of routine then, detectives went to his house, but Collins was not there and did not return for two days. In the interim, investigators learned that Collins had been a member of Theta Chi fraternity. At the next stop, they learned from fraternity brothers the name of one of Collins' old girlfriends whom they then visited. Amazingly, on the day Karen Sue Beineman disappeared, the former girlfriend had seen Collins riding his motorcycle on the same block, at roughly the same time, dressed as witnesses said the mystery cyclist was dressed. Things were heating up. Detectives asked the woman if she had a picture of Collins, and she was able to produce one showing him posing next to a Christmas tree. The police then took the picture to the wig shop. When Joan Goshe saw it, she exclaimed, "That's him." The process was methodical and not very dramatic, but it worked.

Collins was taken in for questioning on Sunday, July 27. He was interrogated at length and was cooperative throughout—so much so, in fact, that investigators were beginning to lose interest in Collins as a suspect. He even agreed to take a lie detector test, but since facilities were not available then, an appointment was made for testing the following day. When detectives arrived to pick up Collins at the designated hour, however, they were met by his attorney who said Collins was no longer willing to submit to the lie detector test and who subsequently admonished the police either to arrest Collins or leave. Lacking incontrovertible proof, the officers departed.

Coincidentally on Tuesday, July 29, Collins' uncle, David Leik, a corporal on the State Police force, returned to his home in Ypsilanti from a vacation in northern Michigan. Leik and Collins were quite close, and while they vacationed John had been given keys to the house so he could feed the family dog. When they returned, Leik and his wife, Loretta Collins' sister, noticed "things not as they should be" in the basement. In particular, there were paint spots on the floor as if someone had used a spray can. Underneath the paint were black spots, which turned out to be blood that matched Karen Sue Beineman's type. One of the spots also preserved a fingerprint of John Norman Collins.

On Thursday, July 31, Collins was again picked up, and this time was booked for the murder of Karen Sue Beineman. There was, in addition, evidence tying him to several of the other murders. Although his car had been cleaned thoroughly, blood and hair matching Alice Kalom's were found in the trunk. Collins often visited fraternity brothers who lived in an Ann Arbor apartment across the hall from a unit frequented by Maralynn Skelton. A fellow rider placed Collins in the car that picked up Joan Schell and stated further that the two had plans to get together after the other men were let out. Trying to provide a reason why the witness had not come forward sooner, Chief Krasny said, "I believe it is a case of 'wheels beginning to spin' and the person who knows he was in a car with Collins and picked up a girl now believes the girl might have been Schell."[52] Not only was Collins a neighbor of Mary Fleszar but also he had an office across the hall from hers in a university department where they were both employees. Finally, there was considerable evidence connecting Collins with the murder of seventeen-year-old Roxie Phillips who had been strangled, raped, and dumped on a lovers lane in Salinas, California.

Prosecutors elected to proceed with their best case since, as an Ypsilanti policeman put it, "If the court acquits Collins of this murder we'll charge him with another. Or if Collins is sent away for 20 years when he gets out he can then be charged with another murder."[53] After the longest trial in Washtenaw County history, involving fifty-seven witnesses, seventeen days of testimony, and twenty-seven hours of jury deliberation over three days, John Norman Collins was convicted of first degree murder in the death of Karen Sue Beineman. Upon learning of the verdict, the victim's mother said, "God was on the jury. I'm convinced that he was the main member of the jury."[54]

Collins refused to testify in his own defense at the trial but before sentencing told the court that he had not murdered or ever even met Miss Beineman. Significantly, he chose a forum for his protestation of innocence that did not allow cross-examination. He received the mandatory sentence under state law of life in prison without parole to be served in "solitary confinement at hard labor" and was immediately transferred to the Southern Michigan State Prison in Jackson where he became prisoner #126833.

In the years following, Collins tried unsuccessfully to obtain a new trial. Each of the three appeals, including the last before the Michigan Supreme Court, determined that the original trial had been fair and so allowed the verdict to stand.

The State of California began proceedings to extradite Collins to stand trial for the murder of Roxie Phillips. However, the effort was abandoned in 1972 because, according to the Monterey County district attorney, the case did not warrant priority attention. Michigan officials who helped build the California case were angered by the decision. Prosecutor Delhey commented, "If this was a minor crime, a larceny or something like it, they might be justified. But murder is an extremely different ball game. If nothing else I think their timing is poor."[55] Sheriff Harvey saw a more crass motive: "Apparently they're balancing a human life against money and the money wins out."[56]

Having exhausted the normal avenues to win release, Collins tried several more creative strategies. On at least four occasions he attempted to break out of prison, once by tunneling, or was found with contraband, including a hack saw, drill bit, and 27–foot rope. In 1981 he legally rechanged his name to Chapman and, thus disguised, applied to be transferred to a Canadian prison under provisions of a 1978 treaty permitting citizens of either the United States or Canada to serve out their sentences in their home country. Significantly, under Canadian law Collins would have been eligible for parole fifteen years from the date of his conviction, in August 1985.

The authorizing paperwork was signed and the transfer only days away when a fellow prisoner wrote the *Detroit Free Press* and blew Collins' cover. The resulting newspaper story on January 15, 1982 was retold in thirty-three newspapers and on eighty-five radio and television stations across Michigan. On January 20 the Michigan Department of Corrections abrogated the transfer order. An outraged Loretta Collins responded, "It's politics, dirty politics. John's hopes were raised, then they slammed the door in his face. It's inhuman."[57] Somehow a little inhumanity seemed appropriate for the coed killer.

EPILOGUE

After the trial, Sheriff Douglas Harvey was voted out of office and began a second career as a truck driver. Peter Hurkos, the psychic detective, played himself in the movie *Now I Lay Me Down to Sleep* about the coed killer case. He died of heart failure in 1988 at the age of 77. No tip to the Secret Witness program ever identified Collins as the murderer, and, although Joan Goshe attempted to claim the funds, no reward money was paid to anyone.

Collins remains in prison, spending twenty-three hours a day in a 7 by 12 foot cell. He busies himself with correspondence, mostly to women, and receives three visitors a month, also female. His most frequent visitor is

Reverend Marlene Thompson of Sister Dora's National and International Church of Love. Collins' power to spellbind apparently still intact, Reverend Thompson is convinced he is innocent.

So how then did John Norman Collins lure women to their deaths? In the days following the arrest, it was learned that four other EMU coeds had been offered a ride on a motorcycle by a young man they did not know. All were approached in the same area where Karen Sue Beineman was last seen alive, on the same day and at the same time. After one woman spurned the motorcycle rider, he reportedly became angry and said, "What's the matter? Do you think I'm the killer?" Four women, it seems, narrowly escaped death at the hands of a man who simply offered rides to anyone he passed until someone said yes. It was no more magical or mysterious than that.

The Media and the Murderer

DAVID RICHARD BERKOWITZ: THE SON OF SAM
New York, New York (1976–1977)

"He who would be God with the lives of young women can also use his great power to direct the newspapers to write what he wants and when he wants it."
—Jimmy Breslin
The Daily News, July 28, 1977

On November 8, 1993 the first of three interviews with David Berkowitz was broadcast on the television magazine "Inside Edition." During the segment Berkowitz revealed that while he had been present at all of the "Son of Sam" shootings he was not the executioner in every case. He further suggested that police were aware others were involved in the murders. "I did not pull the trigger at every single one of them. And, I believe the police know that,"[1] he said.

For the first time Berkowitz confirmed what had long been suspected: the Son of Sam murders that transfixed New York City residents in 1976 and 1977 were not entirely the work of a lone, psychotic gunman but rather involved a conspiracy. And yet, the reaction to this potentially startling declaration was virtually nonexistent. The *New York Times*, as an example, carried only a small article about the program on the second page of the Metro Section. The inescapable conclusion was that, while David Berkowitz could still make the news with his pronouncements, he had long since ceased to be news.

Perhaps no serial murderer before or since has been such a complete creation of the press as David Berkowitz, the Son of Sam. During 1976 and 1977 New York City averaged 1,600 homicides and over 40,000 aggravated assaults per year. David Berkowitz contributed minimally to the total, killing just six people and wounding seven others in eight separate attacks over a thirteen-month period. His actions therefore represented only one in every 300 murders and one in 6,000 nonfatal assaults. And yet, his exploits captured the imagination of the city. The record of his deeds filled the tabloids and made headlines day after day.

Media interest in rare, inexplicable, and violent events is, of course, to be expected. After all, man bites dog is still news, as are plane crashes, wars, and natural disasters. But what sets serial murder apart is the interaction between the psychology of the killer and the commercial imperatives of the press. Serial murderers have particular motivations, needs, and means of obtaining gratification that are abetted by media attention.

Serial murderers are not a uniform lot: several distinctly different types can be identified based on their personality dynamics and modus operandi. One type, Organized killers, most closely approximates the popular conception of a serial murderer. Crimes committed by this group are characterized by careful planning, controlled execution, and concerted efforts to avoid detection. The underlying motivation of the Organized serial killer is to perpetuate the gratification derived from the murders by reliving them and escaping arrest to kill again.

Central to the psychological makeup of the Organized killer is the role fantasy plays in the repetitive nature of the crimes. The killer has a mental image of the perfect murder, and each killing is an attempt to realize the ideal. Reality never quite matches the fantasy, however, and another murder is always needed to attempt to reach the goal. Between murders, the fantasy is the killer's principal source of gratification, and extravagant measures are taken to hold on to and prolong it. One common means Organized killers use to relive the events and fill the fantasy is to keep personal items of the victims as souvenirs or trophies.

The media too act as a fantasy enabler and therefore as a catalyst for future murders. Organized killers frequently follow the murder investigation as it is reported in the press and may keep clippings of stories they find especially exciting. Typical of the type, David Berkowitz exhibited an extraordinarily intense interest in his portrayal in the press. As psychiatrist David Abrahamsen recalled after his capture, "He was so controlled and so eager to find out the latest news about himself that he even asked Detective Fox if he would be getting the day's newspapers."[2] Berkowitz was not allowed to see the papers, and in so doing the police may unwittingly have inflicted a punishment more onerous than incarceration.

While Berkowitz's use of the media to fulfill his fantasies was not out of the ordinary, his manipulation of the media was. Most Organized murderers are control oriented, with the ultimate control being the ability to decide between life and death for another person. In Berkowitz's case, the need for control extended to a community level. As serial murder expert Robert Ressler observed: "He liked the idea of becoming notorious, and that was why he communicated with the police and, later, directly with the newspapers.

The power that he held over the city, and over the sale of newspapers, was stupendous, and very exciting for him."[3] Berkowitz exercised control by toying with the emotions of the citizens of New York, and his ego was fed by the fear and anxiety that resulted. Therefore, the media played a dual role for the Son of Sam, acting as both a means for Berkowitz to keep his fantasies alive and as an outlet for him to control the populace.

What put David Berkowitz in a class by himself, however, was his communication with a columnist, the press creating a persona (the Son of Sam) from it, and the fear among the citizens of New York City that resulted. A sense of dread was reinforced when the killer alluded to demons, devils, and evil, awakening anxieties about the supernatural and touching the public consciousness at a primal level. The summer of 1977 would be remembered, the *New York Times* said, for "lightning, looting and lunatics." It was the summer of the great citywide blackout and the year Puerto Rican separatists bombed buildings. Above all else, it was the summer of Son of Sam, when a single man with the help of a handprinted note and an obliging press held the city in the palm of his hand.

THE .44 CALIBER KILLINGS

Unbeknownst to the public, the thirteen-month reign of terror that eventually would be labeled the .44 caliber killings was foreshadowed by an ugly, random, and seemingly isolated example of urban violence that occurred on Christmas Eve 1975. On that night, David Berkowitz started his journey out of obscurity by attacking at least one, and perhaps two,[4] women with a hunting knife. From this first botched murder attempt he learned enough to modify his attack style, making changes that would prove deadly to six people in the coming year.

The incident began when Berkowitz left his apartment in Yonkers, a Hudson River suburb of New York, and traveled six miles to Co-Op City, a collection of thirty-five high-rise, owner-occupied apartment buildings in the northeast corner of the Bronx. Designed originally as an experiment in moderately priced urban living, Co-Op City is a self-contained residential area, boasting its own shopping facilities, transportation system, and schools. More germane to the crimes in question, Co-Op City was the place David's beloved adoptive mother Pearl chose to move her family when their former neighborhood in another part of the Bronx began to decline.

Pearl Berkowitz died before an opening became available in the complex, but David and his adoptive father Nathan carried through with her dream and moved there in 1969 when David was 16. There father and son lived while David completed high school and until he joined the army after graduation. Although his mother had anticipated a better life in the middle-class urban oasis, David was not happy there and made few friends. Thus, possibly because he was familiar with the area or, for more symbolic or psychological reasons, Co-

Op City was the venue for the start of a process during which an obscure postal clerk would be transmogrified into the media monster Son of Sam.

The only known victim of the first attack was a fifteen-year-old high school sophomore, Michelle Forman, who was stabbed six times in the back, head, and face. While the four and one-half inch blade was not sufficiently long to do fatal damage, Ms. Forman was nevertheless so seriously wounded that she required a week of hospitalization for blood loss and a collapsed lung. Following the attack, Berkowitz drove to a diner where he gorged himself on hamburgers and fries, an episode of binge eating that would be repeated after several later shootings.

The Christmas Eve stabbings were eye-opening experiences for the would-be killer. They had been physically exacting. Both women screamed, tried to defend themselves and ward off their attacker, and most significantly, neither died. It was not at all as Berkowitz envisioned it would be. He had expected a simple, uncomplicated attack in which death was administered quickly, efficiently, and impersonally. Berkowitz was genuinely surprised when the women did not cooperate and accept their fate without resistance. He was particularly taken aback by their screams and would later puzzle over the reactions of one: "I wasn't going to rob her, or touch her, or rape her. I just wanted to kill her,"[5] he said.

The unanticipated difficulties encountered in the first attacks forced Berkowitz to modify his modus operandi in one crucial respect. After these attempts, he left New York and briefly visited his father who had retired to Miami. From there he pushed on to Houston where he stayed with an old army friend, Billy Dan Parker. It was Parker who helped Berkowitz circumvent New York City's restrictive firearms laws, selling him for $130 the .44 caliber revolver and 100 rounds of ammunition that would be used in the Son of Sam murders.

The weapon acquired was a Bulldog .44, a five-shot revolver manufactured by the Charter Arms Company of Bridgeport, Connecticut. The Bulldog .44 was an odd choice and may have been indicative of a buyer who knew very little about handguns or, more likely, one who knew a great deal. Never popular, .44 caliber pistols are continually outsold by .38, .357, and .45 caliber models. Considered old-fashioned by the average handgun owner, .44 caliber weapons reached the height of their popularity in the frontier era, a fact that was repeated and romanticized by the press who dubbed it the "Wild West" weapon. Because of its heritage, .44 sales were concentrated in the southern, western, and southwestern regions of the country, making it an especially unusual gun in New York City.

Even among .44 caliber guns, the Bulldog was unique. Besides Charter Arms, two other companies manufactured competitive weapons, the Smith and Wesson .44 and the Ruger Super Blackhawk. Both of these fired magnum loads, shells with twice the gunpowder and hence twice the power. The Bulldog .44 with its standard load created much lower muzzle velocity. It was, one industry spokesman suggested, a pistol for people who wanted "extra stopping power" but did not want to cause massive injuries that generally accompanied wounds by magnum loads.

But it was precisely this feature that made the Bulldog .44 attractive to handgun aficionados and weapons cogniscenti. Lower muzzle velocity meant a bullet that was more likely to stay in the body of a victim rather than pass through, as was commonplace with magnum shells. It may also explain why so few fatalities resulted from the Son of Sam shootings even at point blank range, including three victims who survived despite being shot in the head. Because of this unique feature, the weapon was popular with sky marshals who needed to incapacitate a would-be plane hijacker but not at the expense of puncturing the fuselage of the jet after the bullet left the target. Of course, this predilection led almost immediately to speculation that Son of Sam might be a former sky marshal.

Supporting this view, or more generally the idea that its wielder was proficient in the use of firearms, the Bulldog .44 was for the average person a difficult weapon to manage. The relatively large bullet fired from a light, 18–ounce gun with a short, 3-inch barrel caused significant recoil—so much so that, as a gun instructor pointed out, hitting anything with it beyond a few yards required considerable practice. To counteract its recalcitrance, Berkowitz adopted a crouching, two-handed firing stance. Police quickly noted that the shooting style was peculiar to military or police training, leading to speculation that Son of Sam might be one of the 1,600 police officers recently laid off by the city or a recently discharged veteran.

According to the Bureau of Alcohol, Tobacco and Firearms, in 1977 alone nearly 2 million handguns were manufactured in the United States, and once produced and sold they joined the over 39 million handguns already held by private citizens. By comparison, the total production of Bulldog .44s from their introduction in 1972 until 1977 numbered only 28,000 units. Thus, only one in every 1,500 handguns owned in the United States was a Bulldog .44. Not surprisingly then, at the time of the murders only 400 permits had been issued in New York City for Bulldog .44s. As head of the investigation, Deputy Inspector Timothy Dowd noted, "This gun—it's good as a signature"[6] and indeed, while at large Berkowitz was more commonly referred to as the .44 Caliber Killer than as the Son of Sam.

In the early morning hours of July 29, 1976, within two months of acquiring the weapon that would personify him, David Berkowitz committed the first in a series of eight Son of Sam shootings. The victims were eighteen-year-old Donna Lauria and nineteen-year-old Jody Valenti. The young women had just returned from a disco and were sitting in a car outside Donna Lauria's home in the Pelham section of the Bronx quietly talking. Donna's father walked by and reminded her that it was late, 1 A.M., and that she had to work the next day. He then went into the house, and several minutes later Donna started to follow.

As she exited the car, Donna caught sight of a man standing on a curb nearby watching her. She turned to Jody and said, "What does this guy want?" Berkowitz meanwhile walked across the street, pulled the Bulldog .44 from a paper bag, assumed the crouching position, and fired five shots. Donna Lauria was struck in the neck and, as she raised her arms to shield herself, in the elbow, with the bullet subsequently traveling down the length of her arm. Her limp body slumped back, coming to rest partially inside the car. Jody Valenti was hit in the thigh by a third shot, and she then laid on the horn to summon help. Berkowitz, his weapon empty, walked calmly to his car parked a short distance away and drove off.

The first person on the scene was Donna's father, Michael Lauria, who was returning to the street to walk the family dog. Donna Lauria died with her father at her side in an ambulance on the way to the hospital. Berkowitz, for his part, drove directly to his apartment in Yonkers. Along the way he passed several toll booths on the Hutchinson River Parkway. In the fever of the moment, he had forgotten to hide the murder weapon, and although it lay in plain sight on the seat beside him, no one noticed. Once inside the apartment, he went straight to bed and slept soundly until morning.

The next day Berkowitz bought all the major newspapers and eagerly read the descriptions of his exploits. Only then did he learn that he had carried out his mission, that he had, in fact, committed murder. From the very start therefore, the press played a pivotal role in the murder ritual, allowing Berkowitz to relive the event, savor the details, and fuel his fantasies. Interestingly, each newspaper's reporting of the first shooting provided a preview of how it would cover the story. The *New York Times* discussed the attack in the context of an increase in shootings citywide. The *Daily News* carried a detailed account of the incident on page 3, emphasizing the reaction of Donna Lauria's father. The city's other tabloid, Rupert Murdock's *New York Post*, ran the story on page 1 under the headline "Bronx Girl Slain in Car," adding details about the victims and their families inside, from the start selling newspapers with the lure of violent crime.

In all, there were eight Son of Sam shootings that took the lives of six young people and grievously wounded seven others. Unlike other serial murder cases in which the roster of dead was given in tabular form, news summaries of the killings were presented in visual form, with the site of each attack superimposed on a map of New York City. Figure 5.1 gives the final map produced after Berkowitz was captured. Printed with the map was a detailed description of the shootings such as Table 5.1 given in the *New York Times* the day after the last attack. (Note that Stacy Moskowitz was still alive at the time it was printed.)

Although there were minor variations in the circumstances surrounding the murders, the method of execution was strikingly similar in all cases, and later attacks mirrored the first in nearly every detail. Death at the hands of Son of Sam followed a brutally parsimonious choreography. Berkowitz drove

Figure 5.1
Son of Sam Chronology

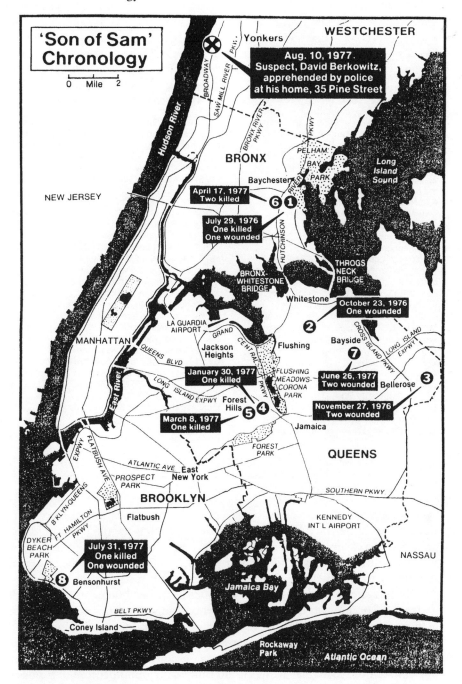

'Son of Sam' Chronology

0 Mile 2

WESTCHESTER

Yonkers

Aug. 10, 1977.
Suspect, David Berkowitz,
apprehended by police
at his home, 35 Pine Street

NEW JERSEY

BRONX

PELHAM BAY PARK

Long Island Sound

Baychester

April 17, 1977
Two killed

6 **1**

July 29, 1976
One killed
One wounded

THROGS NECK BRIDGE

BRONX-WHITESTONE BRIDGE

Whitestone

October 23, 1976
One wounded

2

LA GUARDIA AIRPORT

MANHATTAN

Jackson Heights

Flushing

Bayside

7

January 30, 1977
One killed

FLUSHING MEADOWS-CORONA PARK

June 26, 1977
Two wounded

Bellerose

3

Forest Hills

5 **4**

November 27, 1976
Two wounded

March 8, 1977
One killed

Jamaica

FOREST PARK

QUEENS

ATLANTIC AVE

East New York

PROSPECT PARK

BROOKLYN

SOUTHERN PKWY

Flatbush

KENNEDY INT'L AIRPORT

DYKER BEACH PARK

July 31, 1977
One killed
One wounded

NASSAU

8 Bensonhurst

Jamaica Bay

BELT PKWY

Coney Island

Rockaway Park

Atlantic Ocean

Table 5.1
List of Killer's Victims*

Following is a list of the victims of the killer who calls himself "Son of Sam."

1.   Eighteen-year-old Donna Lauria of 2860 Buhre Avenue in the Westchester Heights section of the Bronx was shot in the back and killed at about 1 A.M. on July 29, 1976 while sitting in a parked car outside her home. Jody Valenti, 19, of 1918 Hutchinson River Parkway was wounded in the left thigh as she sat in the car with Miss Lauria.

2.   Carl Denaro, 20, was wounded in the head Oct. 23 as he sat in a parked car with Rosemary Keenan on 160th Street between 32nd and 33d Avenues in Flushing, Queens. The injury required doctors to place a steel plate in his skull. Miss Keenan was uninjured.

3.   Joanne Lomino, 18, of 83-31 262d Street, Bellerose, Queens, was shot in the back of the head at about 12:40 A.M. on Nov. 27, 1976 while sitting on the porch of her home with a friend. She is now paralyzed from the waist down. Donna DiMasi, 17, of 86-31 262d Street, Floral Park, Queens, was shot through the neck, Nov. 27, 1976 while sitting on the porch with Miss Lomino.

4.   Christine Freund, 26, of 58-18 Linden Street, Ridgewood, Queens was shot to death at 12:30 A.M. last Jan. 30 as she sat in a parked car near the Long Island Rail Road station in Forest Hills, Queens. With her, and unhurt, was John Diel, 30.

5.   Virginia Voskerichian, 19, of 69-11 Exeter Street, Forest Hills, Queens was shot to death at about 7:30 P.M. last March 8 as she walked in front of 4 Dartmouth Street on her way home from college. She was slain a half block from where Miss Freund was killed five weeks earlier.

6.   Valentina Suriani, 18, of 1950 Hutchinson River Parkway in Baychester, the Bronx, and Alexander Esau, who lived with his father at 352 West 46th Street, were shot to death at 3 A.M. last April 17 as they sat in a parked car in front of 1878 Hutchinson River Parkway near Miss Suriani's home.

7.   Judy Placido, 17, of 2208 Wickham Avenue in the Pelham Bay section of the Bronx, was shot in the right temple, right shoulder and back of the neck as she sat in a parked car with Salvatore Lupo at 3:20 A.M. on June 26, 1977 outside 45-39 211th Street, Bayside, Queens. Mr. Lupo, whose address in Maspeth, Queens, was withheld by the police, was wounded in the right forearm.

8.   Robert Violante, 20, of 1972 Bay Ridge Parkway in the Bensonhurst section of Brooklyn, was shot in the head at about 2:50 A.M. yesterday as he sat in a parked car with Stacy Moskowitz in a lovers' lane area near Dyker Beach Park in the Bath Beach section of Brooklyn. Mr. Violante was critically wounded. Miss Moskowitz, 20, of 1740 East Fifth Street in the Flatbush section of Brooklyn, was shot once in the head and also was critically wounded.

*Numbers correspond to sites on the map in Figure 5.1.
Source: *New York Times*, August 1, 1977. Copyright © 1977 by The New York Times Company. Reprinted by permission.

aimlessly until he spied a parked car with two young people inside. He approached the car from behind, stood a few feet away, fired four to five shots, and then hurriedly walked to his waiting car and drove away. The principal exceptions to the pattern were the murder of Virginia Voskerichian, who was shot as she walked from a subway station to her home, and the attack on Joanne Lomino and Donna DiMasi, who were shot as they sat on a porch.

In every instance, the attacks were over in seconds, and because most came from behind, without warning or motive, the victims could provide only the barest descriptions of their assailant. As a consequence, the mysterious killer was known by his singular weapon, the Bulldog .44, and because of it police knew very early, after the third shooting, that the crimes were connected. Moreover, since the same weapon was used each time, it lent support to the prevailing notion that a solitary, psychotic gunman roamed the streets. Finally, the Bulldog .44 became the focal point for the popular imagination, the shorthand means the public could use to distinguish the .44 caliber killings from the level of violence indigenous to the city. Most importantly, it became a moniker the media could merchandize.

THE .44 CALIBER KILLER

The .44 Caliber killer was born Richard Falco on June 1, 1953. His mother, Betty Falco, had been estranged from her husband Anthony for many years and was carrying on a long-term affair with a married man, Joseph Kleinman. To protect the anonymity of the biological father, Betty used the name of her husband on the birth certificate. Kleinman showed no interest in the newborn and refused to support the child, thereby forcing Betty to give him away. He was adopted by a childless couple, Nathan and Pearl Berkowitz, and was renamed David.

David was aware that he was adopted from the age of 7, but the knowledge seems to have had little effect on his relationship with his parents. By all accounts, the parents were loving and provided for the boy to the point of spoiling him. David was particularly attached to his mother Pearl and was personally devastated at the age of 14 when she died. After her death, his relationship with his father remained strong, and the elder Berkowitz stood by his son throughout the Son of Sam ordeal.

As a child, David was an exceptionally handsome boy. He was big, strong, but at times overweight. In terms of his later development, much has been made of the fact that on occasion he was cruelly teased by other children who called him a "fat Jew boy." But if there was a negative side to his size and weight, there was also a positive one. David excelled at sports and was a much sought-after baseball player.

In addition to his physique and the emotional toll he paid for it, a number of other experiences and behaviors have been pointed to as premonitory in the light of subsequent events. As a boy, for instance, he started a "girl haters club," but if membership in such a group were predictive of a person who would kill repeatedly in later life, serial murderers would be not nearly as rare as they thankfully are. Other examples include his fascination with fires that led to his nickname "pyro." It would prove a life-long infatuation. After his arrest he was found to have kept a meticulous and detailed diary of nearly 2,000 fires, and, indeed, he may have set many of them.

In high school David was an above-average student until his mother's death, at which point his performance and grades dropped considerably. His desire for attention (a need to stand out he shared with John Norman Collins and Jeffrey Dahmer) was evident in school where he earned a reputation as a "prankster." Nonetheless, those who remember him from these days were most apt to describe him as a loner. A jumble of contradictions, he was also remembered as conformist, as liking uniforms and being civic minded, as indicated by his volunteer work for the emergency medical services.

Following high school he attended Bronx Community College briefly. Then in 1971 he enlisted in the Army and was stationed in Korea. He joined the service a conservative, patriotic zealot, but while in Korea a complete transformation took place. He began to experiment with drugs, took LSD, became a pacifist, underwent a religious conversion, and was reduced in rank once. The changes were documented in letters to Iris Gerhardt, a young woman from Co-Op City whom he had dated. The letters became famous in their own right several years later when they were sold to the newspapers and became the basis for a number of articles, including "Sam Letters: From Here to Insanity," "Sam Changed after LSD Trips," "How I Became a Mass Killer," and the most famous of all penned by Jimmy Breslin, "Sam Struck Out with Girls . . . So He Struck Out."

Also while in the service, David learned to handle weapons, earned the middle marksmanship rank of "sharpshooter," and bragged about his proficiency in his letters to Iris. Even during these years his thirst for attention was unabated. He was fond of decorating his uniform with optional insignia that could be purchased at base stores and because of which he was known as a "PX hero" by fellow soldiers.

Honorably discharged in 1974, he again went to live with his father in Co-Op City. Nathan by this time had remarried. David disliked his new stepmother, and because of the animosity between them, he moved into his own apartment in 1976. Over this period he worked a succession of jobs without incident, and with each job change he improved his earnings. In his last job as a postal worker, his annual salary was $13,000, which was quite respectable in 1976.

Nevertheless, his after-hours behavior began to deteriorate. He was in frequent conflict with neighbors, usually over barking dogs. David left his first apartment in New Rochelle precipitously, not even bothering to reclaim his security deposit, and moved to Yonkers. There, run-ins with neighbors resurfaced, as did a number of mysterious assaults on those who lived nearby. He shot a neighbor in the leg with a .22 caliber rifle, killed a local dog with a .44 caliber pistol, and set a fire, in which he planted several .22 caliber bullets, in front of the door of a person's apartment who had, he believed, given affront.

Also in 1976 David began a fateful effort to find his natural mother. Demonstrating considerable ingenuity and perseverance, he was able to trace her through long-expired telephone directories. He then went to her residence, left a note in the mailbox identifying himself and asking to get together, and went home to await an answer. His efforts were rewarded when Betty Falco called and happily agreed to meet the son she had never known. An added surprise awaited David. When he arrived at his mother's home, he was greeted by his much older half-sister Roslyn. The initial meeting appears to have been gratifying for all concerned and was followed by several more contacts, including one after his arrest when Betty visited David in jail.

Berkowitz biographers have read great meaning into his meetings with his mother and half-sister, interpreting them as somehow disappointing or anticlimactic and therefore the precipitating events that propelled him to murder. Similarly, much has been made of the illegitimacy of his birth. He was the bastard son of one man and the name of another appeared on his birth certificate, neither of whom was was the man who raised him and whom he knew as father. Rejection on such a basic level, it is suggested, caused Berkowitz to kill and to select victims from very specific groups.[7]

His motivations will doubtless be debated without resolution for years to come, but clearly he derived emotional gratification from the act of killing and the furor it caused. Murder was the means he used to settle old scores, the perceived slights that preoccupied his paranoid worldview, and for gaining the attention and notoriety that were missing in his life. One entry in his diary is revealing. He wrote about a visit to a shopping center and in the process provided a glimpse of his underlying motives, "I went there to look for a friendly face and I found none. I only wish I had a machine gun. Then I could make people notice me. It's obviously the only way."[8] The delusional ideation was forming, and the pathological need to stand out was already present. The act of murder was just a short step away.

The significance of his need for attention was not lost on those who came in contact with him either professionally or tragically. Dr. David Abrahamsen, who got to know the killer in meetings and through extensive correspondence, commented on the centrality of attention seeking in the murders.

His intense desire—his craving—to expose and display himself, which consciously or unconsciously had become a raison d'être for him, stimulated his tendency to exaggerate which, already present in childhood, became a significant part of his young life, and gradually took an aggressive and violent form. He had to be noticed, attract attention, create a sensation, at once and all costs.[9]

Stacy Moskowitz's mother could see it when she first laid eyes on him. "Look at him. Look at that smug smile. He's thrilled to death. He's never had so much attention in his life. I felt like killing him,"[10] she said when he appeared in court.

When captured, David did not for a minute want his identity to go unknown, as the dialogue with the arresting officer indicates.

Berkowitz: Well, you got me.

Officer: What have I got?

Berkowitz: I am Son of Sam.

Whether fame was the initial or primary reason Berkowitz murdered may never be known, but what is certain is that his elevation to celebrity status by the press was profoundly satisfying for the former spoiled child who was now an unknown postal clerk. This need for attention must therefore have figured prominently in the shootings.

CODE .44

Viewed in the context of other serial murders, the reaction of New York City residents to Son of Sam was, in the words of Yankee great Yogi Berra, déjà vu all over again. All the stages of collective response that were prominent in the Boston Strangler and Coed Killer cases were evident once more: police appeals for assistance, contributions from all manner of experts, identification of common denominators, supernatural explanations, and attribution of special powers to the killer. Overlying the universal framework of experience was a particular style, a local panache that could be seen only in New York.

Three hundred policemen, 75 detectives, and 225 patrolmen were assigned to the Son of Sam task force, who, according to their leader, Deputy Chief Inspector Timothy Dowd, had "nothing to do but catch this person." Officers worked round the clock and on weekends. Another 300 not assigned to the task force asked to work overtime without pay, and 136 laid-off officers were rehired to bolster the investigative team. Even IRS agents volunteered to join the hunt in off-hours. In spite of the donated labor, by April 1977 the cost of the investigation was staggering, nearly $2 million, with the tab exceeding $16,000 per day, a bill the bankrupt city could ill afford to pay.

The mayor and police officials appealed first to the public to supply information, telling citizens, "Don't use your judgment as to whether what you have is important or not. Just come forward and tell the police."[11] Five special phone lines were set up to handle the tips, but after the Moskowitz shooting, over 1,000 eager informants per hour got busy signals when they called. If a sense of civic responsibility did not induce witnesses to come forward, nearly $40,000 in rewards might, much of it proffered by the media, including $10,000 each from WABC-TV and the *Daily News* and $5,000 from *Screw* magazine.

Next, police called on psychiatrists to yield patient confidentiality to civic duty and report suspects. None delivered the killer, but instead, scores of psychiatrists gave profiles of the likely killer, some of which were to prove remarkably accurate. Among other attributes, they suggested that Son of Sam was a loner, had been rejected by his mother, was college educated, and had behavior typified by exaggerated conformity. Less insightfully, they claimed he was a woman hater and that his victims were symbolic; the shootings, one psychiatrist proclaimed, were "his orgasm." As the investigation wore on, one authority postulated that the killer had modified his means of obtaining sexual satisfaction from the act of murdering to evading and taunting the police. But no matter how perspicacious some profiles turned out to be, none contributed to the killer's capture.

The police tried every investigative technique imaginable. Seven thousand men were suspects, 1,500 considered top priority were questioned, and 12, known as the "Dirtiest Dozen," were put under twenty-four-hour watch. Special surveillance procedures were instituted, including a radio signal "Code .44," which was to be broadcast whenever the next shooting occurred so that investigators could be on the site without delay. Psychiatric patients were checked, witnesses were hypnotized to obtain repressed information, and people attending the victims' funerals were photographed. Couples were prohibited from sitting in parked cars. Decoy patrols of police took their place. The city was blanketed with 25,000 copies of the final composite drawing, the fourth, of the killer. Enterprising New Yorkers did the authorities one better, selling the composite on T-shirts with the inscription "Son of Sam Get Him Before He Gets You"—only in New York.

The Department of Motor Vehicles provided a ready-made source of information and the potential to zero in on the killer. Initially, the police decided to check white males between 20 and 30 years of age who, in the previous few years, had registered cars in the Bronx or Queens, but they abandoned the effort when they learned there were 235,000 in Queens alone. A witness to one crime recalled a number on the license plate of what was thought to be the getaway vehicle, thereby narrowing the field to a mere 1.7 million possibilities. Despite the daunting odds, registrations were checked in New York, Connecticut, New Jersey, and Vermont, and vehicles owned by the U.S. government were also scrutinized.

Throughout much of the investigation, the only solid lead was the murder weapon, and police pursued it with a single-minded intensity that rivaled the killer's compulsivity. An attempt was made to survey all 166,000 gun dealers in the United States to determine which sold Bulldog .44s and who their customers were. Another questionnaire was sent to the 28,000 owners of the handgun. Two thousand government agencies, businesses, clubs, and groups whose employees or members had access to Bulldog .44s were contacted. All 400 Bulldog .44s legally registered in the city were obtained and test fired. Also checked were the 150 people who bought ammunition for .44 caliber handguns. In desperation, authorities even tried to track the 667 guns that were stolen from the Charter Arms factory before they were commercially distributed. But try as they might, there was no way for the police to trace a firearm transaction between friends.

Residents of the city were not above taking matters into their own hands. Five hundred people attended a community rally in Forest Hills after the first shooting there and after the second vigilante groups roamed the area. Night patrols were set up in Brooklyn, and when one unfortunate man, in the process of being arrested, was rumored to be Son of Sam, police had to spirit him away before he was beaten to death by an angry mob. Home-owners eliminated ambush opportunities by cutting hedges. Women turned down dates, carried whistles, rode bikes, and dressed like men. And in a city where most people understood intuitively that the best defense was the long odds of becoming a victim, they met the threat with stoicism and gallows humor, such as one oft-repeated witticism, "with a little luck, he'll try Williamsburg next and get mugged."[12]

Numerologists had a field day trying to find cryptographic meaning in the sequence of shootings. Following a fad of the day, a chewing gum technology researcher tried to predict future murders by calculating the biorhythms of the killer. This was a nearly impossible task given that the methodology required knowledge of the offender's birthdate. Undeterred, the prognosticator assumed that the first attack took place on a triple critical day, and he worked forward from there. Others tried to find a hidden pattern in the dates of the crimes or the number of days between them, which, for any reader wanting to give it a try were 86, 35, 46, 37, 40, 70, and 35.

Besides the Bulldog .44, a number of common denominators were readily apparent. Most of the shootings involved young couples parked in quiet areas or lovers lanes near major interborough traffic routes. Some of the victims went to the movies or discos before the attack, leading to speculation that they may have been targeted while inside. Geographic similarities were striking in some instances, such as Virginia Voskerichian and Christine Freund being gunned down within 100 yards of one another. It was also noted that Valentina Suriani and Judy Placido attended the same high school. The police diligently pursued these angles as well, profiling the victims and interviewing their acquaintances to find other connections.

The most obvious common denominator, and the one given most popular credence, was the fact that many of the victims had shoulder-length brown hair. As early as the third shooting, on March 12, the *Daily News* trumpeted: "Victims' Hair Style a Link in 3 Killings." The pattern was so indelibly imprinted on the public psyche that when Alexander Easu was shot and killed, it was suggested that since he too had long hair he had been mistaken for a woman. The notion that the killer sought targets only with specific physical characteristics was so widely held that women across the city took steps to protect themselves. Hair salons did a land office business as thousands of women had their hair cut or dyed.

With confidence in the pattern so firmly established, it was particularly unnerving for the community when the last shooting took place in a formerly safe borough, Brooklyn, and involved a woman with short, blond hair. One terrified woman expressed the more pervasive sense of dread: "It's scary. It's like he's saying he can strike anywhere."[13] Inspector Dowd agreed: "We now have an entire city to protect. Sam is now telling us he will strike anywhere."[14] *Daily News'* reporters Brain Kates and Thomas Collins summed up the wider fear with the simple statement, "Now Son of Sam strikes in Brooklyn, too."

Of course, reactions to the .44 Caliber Killer were not without spiritual undercurrents. There were the usual calls from mystics and astrologers offering celestial assistance. One organization of clairvoyants, the Middle Science Commune of Greenwich Village, proposed something of a transcendental duel. In an open letter to the killer, the commune proposed to use their psychic power to drive off the demons that tormented him. Finally, in one of the more bizarre examples of transference on record, the speculation that the killer was actually a visitor from outer space gained currency in some quarters for a time.

But it was the communications from the killer that shifted the investigation into high gear and inflamed mass hysteria. The first note was left beside the murdered bodies of Alexander Esau and Valentina Suriani. Addressed to one of the leaders of the investigative team, Captain Joseph Borrelli, it was termed "wild, rambling and incoherent." Ironically, the note did contain one clue that could have broken the case, partial thumb and palm prints. Berkowitz had been fingerprinted when he applied for a firearm permit, but at the time there was no automated means to match the print to the millions already on file.

Instead, the quasireligious references and allusions to demon possession in the note sent the investigation off in countless unproductive directions. The choice of words led to the conclusion that the killer had a Catholic or Episcopalian upbringing; actually, Berkowitz was a Baptist convert raised as a conservative Jew. Drawing parallels to the Tate-La Bianca murders, many sought similar religious terminology in the music of the Beatles and Rolling Stones and found it in the nearly imperceptible background refrain of a Jimi Hendrix song that went, "help me, help me, help me, son of Sam, son of Sam." The Book of Samuel was scrutinized to determine how many sons the patriarch had. Also checked were all the Samuels living in the Bronx and Queens.

Graphologists and psycholinguists studied the note, finding a host of new suspects based on how it was written. Because of the stylized printing, the tilting of the I, E, and T's, the killer was believed to be a draftsman, a cartoonist, or, since he had filled in the caret used to insert a word, a printer. The note used the initials, NCIC, of a little known federal agency, the National Crime Information Center, and referred to the police in their own argot as "the guys." As a consequence, authorities speculated that the killer was a recently laid-off cop who wanted to prove he was better than the officers retained. Lastly, in a somewhat self-serving interpretation, reporters suggested that Son of Sam was a journalist because of his superior grammar and flawless punctuation. As Jimmy Breslin put it, "Whoever he is, he is probably the only killer I've ever heard of who understands the use of a semi-colon."[15]

Then in the last days of the pursuit, police received what may be the most unusual and fascinating offer to help in the annals of crime. "Mobsters Join

Figure 5.2
Note Left at Suriani and Esau Murder Scene

Dear Captain Joseph Borrelli,

I am deeply hurt by your calling me a wemon hater. I am not. But I am a monster.

I am the "Son of Sam." I am a little brat.

When father Sam gets drunk he gets mean. He beats his family. Sometimes he ties me up to the back of the house. Other times he locks me in the garage. Sam loves to drink blood.

"Go out and kill," commands father Sam.

Behind our house some rest. Mostly young--raped and slaughtered--their blood drained--just bones now.

Papa Sam keeps me locked in the attic too. I can't get out but I look out the attic window and watch the world go by.

I feel like an outsider. I am on a different wavelength then everybody else--programmed too kill.

However, to stop me you must kill me. Attention all police: Shoot me first--shoot to kill or else keep out of my way or you will die!

Papa Sam is old now. He needs some blood to preserve his youth. He has had too many heart attacks. "Ugh, me hoot, it hurts, sonny boy."

I miss my pretty princess most of all. She's resting in our ladies house. But I'll see her soon.

I am the "Monster"--"Beelzebub"--the chubby behemouth.

I love to hunt. Prowling the streets looking for fair game--tasty meat. The wemon of Queens are prettyist of all. I must be the water they drink, I live for the hunt--my life. Blood for papa.

Mr. Borelli, sir, I don't want to kill anymore. No sur, no more but I must, "honour thy father."

I want to make love to the world. I love people. I don't belong on earth. Return me to yahoos.

To the people of Queens, I love you. And I want to wish all of you a happy Easter.

May God bless you in this life and in the next. And For Now

FOLLOWING NOT
RELEASED BY POLICE

I say goodbye and goodnight.

Police: Let me haunt you with these words;

I'll be back!

I'll be back!

To be interrpreted as--Bang Bang, Bang, Bank, Bang--Ugh!!

Yours in Murder

Mr. Monster

Source: Klausner, Lawrence D. *Son of Sam*. New York: McGraw-Hill, 1981. Reprinted with permission of Lawrence D. Klausner.

Hunt," blared the *Post*. Mafia chieftan Carmine Galante, it was reported, had ordered 5,000 soldiers to the streets to find the killer, his motive ostensibly being to protect his own daughter. Reacting to the news reports, Mayor Beame said, "We have the finest police department in the world—we don't need the help of the mob."[16] Police Commissioner Codd was less adamant; "I'd have to see what they are offering,"[17] he stated. Law enforcement and criminals alike were after the .44 Caliber Killer—only in New York.

THE SON OF SAM

The Son of Sam was born on April 17, 1977, when David Berkowitz left a hand-lettered note (see Figure 5.2), at the scene of the murder of Valentina Suriani and Alexander Esau. He had become enamored with his own reviews, followed the progress of the investigation in the papers, knew all the key officers involved in the case, and viewed them almost as valued friends. As he later recalled, "I read about this group they had started to get me. It was in the papers and on television. I remember Borrelli and Dowd. I followed them from that day on. Whenever anything was written about them, I read it."[18] As a consequence, Berkowitz fixated on a newspaper quote, incorrectly attributed to Captain Joseph Borrelli, which referred to the mystery killer as a woman hater. Taking umbrage at the suggestion, he addressed the note to Borrelli and began, "I am deeply hurt by your calling me a wemon hater. I am not. But I am a monster. I am 'Son of Sam.' I am a little brat."

When released to the press, the note became an immediate sensation, forever changing the nature of the case while putting the killer in a realm few others would ever inhabit. The significance of what had just happened was not lost on the mayor of New York, Abraham Beame, who said

I'll never forget that morning. I knew the press was going to have a field day. Son of Sam. I even liked the name and that in itself was terrifying. I knew it would stick . . . would become his trademark. There had been six attacks, all laid at the feet of a single individual, and you could see it all building, the fears of the people, including my own, and the headlong rush of the press to create a personality, someone they could build a story around.[19]

The killer had personalized himself. He had revealed his thinking—his motivations. The public knew how he viewed himself. He was driven; even more, he was "commanded," "programmed" to kill. By his own admission, he was out of control, an "outsider" on a "different wavelength from everybody else."

But there was more. Belief in the supernatural and evil causation has been identified here as a common thread that runs through serial murder cases to explain the reasons for the killer's actions and as the means by which he will be brought to account. The Son of Sam tapped this subliminal current of belief with the terminology and phrases in the note. In so doing he confirmed what people suspected in the deepest recesses of their minds, awakening anxieties felt even by those too urbane, rational, and sophisticated to voice them.

He admitted to being a "Monster"; he was the devil "Beelzebub" and a "chubby behemouth." He was forced to "prowl" like an animal, to "rape and slaughter" and "drain blood" like a vampire. Conversely, he presented images of benevolence and divinity; "happy Easter," he said, and "May God bless you." The Son of Sam was, furthermore, a slayer of evil since by his simple equation wemon = demon.

Berkowitz—the Son of Sam—touched potentiating emotions and sent a shock wave of fear coursing through the community, greater certainly than would otherwise have been the case without references to the supernatural. The source of the allusions may have been this involvement in satanism as biographer Maury Terry has proposed. But if his subconscious need was to garner attention and control the populace through fear, he succeeded beyond his wildest fantasies.

The note changed on a fundamental level how the public viewed the killer. Dr. David Abrahamsen saw the significance of the quasireligious utterances

for mass psychology and succinctly enumerated the psychological underpinnings of transference that converted much of the citizenry to the killer's
side.

We were fascinated. Fascinated with the demons and fascinated with the killer's
mystery. Our own hostile, frustrated, and aggressive feelings, hidden or dormant, are
often mobilized and activated by any violent act, be it murder or execution. Through
conscious or unconscious feelings we participate; without really knowing it, we become, in a strange way, partners to the crime. Thus, some people came to identify
with "Son of Sam." Some secretly admired him, even came to root for him as he
continued to elude capture for such a long time.[20]

The killer had become a hero in the eyes of many. It was not difficult next
for the press to make him a star.

Significantly for the way the police would handle the case, an element of
remorse seemed to creep into the message; "I don't want to kill any more,"
he claimed. Police and press seized on the glimmer of hope. On April 19,
the *Daily News* published the first in a series of increasingly personal pleas
to the killer to give himself up. "The News is appealing to the killer of
Valentina Suriani and Alexander Easu to give himself up before he commits
any more crimes or is killed or wounded himself. If he has any reservations
about turning himself in to police or other authorities, we urge him to surrender to The News. We will undertake to deliver him safely to police,"[21]
they wrote.

A few days after the *Daily News* effort, the police tried for themselves.
Addressing the killer by his new name, they attempted to sympathize with
his condition and assuage any emotional damage they may have caused. "Son
of Sam: we now know you are not a woman hater—and know how you have
suffered. We wish to help you and it is not too late. Please let us help you.
Call Capt. Borrelli or Inspector Dowd at 844–0999 or write them at the
109th Precinct, Flushing, N.Y."[22] Son of Sam was silent for six weeks.

Although the police had addressed all of the killer's concerns, the note
had not been released in its entirety. Berkowitz seems to have been disappointed by this omission, and perhaps he even felt slighted. So the next
message (see Figure 5.3) was sent to the press, to *Daily News* columnist
Jimmy Breslin in particular, where it was sure to be published. The killer
bestowed on Breslin and his employer a gift of unprecedented proportions,
and the recipient and the *Daily News* began a masterfully conceived, coordinated campaign to wring every ounce of circulation out of the bequest.
Beginning on Friday, June 3, and extending over the next five days, the paper
stage-managed release of the note and its contents as if directing a Shake-
spearean drama, building suspense initially, reaching a climax on the third
day, and finally winding down to a gentle denouement.

The first day the paper ran a teaser article under the headline, "I'm Still

Figure 5.3
Son of Sam Letter to Jimmy Breslin

Hello from the gutters of N.Y.C. which are filled with dog manure, vomit, stale wine, urine and blood. Hello from the sewers of N.Y.C. which swallow up these delicacies when they are washed away by sweeper trucks. Hello from the cracks in the sidewalks of N.Y.C. and from the ants that dwell in these cracks and feed on the dried blood of the dead that has settled into the cracks.

J.B. I'm just dropping you a line to let you know that I appreciate your interest in those recent and horrendous .44 killings. I also want to tell you that I read your column daily and find it quite informative.

Tell me, Jim, what will you have for July Twenty-Ninth? You can forget about me if you like because I don't care for publicity. However you must not forget Donna Lauria and you cannot let the people forget her either. She was a very sweet girl but Sam's a thirsty lad and he won't let me stop killing until he gets his fill of blood.

Mr. Breslin, sir, don't think that because you haven't heard from (me) for a while that I went to sleep. No rather, I am still here. Like a spirit roaming the night. Thirst, hungry, seldom stopping to rest; anxious to please Sam. I love my work. Now, the void has been filled.

Perhaps we shall meet face to face someday or perhaps I will be blown away by cops with smoking .38's. Whatever, if I shall be fortunate enought to meet you I will tell you all about Sam if you like and I will introduce you to him. His name is 'Sam the Terrible.'

Not knowing what the future holds I shall say farewell and I will see you at the next job. Or should I say you will see my handiwork at the next job? Remember, Ms. Lauria. Thank you

In their blood
and
From the Gutter
'Sam's Creation' .44

Here are some names to help you along. Forward them to the Inspector for use by N.C.I.C.:

'The Duke of Death'
'The Wicked King Wicker'
'The Twenty-two Deciples of Hell'
'John Wheaties - Rapist and Suffocater of Young Girls'

PS: J.B. please inform all the detectives working on the slayings to remain

PS: J.B. please inform all the detectives working on the case that I wish them the best of luck Keep Em digging, drive on, think positive, get off your butts, knock on coffins, etc.

Upon my capture I promise to buy all the guys working on the case a new pair of shoes if I can get up the money

Son of Sam

Source: "Breslin to .44 Killer: Give Up Now!'", *Daily News*, June 5, 1977. © Copyright *Daily News*, L. P. Reprinted with permission.

Here & I'm Not Asleep Says .44 Killer." It acknowledged the existence of the note and mentioned parts of it such as the murderer's statement that he could not stop killing, did not want publicity, and was a regular reader of Breslin's column. The next day, Saturday, June 4, they turned up the heat. Investigators had vetted the note, the paper stated, had confirmed it was from Son of Sam, and, implying they were working in concert with police, revealed that the *Daily News* "withheld publication until now *at* the request of the special task force assigned to the case." Turning to their chosen columnist, the paper announced that the killer wanted to meet Breslin "face-to-face" and promised that the columnist would respond the next day.

The pinnacle was reached on Sunday, June 5, when the much-ballyhooed response was given under the banner headline, "Breslin to .44 Killer: Give Up Now." The author began with a description of Michael Lauria's reaction to the note, his daughter Donna having been prominently mentioned in its contents. Then after complimenting the killer for being a good writer, Breslin reprised the letter in its entirety. Finally, reversing the bond the killer seemed to have for him, Breslin asked Son of Sam to surrender to him personally.

The only way for the killer to leave this special torment is to give himself up to me, if he trusts me, or to the police, and receive both help and safety.

If he wants any further contact, all he has to do is call or write me at The Daily News. It's simple to get me, the only people I don't answer are bill collectors.[23]

It was gruff, emotional, and macho, quintessential Breslin and a tactic that would inspire imitators and critics alike.

Breslin's appeal for the killer's personal capitulation was mimicked by fellow *Daily News* columnist Pete Hamill and the *Post*'s Steve Dunleavy. Their colleagues would attack all of them for the patently self-serving ploy. Forced to defend their actions, Breslin responded that a journalist's role is dictated by the killer, and he had simply been reactive. Hamill claimed to have discussed the issue with psychiatrists, who urged him to issue the appeal; therefore he had "no regrets." Dunleavy said the situation was so unusual that there were no journalistic rules covering it. Besides, he said, his appeal was no different from an open letter to a head of state. David Berkowitz—the Son of Sam, serial murderer elevated to the level of a head of state—only in New York.

Saving the best for the big (and expensive) Sunday edition was a master stroke. The first edition sold out in an hour. The paper had record sales surpassed only by sales on the day Berkowitz was arrested. Over 1 million copies of the paper were sold, which meant that about one out of every four adult New Yorkers bought the *Daily News* that morning. It is hardly likely they were disappointed by what they read.

In the days following publication of the text, the paper printed a facsimile of the note showing the stilted block lettering. Also reproduced was a cryptic sign given on the bottom of the note made by combining symbols for man and woman with a cross and an S. In another article entitled ".44 Killer Taunts Cops with 'Clues,'" the paper delved into the significance of the names provided by the killer such as "The Wicked King Wicker." In yet another article, private handwriting experts hired by the *Daily News* to study the note labeled Son of Sam as "not too bright." Every aspect of the note was revisited, analyzed, and interpreted.

Although the *Daily News* and Berkowitz would be savagely, at times perhaps enviously, attacked for their exploitation of the situation by others in the industry, it is difficult to find fault with their actions. For reasons probably unknown even to themselves, they had been given the media merchandising opportunity of a lifetime. While serial killers occasionally leave notes for the police, few if any others have communicated directly with the press. What makes David Berkowitz truly unique among compulsive killers therefore is that he bypassed the police, went straight to the press, and did so apparently with deliberate goals in mind. Again, Dr. David Abrahamsen provides a cogent analysis:

The killer started a dialogue with his public, initiated a cat-and-mouse game with the police, created a bizarre tie with the world. The victimizer wanted to talk with his victim, wanted to make sure they were "hooked." The overtones of his nom de guerre, "Son of Sam," made him perversely seductive, titillating the fascination and fears of the public, challenging authority, and cleverly manipulating the news media. No doubt about it: the killer was calling the shots.[24]

The news media were, quite naturally, willing participants in the manipulation, choosing to do the killer's bidding for their own financial gain.

While at large, the Son of Sam never wrote again, and no columnist was again so blessed. Instead, Breslin's plea for surrender was answered with another shooting on June 26. The new assault rekindled interest in the Breslin note as one of the only sources for predicting future attacks, and the letter was scanned with a new sense of urgency to determine what the killer might do next. And it did contain hints and vague suggestions. In the message to Breslin, Son of Sam had written rhetorically, "Tell me, Jim, what will you have for July 29th?" Then he admonished the columnist not to "forget Donna Lauria and you cannot let the people forget her either," and again "Remember Ms. Lauria." The question and reminders were widely interpreted to mean the killer was planning an attack on the anniversary of the first shooting. This belief was legitimized when Mayor Beame announced on July 10 that extra police patrols would be added for the anniversary weekend.

Taking the impending date as a point of departure, Breslin wrote another of his famous, some would say infamous, columns, this time an open letter to the killer called "To the .44 Caliber Killer on His 1st Deathday." In it the author initially reprised portions of the nonpareil communique from Son of Sam in which the anniversary date and first victim were mentioned. Then he wondered aloud, "Will he go out and kill—is the date that significant? Or will he sit alone, and look out his attic window and be thrilled by his power, this power that will have him in the newspapers and on television and in the thoughts and conversations of most young people in the city?"[25] Critics pointed out afterward that the killer never gave any indication in his note that he would attack again on the anniversary date, but they would suggest Breslin had challenged him to do so. Thus when Son of Sam did strike two days later, the storm of protest was ready to break.

IMPACT

It was clear that the killer thrived on media attention, but did it influence him? Was his behavior changed in any way? And, if so, did the changes represent a new or greater threat to the citizens of New York? Questions of this sort began to be voiced openly in the wake of the Moskowitz shooting. There was a growing feeling that the media emphasis on the "1st Deathday" might have served as the impetus for the murder just past and may have caused the fateful break in the Bronx–Queens long-brown-hair pattern.

Yet when consulted, eminent psychologists could not state conclusively what the media effect might be. Most agreed that the killer was paranoid, and true to the type his ego was overinvolved. As a consequence, psychologists suggested, he enjoyed publicity immensely, followed the case carefully in the newspapers, and reveled in teasing the police. Less certain was whether the media provoked or inspired the murders. In this regard, psychologists saw contradictory possibilities. First, they maintained that it did goad, if not compel, him to murder, but conversely, if there was no publicity, the killer might be forced to do something drastic to gain attention. As he often did in the Son of Sam case, Dr. David Abrahamsen gave the most incisive summary of the matter. "The publicity feeds his self-esteem and it is very hard to gauge how much or how little you should write about this. He enjoys it very much."[26] Regardless, all agreed he would continue to kill until caught, and hence, there was "no guilt to be thrown on the media for that."

If the effect of the press on the killer was unclear, its impact on the investigation was straightforward and became more negative as the case wore on. Initially, investigators, like the killer, seemed to bask in the media glow and take the reporters' presence in stride. They offered interviews freely, allowed reporters to view and write about their methods, and seemed at times to treat the press as a quasi-official publicity arm. An article titled "TV Finds No Kojak or Columbo at the 109th Precinct," published in the *New York Times* in late June, documents how inured the police had become to the media presence: "Newspaper photographers roamed about taking pictures of the squadroom. The sergeant is now used to media methods, so he tolerantly sat for 'cutaway' shots the TV people need, a silent posed picture of newsman and detectives in apparent interviewing."[27]

The city administration, quite simply, used the press to assure the public that everything in its power was being done to catch the killer. As time went on, however, the assurances had the opposite effect. Far from being calmed by police efforts, the public felt more endangered by a killer who struck at will, despite the best efforts of the nation's largest police force. Published descriptions of the massive investigation had the counterintended effect of making the killer seem more invincible and the public more vulnerable as a result. These feelings were reinforced by a press that bypassed official channels and communicated directly with the killer. The implication was clear: the killer was in charge, and the police were impotent and incidental.

Further complicating the investigation was the intrusive nature of the media's pursuit of new stories. The press tried all manner of tricks to get close to those involved, and the ruses became more outrageous and potentially illegal with the passing weeks. The *Post*, for instance, sent an Armenian photographer to the Voskerichian residence to interview the family and later hired Stacy Moskowitz's mother Neysa as a temporary employee so she could gain entry to court. And, of course, in the process the paper was able to get choice quotes from a victim's mother. In the emergency room at the hospital where dying Stacy Moskowitz and maimed Robert Violante were taken for treatment, reporters were so numerous that orderlies had difficulty wheeling gurneys down the aisles. On another occasion, a television crew set up shop and began to interview undercover policemen who were busy staking out a suspect, causing a crowd of neighbors to gather and one young boy to call out, "I'm going to be on the news." So much for unobtrusive observation.

While having the media underfoot was only a nuisance, the effect on witnesses was more chilling. An eyewitness to the Moskowitz shooting had narrowly escaped death himself by moving his car from under a street light just minutes before the attack—his place had been taken by Robert Violante. Police protected the man's identity, referring to him only as Tommy Z, and sequestered him for fear of reprisals. Nevertheless, his whereabouts were found out by WABC-TV who interviewed him on "Eyewitness News." Worried that the program might discourage others from coming forward, Chief Inspector Dowd appealed to reporters to stop going after witnesses. In their defense, a spokesman for WABC-TV responded, "We are very careful in the selection of information we broadcast not to give clues whatsoever to Tommy Z's identity. He was interviewed with his back to the camera in the dark."[28]

Protestations to the contrary, it is known that witness Cacilia Davis, who provided the case-breaking clue that the getaway car was ticketed just before the murder, waited four days before coming forward because she feared being identified in the press and being stalked by the killer in return. Davis was awarded part of the reward offered by WABC-TV. Because her information was so crucial to resolving the case and hence overcoming her fear was so vital, and possibly out of a sense of responsibility for the delay, the television station gave an equal share to the neighbors who were finally able to persuade her to go to the police.

By the end of the investigation, the press had become a virtually unmanageable force answerable only to itself and its circulation figures. One investigator vividly describes the inextricable commingling of police and press interests:

Our biggest beef was the press. They knew everything. Some of those reporters have friends on the top floor of One Police Plaza. Favors were commonplace. At the 109th, reporters were always looking over our shoulders. It was impossible to keep anything secret. It got to a point, like a joke, we'd say that we'd look in the News or Post for just what we were going to do the next day.[29]

The investigative officers felt betrayed by their own superiors whom they viewed as being too cozy with the press, and as a result their efforts had been hampered. Expressing the ultimate frustration, one police informant said, "It was all so impossible. Those yellow press passes were more powerful than our shields."[30]

The relationship was not completely exploitative, however. The press did cooperate with the police and withheld critical information at their direction. It was not revealed until after the suspect's arrest that finger and palm prints were left on the notes to Captain Borrelli and Breslin. In addition, the press, at the request of the police, did not print a page of the note to Captain Borrelli. The missing information could then be used to identify the real killer from the garden-variety confessors who surrendered themselves.

Conversely, local officials used the press as a conduit for information they wanted to convey to the police. Early in the ordeal, requests for information from citizens and for psychiatrists to report suspicious patients were communicated through the media. Noting the killer's obvious attention to the media, the police used it to solicit his surrender and offer him safe passage. When the tactic failed, investigators may have given tacit approval for the papers to challenge the killer. As Lieutenant John Power was quoted as saying, "I'm a big guy for going on the offensive. I figure he's going to kill again, let's get him so angry that when he goes out, he'll slip up. Hell, I know we're responsible. But I think we could really throw him off if we forced him out. Dare him. He's calling all the shots now."[31] According to the *Daily News*, "Power said it would be up to the news media to issue the dare." Or perhaps, it was only an attempt ex post facto on the part of the paper to justify their actions, given that the quote from the officer appeared on July 29, one day after Breslin's 1st Deathday column.

Mayor Beame used a press conference as well to sound the all clear following the killer's arrest. Although the media would be criticized for not being diligent about qualifying descriptions of the killer with terms like "alleged" and "suspect" to indicate his legal status of innocent until proven guilty and without which it was feared news reports would give the impression to the public of guilt before trial, the mayor had no such compunctions. Early in the day on August 10, he proudly announced to the waiting media, "I am happy to announce that the people of the City of New York can rest easily this morning because the police have caught the person known as Son of Sam."[32]

Thus, throughout the Son of Sam chase, the authorities, killer, and press were locked in a bond of mutual exploitation. The police and city government used the media to further their investigative efforts, manage the information flow to the public, and influence mass perceptions of the case. For the killer, media accounts of the murders were a means to relive the events, replenish fantasies, and garner attention, awe, and adulation from a captivated citizenry. The press played the willing partner to both parties, reaping a circulation bonanza in the process.

Questions pertaining to media impact continued after Berkowitz's arrest. Of particular concern was how the extensive reporting affected the judicial process and the defendant's right to a fair trial. As presaged during the investigation, both the killer and public officials would use the media to further their ends.

Even the trial judge was not above using the newspapers to send messages to the public. In October 1977 Judge John Starkey created a media sensation that would ultimately destroy his career. In an interview with the *Post*,[33] the justice said he would not accept a plea of guilty by Berkowitz if he continued to say the crimes had been committed at the direction of demons. But he was afraid the jury would get the wrong idea from an insanity ruling, as he told the interviewer.

Judge: Well, it's an archaic principle of law that the jury must have no concern with sentencing. And so, if Berkowitz goes to trial, and takes an insanity defense I cannot let them know he won't walk.

Nevertheless, the resourceful justice had found a way out of the box.

Interviewer: If they don't know that, why should Berkowitz bother with an insanity defense?

Judge: Oh, they'll know.

Interviewer: How?

Judge: You're going to tell them.

Not only had the judge demonstrated that he had already arrived at a decision in the case, but also his statements were tantamount to an admission that he would use the press to manipulate the judicial process. Wilting under the firestorm that followed, Judge Starkey said, "I'd like to try the case without being bothered by the press or the public. I'd like to be able to do what I think is right without the pressure of public opinion, formed or molded." And he added: "I'm beginning to think of taking myself off [the case]. My wife is very much annoyed. She shuns publicity. And when the story broke, over the last week, she had to cancel her beauty appointment."[34] Judge Starkey, having committed media suicide, removed himself from the case several days later.

During the trial phase, Berkowitz also continued his efforts to manipulate the media, this time for a more utilitarian purpose—to establish a basis for a legal defense after he was caught and for more favorable treatment by authorities if convicted. As serial murder expert Robert Ressler observed, "The Son of Sam business, and the assertion about the talking dog . . . had been his way of signalling the authorities that he was insane. In other words, it was a construct made for the purpose of attempting to avoid proper prosecution for his crimes."[35] Berkowitz continued the charade throughout the court proceeding, using the newspapers to convey examples of his insanity to the public that would ultimately judge him.

When the court determined that he was mentally competent to stand trial, Berkowitz used one more public outburst to try to scuttle the proceedings. As he was brought into court, in front of the victim's mother and attendant media, the killer began to chant "Stacy was a whore," and "That's right. I'd kill her again," until an outraged judge had him taken away.

Although the trial was postponed and more psychological tests were ordered, the court was wise to the trick. Suspicions that Berkowitz acted to cast doubt on the previous competency ruling were confirmed when county psychiatrist Schwartz revealed that Berkowitz had told him he planned a "surprise" for the court date. Berkowitz was returned to court within two weeks. Fed up with the game, the judge was prepared to brook no interference from the defendant. Seeing a strategy bankrupt of any further opportunities for manipulation, Berkowitz pleaded guilty to six counts of Felony B Murder and was sentenced to twenty-five years to life on each of the six counts.

BACKLASH

The arrest of the .44 Caliber Killer was greeted with a long, cathartic outpouring of information. Yet for all his skillful manipulation of the media, the one thing the killer could not beautifully stage-manage was his arrest. Apprehended in the dead of night, the story broke on a city asleep or about to retire. As a consequence, the initial reporting windfall fell to the fastest media, radio and television, while newspapers, which had done so much to create the killer's persona and sustain public preoccupation with the murders, were left to pick over the bones of the story in the days following.

The CBS station, Channel 2, broke the story at 12:35 A.M., August 11, and subsequently provided detailed reports at 2:30 A.M., 4:30 A.M., and 4:45 P.M., in-between giving nine brief reports. NBC's Channel 4 carried the story beginning at 12:53 A.M. On seven separate occasions over the next two hours, news ribbons, known in the trade as flashcasts, were broadcast across the bottom of the screen. A detailed report was given at 3:05 A.M., and at 3:45 A.M. a tape of Berkowitz being led into police headquarters was telecast. ABC News, Channel 7 locally, added a 90–minute segment to its regularly scheduled programming, while executive Roone Arledge, then in the process of trying to upgrade the network's news product, spent the day at police headquarters because, he said, "I believe in being where the action is."

During the daylight hours, the news flashed around the globe; announcements interrupted broadcasts in Los Angeles, Tokyo, Frankfurt, and London. Locally, bulletins appeared regularly, official news conferences were broadcast live, and radio stations WNBC, WABC, WCBS, WNYC, WHN, WNEW, and WMCA carried extensive reports. The media storm was inescapable. The public was buried under an avalanche of facts about the crimes, the arrest, and emerging details of the killer. Public reactions, such as the obligatory comments by stunned neighbors, were equally newsworthy. As the *Daily News* characterized it, "Interviews—with ordinary people, with authorities, with reporters—were carried throughout the day, putting brush strokes on an event that turned television for one day into one long 'Police Story.' "[36]

Without the resources of the networks, major independent stations struggled to keep pace. Even so, each of the three independents devoted their evening news programs to the arrest, and two carried special reports during the day. Only Channel 13, the public television station, failed to offer anything out of the ordinary. Instead it relied on a previous MacNeil/Lehrer report, "Son of Sam: Anatomy of a Murder Investigation," which had been broadcast two weeks earlier on the anniversary of the first shooting.

Newspapers, when they were finally able to publish, sold copies in record numbers. The *Daily News* sold 2.2 million papers, nearly 20 percent above its normal circulation of 1.85 million. The *Post* did even better. Telling the whole story in a one-word headline, "Caught," in red letters, the *Post* increased circulation by two-thirds, from its normal 600,000 to a million copies. Reporters, by now celebrities in their own right, were in high demand. A panel of newspaper reporters provided analysis on the ABC program, the "Stanley Siegel Show," and Jimmy Breslin and Dick Schaap, already writing a book about the case, were interviewed on *Today*. For everyone in the media, it was a day to remember.

But even before the final news blitz, the public seemed to be tiring of the constant media hype. A series of interviews of Brooklyn residents conducted by the *New York Times*[37] immediately after the last shooting uncovered a wellspring of skepticism about the press' handling of the case. More specifically, it was observed that collective sentiments and fears were being manipulated to the benefit of the media and the detriment of the community.

Noting that reactions to the crimes were out of proportion to the actual threat, *Times* reporter Richard F. Shepard mused, "In an age where random murder is an everyday occurrence, where the police blotter daily moans a litany of violence, it is almost phenomenal how the .44–caliber killer has seized the public imagination and fears." When asked why this should be so, many residents noted that the shooting of a blonde in Brooklyn represented a radical departure in the pattern they had come to rely on for security. Many also pointed to the press' role in whipping up concern and inflaming popular passions. One man said, "Why is it so talked about? Because they are publicizing it so much." A second intoned: "It is overpublicized. The people know about it, and he knows about, the killer. It makes him feel better to know that he's being talked about." A third woman remarked, "I think the publicity played a part."

The repressed resentments and latent hostility toward the press broke full force when the threat was removed. Letters to the editor poured into the *New York Times* in the weeks following the arrest. One letter quoted Mark Twain to make a point about publicity and the likelihood of getting a fair trial, but most focused on two issues, exploitation and profiteering. A Rutgers University psychology professor called the media to account for its appeal to the public's baser sentiments. "I am revolted and enraged at the irresponsible manner in which the public media are dealing with the capture of the alleged .44–caliber killer. For the most part, they are pandering to the sadism that is all too close to the surface in all of us instead of focusing upon the questions which cry out to be raised,"[38] she wrote.

One writer described the case as a "grisly windfall for the exploiters." Another called the press reaction a "sweepstakes syndrome of shame," adding, "The stench at the beginning of the already excessive, perhaps self-perpetuating 'Son of Sam' sweepstakes is strong." Continuing with an air of resignation, he noted: "Promoters, publishers and authors of print and media, lawyers, businessmen of all kinds are sadly racing to scoop up their share."[39]

And yet, the criticisms of the public paled in comparison with the attacks the press leveled against itself. The most lighthearted of this criticism was provided by the comic strip *Doonesbury* in a four-part lampoon of the *Daily News* (see Figure 5.4). With distinctive droll wit, author-illustrator Garry Trudeau took withering aim at the tabloid and its feature columnists. Using a publicity-seeking serial killer wannabe, "Son of Arnold and Mary Leiberman," as a foil, the series satirized the standard practice of interviewing acquaintances of the killer, communications by columnists directed to the killer ("Well, would you care to speak to Mr. Hamill?" "Hamill? Gee, I don't know. I thought his pleas to Sam kind of rambled"), and the rush by media personalities, especially Jimmy Breslin, to cash in on their notoriety ("'Breslin to Tinseltown: Drop Dead!' 'Nixes 100 G's!' God love him, he held out for creative control!").

The management of the *Daily News* found the strip not to their liking and refused to carry the four installments, substituting a previously run *Doonesbury* in its place. This sent the staff at the paper's major competitor, the *Post*, into paroxysms of joy. The *Post* published the strip and crowed, "It seems that today's strip of the Pulitzer Prize winning cartoon hit a bit too close to home for the 42nd Street bunch."[40] Turning up the heat over the next few days, the *Post* accused the *Daily News* of pressuring UPI to keep the strip out of their hands and then published the telephone number of the *Daily News* for any subscriber who wanted to complain about the missing cartoon. And when the series had run its course, the *Post* got in a final dig: "On Monday, the News will be running the regular Doonesbury again—so long, that is, as it does not offend the strange sensibilities of the folks on 42nd Street."[41] Considering what would be revealed about the *Post*'s improprieties in the coming months, they might have been well served to remember the aphorism about glass houses.

The *New York Times*[42] took a more sober, almost scholarly approach, stating: "As the case itself began to recede from the public consciousness in recent days, the coverage grew as a subject of debate among journalists and the public at large." Author Carey Winfrey then gave a thorough analysis of the issues raised by the case, including the degree to which constitutional guarantees of freedom of the press also implied other responsibilities, the difference between reporting and exploiting the news, the propriety of reporters becoming part of the story they were covering, the conflict between the public's right to know and the defendant's right to a fair trial, reporters violating the law to get a story, and the ethics of checkbook journalism.

Special attention was given to the Breslin anniversary column and its implications of an imminent attack. Describing the media frenzy accompanying the date, Winfrey concluded: "The shooting, coming as it did in the wake of so much press attention and speculation unleashed some of the most aggressive, competitive and, in the view of some critics, tasteless journalism to be seen in New York City in many years." Equally tasteless in the author's view was the "orgy of dubious detail," such as interviews with classmates, high school yearbook pictures, and copies of adoption papers that accompanied Berkowitz's arrest.

The most savage attack, however, came from the city's paragon of proper conduct and arbiter of good taste, *The New Yorker* magazine. Devoting much

Figure 5.4
Doonesbury Lampoon of Son of Sam Coverage

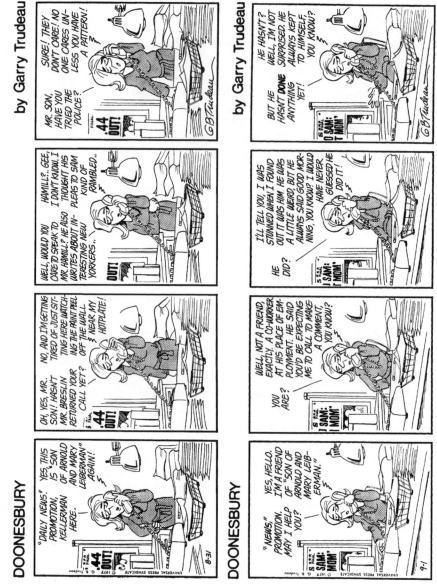

118

of "The Talk of the Town" column[43] to the reportage, it began with a simple observation: "The Son of Sam has killed six people and wounded seven, and he has sold a lot of newspapers." It then catalogued a number of deleterious effects resulting from the coverage. The chief concern was the impact the publicity may have had on the killer and his imitators: "By transforming a killer into a celebrity, the press has not merely encouraged but perhaps driven him to strike again—and may have stirred others brooding madly over their grievances to act. He has a public reputation now, and must live up to it." In the list of sins was the presumed influence of the press on investigators. Publicity had politicized the process, *The New Yorker* maintained, thereby leading to a misallocation of resources that raised the level of danger for all city residents. "It was clear that three hundred policemen couldn't accomplish much more than ten could. But the press has created a political issue, and now the Mayor and Police Commissioner had little choice but to act politically. The assignment of the additional officers left residents of the city with less protection than before." Finally, the magazine suggested that the judicial process would be irreparably biased once the killer was arrested and brought to trial: "And by transforming a person who has killed or wounded thirteen people into a seemingly omnipotent monster stalking the city the press has created the kind of public and official hysteria that . . . will make a fair trial of an accused killer nearly impossible."

The New Yorker took special exception to the reporting practices of the press and saved its most unrestrained invective for one practitioner, Jimmy Breslin. Reporting surrounding the anniversary of Donna Lauria's death had been characterized as "non-news"—rehashed details of the past murders and victims' families, misleading headlines and stories, and a flood of information "that would have been of the greatest interest, and help to the killer," the magazine charged. The pressure to report anything that day had been inspired by Breslin's anniversary column in which he reprinted part of the letter he received from the killer nearly two months before. Although the letter made no mention of killing again on the 29th, Breslin implied Sam would go "find a victim." *The New Yorker* noted that Breslin was "the journalist most likely to be read by Son of Sam" and that "Journalism schools could use these paragraphs as examples of journalistic irresponsibility." Commenting on potential police complicity in the reporting excesses, *The New Yorker* added: "A couple of days after the murder, the News reported that the police had admitted using the press to taunt the killer, and thereby 'smoke' him out. If that were true, it was a case of double irresponsibility, which may have caused another death." The columnist responded to the sharp reproof by the eminent periodical in characteristic Breslin style: he stated that blaming his anniversary article for the Moskowitz shooting was the equivalent of blaming the Johnstown flood on a leaky toilet in Altoona.

Certainly, some of the excesses mentioned by the media critics contributed to the public's disaffection with the press. After the arrest, information about

Berkowitz was at a premium, and for some people nothing, including breaking the law, could deter their headlong dash to obtain it. Just a day after Berkowitz surrendered, as an example, four newsmen, two reporters for the *Washington Post*, a freelance photographer for *Time*, and a staff photographer for the *Daily News*, were arrested when they were found inside his apartment, though it had been officially sealed by the police. The men, having entered through a fire escape, were charged with criminal trespass, a Class A misdemeanor carrying a potential penalty of one year in jail and a $1,000 fine. However, six months later the court decided that police did not have control or custody of the apartment and hence no criminal trespass occurred. Charges were dismissed.

Then came one of the strangest interludes in a case that had its share of the extraordinary. Attorney Phillip Peltz unexpectedly filed papers to represent the defendant at his arraignment in Brooklyn Criminal Court on August 11. Unlike the other attorney present, Leon Stern, who had been retained by the family, Peltz had not notified the presiding judge in advance but simply came to the proceedings. When pressed as to how he became involved, Peltz was evasive, saying at various times that an unidentified person had called him, that a family member had hired him, and that he had responded to a message left on his answering machine. Nathan Berkowitz was not amused and in a shouting match in court, at a later hearing, ordered Peltz off the case.

Nevertheless, Peltz could authenticate his claim with a document signed by the defendant himself, appointing him defense counsel and, more importantly, giving Peltz power of attorney and full title to literary and press memoir rights. Somehow, and it was never made clear, following the arrest, Peltz, possibly on the strength of chutzpah alone, talked his way past guards at Kings County Hospital, met Berkowitz, and ingratiated himself to the prisoner. He left with the necessary legal papers and something potentially much more valuable, tapes of their conversations.

After the arraignment, Peltz appeared on a news show and spoke eloquently of the need to protect Berkowitz's "precious rights" to a fair trial, while all the time trying to sell his taped conversations with the accused. Peltz and his partner Ira Leitel next went to the *Post* where they offered to sell newspaper serialization and book rights to the tapes and all subsequent recordings for $100,000, of which Berkowitz was to receive two-thirds and Peltz a third. *Post* associate city editor Peter Michelmore declined, calling the offer "absurd and distasteful." This was an interesting display of situational scruples, given what the *Post* generally and Mr. Michelmore specifically would try in the coming months. *Post* owner Rupert Murdock concurred in the decision and was said to want nothing to do with "these people." Undeterred, Peltz showed up at the *Daily News* ten hours later with an offer to sell the tape for immediate use, providing it appeared in a Sunday edition. The perishable commodity now was priced at a bargain $50,000.

Reports of the rebuffed offers to sell the purloined tapes appeared daily in the paper. When asked if he had tried to sell the tape, Peltz responded "not to my knowledge." But with the strong scent of impropriety in the air, the State Supreme Court stepped in, barring the police and media from disclosing any conversations with the accused killer.

This time, however, people were beginning to ask ugly questions about Peltz and his authority to make deals for Berkowitz. The legal Canon of Ethics prohibits attorneys from trying a case in public before trial and from releasing privileged information without the client's consent, which Peltz seemed to have. However, no court had yet ruled on Berkowitz's mental capacity. All the available evidence indicated that he was insane, and it was not at all clear that he had the mental capacity to enter into the agreement with Peltz or was aware of the consequences of releasing the information. More indicative of Peltz's true nature, it was also discovered that he had been convicted previously of security violations and was facing disbarment.

With the scalphunters closing in, Peltz tried to wrap himself in the mantle of the profession and deflect criticism onto the press by piously abrogating his interest in the tapes: "I want no part of it for to do otherwise would contribute to what I think is an unwarranted view of the profession and myself. While representing David R. Berkowitz I will not be able to respond freely to the unjust charges which have been leveled against me in the press. If I am defending David R. Berkowitz, I cannot defend myself."[44]

A day later on August 16, Peltz resigned from the case and in the process turned over the tapes to a "respected" lawyer for safekeeping, giving up any rights to earnings or commissions. Still blaming the press he once so assiduously tried to do business with, he said, "If I am guilty of anything it is my failure to foresee that anyone who became involved with this case would be the subject of media notoriety."[45] In just a few short days, Peltz's brief race for riches was over. Four months later he was disbarred.

A much more serious breach of the law began on December 5, 1977 when the *Post* ran a picture of Berkowitz napping in his prison cell under the headline "Sam Sleeps." Charges were subsequently brought against freelance journalist and former policeman James Mitteager who, it was learned, had paid guard Herbert Clarke $5,800 to take pictures of Berkowitz and obtain information about him. The plot was uncovered when fellow guard Frank Jost reported Clarke's attempt to enlist him in the scheme. Clarke was granted immunity to testify against Mitteager but was still brought up on departmental charges. Mitteager, in turn, was charged with bribery and rewarding official misconduct, and faced a maximum sentence of seven years in prison on the bribery count alone.

At his pretrial hearing, in April 1979, Mitteager tried to have the charges against him dismissed. Using the empty chair defense, he claimed to have been in the employ of the *Post*, and so he maintained that rightfully the paper, not he, should be on trial. Mitteager further suggested that he had been made the scapegoat because any indictment of *Post* officials would have serious political repercussions. Hearing testimony appeared to bear out his contention.

Post editor Susan Welchman revealed that Steve Dunleavy had asked her if she could obtain a "spy camera" for Mitteager, one that could be easily concealed. Her assumption, she stated, was that it would be used to take illegal pictures. When asked if such a purpose presented a concern, she said, "There are a lot of illegal pictures taken and put in the paper."[46] Metropolitan editor Peter Michelmore, who approved the camera purchase, next disclosed that the *Post* paid Mitteager $13,000, and although he knew someone inside the facility would also be paid, he denied knowing that the money would be used for bribes. Michelmore also testified that he did not inquire into how the camera would be used and did not try to authenticate the pictures. Last on the stand for the *Post* was owner Rupert Murdock. Expenses for such small amounts did not come to his attention and were left to Mr. Michelmore's authority, he claimed. When asked what guidelines he gave his editors, he self-servingly replied, "Seek the truth and if they have any doubts about legality to consult with counsel."[47]

Despite efforts to distance the paper from the brewing scandal, incriminating evidence implicating the *Post* continued to pile up. Editor of the *Soho Weekly News* Allan Wolper told of a conversation with Mitteager in which he repeated Michelmore's comment: "we're paying you and your guy at the hospital." More damning still was the testimony of an investigator, John Zwaryczuk, from the New York State Special Prosecutor's anticorruption office. Zwaryczuk told of having been directed by superiors to "not actively seek" evidence that could "directly" implicate the *Post* in the bribery scheme; he further claimed that high-level officials in the department had directed the investigation and legitimate leads were not investigated. Nevertheless, the judge cited the broad discretion of prosecutors in bringing charges and refused to dismiss the bribery count, ruling that there had been "no invidious discrimination in the case."

The trial in November 1979 added a few fresh tidbits and the opportunity for both sides to present final arguments. Clarke testified that he was aware the pictures would be published by the *Post* but had been told to plead the First Amendment, freedom of the press, if caught. Mitteager claimed that Michelmore and *Post* lawyers had assured him that his actions were not criminal. In final defense, Mitteager summed up his position: "I was inexperienced—I was relying on the Post for guidance and direction."[48] The prosecutor took exception, pointing out that as a former police officer Mitteager should have recognized the illegality of his offer.

With that, the matter was consigned to the arbitrative wisdom of the judicial system. The jury took only a day to make its decision, returning a stinging rebuke to the prosecution and the *Post*—Mitteager was acquitted of the bribery charges. When asked to explain the rationale for the decision, one juror said, "The wrong defendant was on trial—the feeling was the *Post* should have been on trial."[49] Public disgust with media methods, expressed in the judgment of the jury, was complete.

EPILOGUE

In September 1977 Steven Dunleavy of the *Post* wrote a column in which he charged that the Yonkers Police could have stopped Berkowitz earlier if only they had read the clues correctly. How did he know, he asked rhetorically—because David Berkowitz told him in a letter. Lest anyone miss the point that he too had been singled out by the newsmaker of the year, Dunleavy repeated the fact three times in the text of the article.

Nevertheless, the column ruffled few feathers and was almost completely ignored by the public. The simple fact was that following his arrest David Berkowitz became a compulsive communicator, trying to use the strategy that had served him so well in the recent past. Once again he was reaching out to the press in a vain attempt to regain some of his lost glory, to recapture those perfect moments when he baffled the police, terrified the public, and monopolized the press.

Previously, on August 26 he had written Jimmy Breslin, the man on whom he had once bestowed media immortality. Taking a cue from one of Breslin's columns in which the author said he would like to meet Son of Sam someday, Berkowitz wrote:

It has come to my attention that you wish to speak to me. Well, all you have to do is come over to my house at Kings County Hospital. At this time I am unable to visit you.

I am disgusted with the way the press has been spreading lies about me, but perhaps some of these can be ironed out in our meeting. However, I am not one to cry out a case of injustice.

I hope Mayor Beame enjoys dribbling my head across the court.

This is like a circus event with clowns and criminals. Please bring a beer when you come.[50]

In response to the invitation, Breslin was quoted as saying he would visit Berkowitz "at an appropriate time" but could not do so immediately out of deference to the accused killer's rights. But an "appropriate time" never came. Breslin never went to meet the Son of Sam.

The columnist knew instinctively that the engine of publicity is fueled by consumer demand. With their daily purchases of newspapers, residents were voting to be manipulated by the killer and the press, endorsing the media's actions by their expenditures and interest. Conspiracy or not, the public had been led to believe that a lone gunman was responsible for the shootings, so the arrest of a single individual removed the threat instantaneously. Without the implicit threat that he could gun down young people at will, Son of Sam was no longer news. Even the killer seemed to grasp this fundamental truth. He signed his letter to Breslin: "Sincerely, David Berkowitz."

A House Divided

WAYNE BERTRAM WILLIAMS
Atlanta, Georgia (1979–1981)

"It doesn't have to be a white killer just because the children are black. But if the killer is white, it's going to tear this city apart."
—Mary Davis, Black Business Owner
Atlanta Constitution, March 22, 1981

The United States in 1979 was a hostile and threatening place for black Americans. The Ku Klux Klan was rumored to be setting up paramilitary training camps in the South. Racially motivated murders were reported with alarming regularity and seemed to respect no geographic boundaries. Attacks had occurred in Salt Lake City; Indianapolis; Johnstown, Pennsylvania; Oklahoma City; Cincinnati; and Buffalo, where two black cabbies had their hearts cut out. In Boston eleven black women were strangled in a brief three-month period.

It was difficult to avoid the conclusion that the cases were connected or the possibility that they were part of a plan by white hate groups to systematically kill blacks. The situation was sufficiently serious to prompt President Jimmy Carter to act. Launching an FBI probe into the matter, he told *Ebony*:

The possibility exists that there is a conspiracy. An investigation of suspects throughout the country is being conducted to see if there is a tie among these events. The FBI is concentrating on that with the utmost diligence and is making regular reports to me. It's hard for me to form an opinion without having actual evidence to base it on. . . . But, yes, the possibility exists that there is a conspiracy.[1]

And then, bodies of murdered black children began to be discovered in Atlanta. A child disappeared every twenty-five days, the death toll mounting with "clockwork precision." Tensions grew proportionately, as did mistrust, suspicion, and accusations, the symptoms of a population under stress. Against a national backdrop of fear and racial hatred, Atlanta tried to cope with its own adversity, a killer among us.

Atlanta began to evidence the pernicious effects of being presented with an internal threat. Three related processes of social dissolution ensued: a decline in social interaction, an increase in conflict, and the attribution of blame. With respect to the first, individual behavior was modified to minimize vulnerability. Fewer people ventured out, children no longer played in the streets, and isolation replaced communication. Myriad casual social contacts vanished, and the lifeblood of society desiccated. Sadly, the youngest members of the city were the most prone to the impact and evinced the most serious symptoms of living in chronic fear.

A serial killer puts a strain on the existing divisions in a community. Individual mistrust leads to reinforcement of group boundaries, intensification of separateness, and isolation on a collective basis. Tensions already present are exacerbated, old animosities are resurrected, and conflict occurs along natural dividing lines in the population. Atlanta was no exception to the rule. The city that considered itself "too busy to hate" found that it had the time after all. A history of segregation preordained that the conflict would have racial overtones, as much as did the race of the dead children.

The sharpening of class boundaries makes the assignment of responsibility necessary and possible. Scapegoating is the process of absolving guilt by placing blame. For the most part, scapegoats are found among clearly delineated groups in society that differ from the mainstream, minorities, ethnic, and lifestyle groups being examples. The quality of differentness is taken as the implicit reason for the scapegoat's presumed complicity in the crime. Substantiation for the belief may be rooted in superstitions and ancient fears that are reawakened in times of crisis. The fact that the killer often selects victims from the minority group only serves to reinforce and confirm the judgment of the majority.

The scapegoat is an outsider, one on whom scorn can be heaped without remorse. Furthermore, when responsibility is fixed, the source of the threat is known, causing a consequent reduction in fear. The threat is distanced, put beyond where it can do harm, since it is confined to a group with which the majority of the population has only limited contact. Because the scapegoat performs so many psychological and social functions, the process of finding one is nearly universal in communities under stress.

Most often, the scapegoat is a member of a politically or economically disenfranchised group, and hence the dominant group has little fear of retaliation. In the Atlanta child murders, the race being victimized was also the one in political power. Blame was therefore apportioned on the basis of socioeconomic status. Because of their child-rearing practices, lower income blacks generally and the parents of victims in particular were held responsible for the murders. After having suffered the loss of a child, the cruelest fate to befall the victims' families was then to be blamed for their deaths.

All the elements of social dissolution were present in Atlanta, and barring any opposing tendency, the slide toward social disintegration is likely to have continued unabated. But Atlanta weathered the storm, with the people of the city finding the inner strength and resilience to get by. The reaction of Atlantans to Wayne Williams and the missing and murdered children is as much a case study of the factors that hold a community together as it is of the processes that tear it apart.

In this regard, the Atlanta experience stands in stark contrast to the re-action of Milwaukee residents to Jeffrey Dahmer. Both cities had the same problems, changing demographic composition, and shifts in political power. Atlanta had the good fortune to have the killer among us after the mantle of power had been passed to a new racial group. In Milwaukee the transfer of power had just begun. The city was so consumed with its political strug-gles that it was incapable of recognizing the hand of a serial killer behind the bizarre disappearances of gay men. Awareness when it came was accom-panied by vicious fault finding.

But Atlanta had more than just a stable city government that represented the racial realities of its population. It also had a nongovernmental infra-structure and personal assets that could be called on in times of trouble. Above all else, it had the memory of Martin Luther King, Jr., and his legacy of nonviolence. In the last analysis, it was Martin's Town.

THE ATLANTA SNATCHINGS

The unpleasant reality of modern urban life is that children are murdered with some regularity. Atlanta in the last half of the 1970s was no exception. In the four years immediately preceding the start of the serial murder string, thirty-six minors, 17 years old or younger, were killed in the city—ten in 1975, nine in 1976, seven in 1977, and ten again in 1978. Therefore, when thirteen homicides were recorded in 1979, the count was not grossly out of line with what would normally have been expected. Authorities had little reason to suspect that a serial murderer was loose in the community or that two of the homicides committed in 1979 were his first victims.

The rate of murders continued on a steady pace through the first half of 1980 when six homicides were recorded. But while the number of homicides was not widely different from the norm, other statistics were not in balance. Usually children are shot, stabbed, or beaten to death, as were twenty-nine of the thirty-six minors killed in Atlanta from 1975 to 1978. Typically, too, the murderer is a parent, guardian, or acquaintance who regrets killing the child; indeed, the usual child murder is punishment that gets out of hand. The body is left at the scene, and the killer rarely tries to flee. As a result, these murderers are easily apprehended, and most child murders are quickly cleared by an arrest. With respect to the victim, the dead are as likely to be females as males.

In Atlanta a pattern began to emerge that was not consistent with customary experience. The children tended to die more often of asphyxiation. The victims were disproportionately males, and all seemed to have similar physical characteristics—for example, they were small or had a slight build. The bodies had been carried from the murder site and dumped in remote areas, rivers, or in some cases where they could be readily found. No murder weapons were found, and the killer had made good his escape.

These characteristics would eventually become associated with the Atlanta child murders, but they were not obvious at the beginning. The pattern took some time to reveal itself. For instance, of the first twelve victims, the cause of death was unknown in five cases, one had been shot, one stabbed, and one beaten to death. Even the asphyxiation deaths were not uniform—one was done manually, one with a ligature, and in the two other cases strangulation was not certain. What authorities had no way of knowing was that the evidence that would eventually break the case, textile fibers, had already been found on the body of Yusef Bell, the fourth child slain.

The murders were not officially linked until the murder of Clifford Jones, the thirteenth victim. Parents of the twelve earliest victims would take special umbrage in the fact that Jones was a visitor to the city. In their view, police were unwilling to listen to the legitimate fears of Atlanta residents, but only took notice when an outsider was killed. For many this was equivalent to saying the police could not or would not protect segments of the city population. Parents saw the specter of prejudice in the way they were treated, believing warnings about the children were ignored because of their social status. In the words of Yusef Bell's mother Camille, "We've got a black administration now, so it can't be that we're black. It must be that we're poor."[2] Thus, failure to detect and acknowledge the pattern in the murders divided the black community along the lines of social class.

The list of dead children normally associated with the Atlanta child murders is given in Table 6.1, just as it was printed in the *Atlanta Constitution* a week after Wayne Williams was arrested. The list became a public statement symbolizing the city's concern for the missing children. Ironically, it also contained the seeds of the dissension that followed.

The dead children became a political issue, their deaths representing dimensions beyond grief and tragedy. Once police acknowledged that a pattern existed, that many cases were linked, it became impossible not to add all new murders of young blacks to the list. It delimited the boundaries of the tragedy such that when a suspect, Wayne Williams, was arrested no subsequent names were ever added to the list, just as before every child murder had been. Since the list was not added to after the suspect's arrest, it was implicit, but the most compelling, proof of his guilt.

The list created one of the issues that was to dog the investigation and would cause lasting doubts about the trial and verdict. If all of the dead children were automatically added to the list, what had become of the murders that should have occurred as a matter of course? Even if a serial killer were systematically murdering children, some of the children should not have died by his hand. The belief that there were other murderers was impossible to shake. It became a source of controversy among investigators, and when, after Wayne Williams was convicted, police closed twenty-three of twenty-nine cases there was a howl of protest.

Adding weight to the multiple murderer theory were the differences that existed among the first twelve victims. The two female victims were part of this group, and the circumstances of their deaths made their inclusion on the list highly questionable. Latonya Wilson was supposedly kidnapped from her bedroom. In order to do so, it was revealed, the killer would have been forced to climb over the bed of a sleeping sibling, snatch Latonya, and leave without attracting attention. Angel Lenair was found tied to a tree six days after her disappearance, strangled with an electrical cord with panties, not her own, stuffed in her mouth.

The early murders of males were equally variable. Edward Smith was the only member of the list to have been shot. Anthony Carter vanished while playing hide and seek and was subsequently found stabbed to death a short way from his home. Yusef Bell was strangled, his body hidden in a crawl space beneath an abandoned elementary school. Eric Middlebrooks was beaten to death shortly after he testified against several other juveniles in a theft case. The early murders lacked the uniformity in method that would become the hallmark of the Atlanta child snatcher. Whether these murders were related to subsequent ones was hotly debated. Whatever the truth, for the public the list was less the ledger of a solitary psychotic killer than a symbol of forgotten children, less a scorecard of a serial murderer than a cause.

As the list became increasingly invested with emotion and hence more politically potent, the media coverage grew accordingly. The vagaries in the circumstances of the first dozen gave rise to the "two-string" theory and the frightening possibility that the creation of the list and media coverage may have set off a serial murderer. As DeKalb County Medical Examiner Dr. Joseph Burton observed, "I'm not at all sure that we had a single killer methodically snatching children at the beginning of all this. But if that man didn't exist then, we have created him and he is killing now. We are dealing with a suddenly rising number of cases that are connected."[3]

Toward the end of the ordeal, questions would be raised again about how many murders were actually related. In this instance, the reason for doubt was that the last victims were no longer children: they were young adults. Similar to the Boston Strangler case, however, every effort was made to preserve the connection between the slayings. Law enforcement officials were quick to point out that the victims were "childlike adults," diminished

Table 6.1
Atlanta's Murdered and Missing Children

	Victim	Characteristics
1.	Edward Smith	Nicknamed "Teddy," age 14, 5-foot-4, 125 pounds Liked karate, skating, basketball, football
2.	Alford Evans	Nicknamed "Q," age 13, 5-foot-4, 87 pounds Liked basketball, wrestling, karate movies
3.	Milton Harvey	Age 14, 5-foot-0, 95 pounds Liked karate movies, wrestling
4.	Yusef Bell	Age 9, 4-foot-7, 65 pounds School band member
5.	Angel Lenair	Age 12, 5-foot-4, 90 pounds Liked volleyball, skating
6.	Jefferey Mathis	Age 11, 4-foot-8, 71 pounds Liked swimming, bicycling, basketball, football
7.	Eric Middlebrooks	Age 14, 4-foot-10, 88 pounds None
8.	Chris Richardson	Age 12, 5-foot-0, 85 pounds Liked swimming
9.	Latonya Wilson	Age 8, 4-foot-0, 60 pounds None
10.	Aaron Wyche	Age 10, 4-foot-10, 65 pounds None
11.	Anthony Carter	Nicknamed "Tony," age 9, 4-foot-5, 73 pounds None
12.	Earl Terrell	Age 10, 4-foot-7, 80 pounds Liked swimming (Southpark Boy's Club)
13.	Clifford Jones	Age 12, 4-foot-11, 57 pounds Liked sports
14.	Darron Glass	Age 11, 4-foot-9, 75 pounds Liked touch football
15.	Charles Stephens	Age 10, 5-foot-0, 120 pounds Liked building models, drawing

Last Seen/Location	Cause Of Death
Saturday, July 21, 1979, 12 a.m. Church's Fried Chicken, 3667 Campbellion Rd. S.W.	.22 gunshot wound
Wednesday, July 25, 1979, 3-4 p.m. Bus stop Glenwood Ave. at Meadowlake Dr.	Probable asphyxiation/strangulation
Tuesday, Sept. 4, 1979, 10:30 a.m. Bolton Rd.	Unknown
Sunday, Oct. 21, 1979, 5:30 p.m. Fulton St. at Ira St.	Manual strangulation
Tuesday, March 4, 1980, 7:30 p.m. Home	Ligature strangulation
Tuesday, March 11, 1980, 7 p.m. In front of Williams Barber Shop Gordon St.	Unknown
Sunday, May 18, 1980, 10:30 p.m. Home	Blunt trauma to head
Monday, June 9, 1980, 1:30 p.m. Krystal Hamburgers, 3385 Memorial Dr. Decatur	Unknown
Sunday, June 22, 1980, Early a.m. Home	Unknown
Monday, June 23, 1980, 6 p.m. Tanner's Grocery McDonough Blvd.	Asphyxiation Broken neck from fall
Sunday, July 6, 1980, 1:30 a.m. 839 Cunningham Pl.	Multiple stab wounds
Wednesday, July 30, 1980, 3:30 p.m. Lakewood Ave.	Unknown
Wednesday, Aug. 20, 1980, 12:40 p.m. St. James Ave. and Lookout Ave.	Ligature strangulation
Sunday, Sept. 14, 1980, 6:30 p.m. Home	
Thursday, Oct. 9, 1980, 4:30 p.m. Home	Asphyxiation

Table 6.1 (Continued)

Victim	Characteristics
16. Aaron Jackson	Nicknamed "Junior," age 9, 4-foot-8, 84 pounds Liked swimming
17. Patrick Rogers	Nicknamed "Pat Man," age 15, 145 pounds None
18. Lubie Geter	Nicknamed "Chuck, Rosie," age 14, 130 pounds Liked baseball
19. Terry Pue	Age 15, 5-foot-5, 105 pounds Liked basketball
20. Patrick Baltazar	Age 12, 125 pounds Liked electronic games
21. Curtis Walker	Nicknamed "Tank," age 13, 5-foot-0, 75 pounds None
22. Joseph Bell	Nicknamed "Jo Jo," age 16, 5-foot-2, 100 pounds Liked basketball
23. Timothy Hill	Nicknamed "Timmie," age 13, 5-foot-3, 95 pounds None
24. Eddie Duncan	Nicknamed "Bubba," age 21, 5-foot-9, 140 pounds None
25. Larry Rogers	Nicknamed "Little Larry," age 20, 110 pounds None
26. Michael McIntosh	Nicknamed "Mickey," age 23, 115 pounds None
27. Jimmy Payne	Age 21, 5-foot-7, 135 pounds None
28. William Barrett	Age 17, 5-foot-4, 124 pounds None
29. Nathaniel Cater	Age 28, 5-foot-11, 146 pounds None

Last Seen/Location	Cause Of Death
Saturday, Nov. 1, 1980, 7 a.m. Moreland Plaza, Custer and Moreland Rds. S.E.	Asphyxiation/ suffocation
Monday, Nov. 10, 1980, 7:05 a.m. Bus stop, 1100 Black Henry Thomas Dr.	Blunt trauma to head
Saturday, Jan. 3, 1981, 2:30 p.m. In front of Food Giant, Sylvan Hills	Manual strangulation
Thursday, Jan. 22, 1981, 2 p.m. Shoney's, 4975 Memorial Dr. Stone Mountain	Ligature strangulation
Friday, Feb. 8, 1981, 5:30 p.m. Fisherman's Cove Restaurant, 201 Courtland St.	Ligature strangulation
Thursday, Feb. 19, 1981, 4:30-6:30 p.m. Near Byron Gun Club on Bankhead Hwy	Asphyxiation/ strangulation
Monday March 2, 1981 Cap'n Peg's, 325 Georgia Ave.	Asphyxiation
Wednesday, March 11, 1981, 2:30-5:30 p.m. Rear of 987 Selts Ave.	Asphyxiation/ drowning
Friday, March 20, 1981 Play room at Techwood and Mills	Unknown
Monday, March 30, 1981, Afternoon Westlake & Simpson & Ezra Church	Asphyxiation/ strangulation
About first of April Near his residence	Asphyxiation
Wednesday, April 22, 1981, 10:30 a.m. Home	Asphyxiation
Monday, May 11, 1981, 5 p.m. Kirkwood area	Asphyxiation
Thursday, May 21, 1981, Morning Central City Park	Asphyxiation

Source: "Atlanta's Murdered and Missing Children," *The Atlanta Constitution*, June 28, 1981. Reprinted with permission from *The Atlanta Journal* and *The Atlanta Constitution*.

in capacity due to mental (e.g., slightly retarded) or physical (e.g., small stature) limitations.

In many respects, the murder of Clifford Jones could serve as a proxy for the majority of the Atlanta child murders. The twelve-year-old Cleveland resident was visiting his grandmother in Atlanta. When he disappeared, twelve children had been reported missing, and half of these had been found dead. The threat was real, and aware of it, his mother duly warned him to be careful as he was leaving to go search for returnable cans. Clifford left his grandmother's house on August 20 and simply vanished. In the vernacular, he had been "snatched." His body was discovered the next day.

The cause of death was asphyxiation, but unlike many victims, especially later ones, a ligature was used to strangle the boy. Also different was the condition of the body. There were bruises around his lips and a cut on the inside of his mouth. Bodies of other asphyxiated boys showed no outward signs of struggle; the unmarked corpses earned the murderer the reputation of a "gentle" killer. Nonetheless, it was assumed that the commission of the murders required great strength and that the killer strangled his victims by choking them with an armlock around the throat.

To explain the paucity of physical evidence that the victims resisted their attacker, police hypothesized that the victims were slain just as an ingratiating killer won them over, at the "moment of trust" when they had gone beyond the point of natural suspicion and dropped their guard. The killer was thought to use a trust-inspiring lure to gain compliance, or may have made an initial contact with the victim and arranged to meet again at a later time when the murder was effected.

Jones, like so many other murdered children, had disappeared while trying to earn some extra spending money; he had, said his mother, "got killed for a penny can." As a group, the murdered children were described as "streetwise" or "hustlers" to denote their eagerness to earn pocket change, and it may have been their headlong pursuit that led to their demise. As a simple police experiment graphically demonstrated, "At the height of the killings, police plainclothes detectives drove through some of the neighborhoods targeted in the investigation. The detectives offered youngsters $10 if they would get into the car and come along for an 'odd job.' The police later said that virtually none of the youngsters refused the offer."[4] It was a startling illustration of vulnerability, with terrifying implications for parents trying to protect their children.

GREEN RIBBONS

If records were kept of such things, the response to the Atlanta child murders would lead every category. Police efforts were prodigious, the scope of the investigation colossal. However, the techniques used and the manpower expended by law enforcement were not dissimilar to those in other cases. What distinguished the Atlanta experience was an enormous out-pouring of public support, both local and national, for the murdered and missing children, reactions on a scale that dwarfed other serial murders.

Slow to recognize the threat implicit in the mounting death toll, once the pattern was evident, local law enforcement agencies reacted with all the re-sources they could muster. The Atlanta police assigned ninety-two officers to the case, including twenty-one detectives and eleven undercover officers. The Georgia Bureau of Investigation, the FBI, the Georgia State Police, Fulton and DeKalb counties and even the State Law Enforcement Division from neighboring South Carolina provided additional resources. Just the task force created to oversee the investigation had thirty-seven full-time mem-bers.

The effort expended to catch the killer was staggering. The DeKalb County Sheriff's Office alone spent over a man-year of time investigating the four bodies that were dumped in its jurisdiction. Police went door-to-door gathering information in low-income neighborhoods. Roadblocks were set up, helicopters patrolled the sky, and some suspects were put under twenty-four-hour surveillance. Five years of homicide records were searched, and two computers were used to look for a pattern in the circumstances of the crimes. Funerals were filmed, voice prints analyzed, witnesses hypno-tized, and inmates and juvenile delinquents interviewed as part of their in-carceration processing.

But still children disappeared. The more the police worked, the more frustrated and critical the residents of Atlanta became. As columnist Jack Traver quipped, " 'The city too busy to hate' is increasingly regarded as the burg too bungling to protect its young 'uns."[5] It rapidly became apparent that the organizational and investigative demands of the case went beyond the local authorities' expertise and financial and manpower resources.

Law enforcement officials started to look beyond their own ranks for spe-cial skills, rational and supernatural, that might crack the case. In addition to the FBI, the police asked for help from five "super cops," all of whom had been involved in a successful serial murder investigation. One of the group was Joseph Borrelli, who had been addressed in the infamous Son of Sam note. Medical researchers from the Centers for Disease Control were enlisted to search out common denominators among the victims. Treating the murders as an epidemic and the killer as a lethal biological agent, CDC epidemiologists attempted to gather data in low-income housing projects only to find their interviews cut short by the residents' fear and suspicion.

The authorities even took the unusual step of inviting a well-known psy-chic, Dorothy Allison, to join the team. The supernatural dam having been breached, a host of paranormals poured through. In all, police would receive 1,300 letters from psychics itching for a chance to display their telepathic wares. In the end, appeals for supernatural assistance were tinged with racial preference, as a letter to the editor of the black newspaper, the *Atlanta Daily World*, illustrates.

The highly-publicized use of a white psychic in the investigation of the brutal child murders in Atlanta completely ignores a very vital force in the black South that, if used carefully and respectfully, would produce the killer, the other missing children, and administer justice to the satisfaction of all concerned. Simply use some of the reward money to hire a black specialist to the case a Vodou (Voodoo) priest from Africa, Haiti or the South—and let him do his work.

It would be money well spent; it takes such serious measures to deal with such serious crimes against innocent children, and this case has gone on much too long. Voodoo used this way has righted wrongs as long as black people have lived on earth—blacks of all shades, all levels of belief (especially in Christianity and Catholicism). Its methods may be different but it produces results.[6]

While police dabbled in the metaphysical, ordinary citizens turned for succor to old-time religion. Prayer rallies were held, mothers fasted, and even the NAACP urged everyone to pray daily. Contributing poet for the *Atlanta Daily World*, George Coleman, was inspired by clouds in the form of a cross he had seen in the sky. It presaged, he said, the imminent capture of the killer. In the poem written to document the miraculous sign, he gave a pristine example of the basis for appeals to the supernatural:

> We are angry, Lord, and we are frightened.
> We grieve in every fiber of our being.
> But mostly Lord, we are confused.
> Help us to understand.[7]

With the police work dragging on and no end in sight, the demands on city coffers became unbearable. As a result, Mayor Jackson was forced to make an open appeal to the federal government for funding assistance to cover the extraordinary and unbudgeted costs of the investigation and for skilled manpower to shore up local resources. In the process, a local tragedy was turned into a national cause célèbre.

The radical chic of the 1960s had given way to the liberal chic of the 1970s. As a consequence, it became the height of fashion to demonstrate concern for the missing and murdered children. A cavalcade of stars gave benefit concerts to raise funds for the investigation, including Sammy Davis, Jr., Frank Sinatra, Gladys Knight and the Pips, and the Jacksons. Receipts from the annual Kool Jazz festival were given over to the effort. NFL players took part in basketball games, boxers fought exhibition bouts, and fashion shows were held, all in the name of the cause.

Meanwhile, city officials were inundated by a flood of donations to offset the cost of the investigation, add to the reward money, or aid the families of the victims. Businesses contributed. Coca-Cola, headquartered in Atlanta, gave $25,000; Warner Brothers added to the pot, as did business leaders in Minneapolis and New York. States and municipalities sent funds. The Rhode Island legislature voted a $20,000 appropriation, Columbus, Ohio added another $35,000, and Philadelphia tried to raise a million more.

Personal contributions were equally generous. Burt Reynolds and Kenny Rogers each gave $10,000. Mohammad Ali, noting that a $100,000 reward would not even buy a Rolls Royce, added $400,000 to it. A seven-year-old girl donated her entire allowance—one dollar. Even prisoners sent money— $8 from Illinois, $5 from California, and $86.47 from five inmates in a county jail in Austin, Texas. Instate, a check for $223.69 was received from the Stone Mountain Correction facility with a letter that read in part, "Even though we are confined and our lives are presently tainted by our past antisocial mistakes, we want to let you know that as a group, we are utterly appalled by and totally against the horrendous acts of violence being perpetrated against helpless, innocent children."[8]

Contributions came in from several unlikely quarters. At one point a black businessman observed, "These aren't black or white people doing this. They're sick people. I told a group the other night that I believe even a group like the Ku Klux Klan would cooperate with a problem like this."[9] He was not far off the mark. David Duke, former grand wizard of the Ku Klux Klan and head of the National Association for the Advancement of White People, donated $1,400 to help promote better black-white relations. Former Georgia governor and champion of segregation Lester Maddox ran an ad in the *Atlanta Constitution* offering the killer $10,000 for legal defense as an inducement for surrendering. Senator Strom Thurmond of South Carolina pressured the federal government to send funds. Sympathy for the missing and murdered children made for some very strange bedfellows indeed.

For those who could not send money, there were other outward expressions of caring. Marches and rallies were held in Chattanooga, Baltimore, Washington, and Harlem. Taking a cue from the yellow ribbons tied to trees across the nation to remember the U.S. embassy hostages in Iran, Mrs. Georgia Dean, a sixty-seven-year-old grandmother from Philadelphia, suggested people wear green ones to commemorate the dead children of Atlanta. The idea caught on immediately, although there was some initial confusion about colors. Neighbors of the victims wore blue, Cincinnati residents wore red, in Dayton ribbons were black, while people in Baton Rouge sported red and black ones. Eventually green, symbolizing life, was chosen as the quasi-official color of the crusade.

Closer to home, Atlanta residents were still presented with the nearly impossible task of protecting their children until the madman was caught. The resulting efforts were as mammoth as every other aspect of the case. A mass media campaign was mounted to spread the safety story and was targeted at those most vulnerable. Safety tips appeared on television and billboards; they were also broadcast around the clock on radio and were sent through the mail. At various times 5,000 posters were printed, 85,000 pamphlets produced, and 150,000 computerized telephone calls placed to households throughout the metropolitan area. Mr. Rogers, Ronald McDonald, and the Sesame Street characters acted as safety spokesmen. A local production company created a public safety film featuring "Tommy Tip" and "Sharon Smart." Leaflets were handed out in school, and a music teacher chipped in with an original song, "Kids Know No."

The warnings were ubiquitous, incessant, and strident, and before long people began to wonder whether the barrage of messages was not contributing to a siege mentality and creating more problems than it was preventing. Certainly, there was ample evidence of significant psychological damage being done to the young people of the city. Without the mature defense mechanisms of adults, the children of Atlanta began to exhibit the pernicious consequences of living in a state of chronic fear. Behavioral problems were reported with alarming regularity, chief among them being an increase in sleep disorders such as bedwetting, nightmares, and fear of the dark. Children were more dependent and tentative, clung to parents, became hysterical when not picked up on time, and were unwilling to play alone.

Test scores of 74,400 school children confirmed and quantified the deleterious effects. Atlanta's youngsters, especially blacks and those from low-income families, were found to be more withdrawn and less verbal on intelligence tests when compared with children in previous years. On projective tests, students were less self-confident, registered lower self-esteem, but evinced greater hostility than in the past. According to one school psychologist, "They are even distrusting of the examiner because he or she is a stranger."[10]

The test scores gave stark witness to the primary process of social dissolution, the evaporation of personal trust in one's surroundings and one's fellow man. The process was insidious, slow but cumulative in its impact, so that each person became gradually detached from the social corpus and individual interactions became more constrained and less spontaneous. After the danger was past, the damage lingered, with unknown consequences for the future. One psychologist described the rebuilding job ahead: "How do you teach a child again to trust his environment?"[11]

BLAMING THE VICTIMS

The police, operating solely on probabilities, had every reason to suspect the parents of being the murderers. The grim statistics of child homicide indicate that in the vast majority of instances relatives are the perpetrators. The circumstances of several cases were also highly dubious, particularly that of Latonya Wilson who, it seemed, could hardly have been kidnapped without alerting someone in the house to her plight. The obvious inference was that she had been taken with the complicity of someone in the household or by someone she knew.

It was routine police practice for investigators to concentrate their initial efforts on family members. Clarence Wilson, father of Latonya, was given two lie detector tests and repeatedly questioned. For parents already suffering the loss of a child, it seemed like the ultimate indignity and grossly unfair. Mr. Wilson, who lost his construction job due to absenteeism after his daughter's death, said: "It seems like they're trying to find somewhere to put the blame, and the parents are the easiest out. I think they're trying not to accept that someone out in the streets is doing it."[12] His wife Ella concurred: "I resent it because I feel like they're badgering and accusing me. They're looking for a motive, like someone who has a grudge against us. They're going to have to look further than the parents."[13]

Despite their suspicions, police could find no evidence that any of the parents were directly responsible for the deaths of their children. Lacking indictable proof, the question of parental involvement in the murders subtly shifted emphasis to indirect responsibility. Parents were still accountable for their children's safety, and it was their job to keep them out of harm's way. The fact that the killer could continue to snatch a child with impunity every twenty-five days was a vivid indication that some parents were not living up to their obligations.

The city government decided to take matters into its own hands. To force compliance with minimum safety standards, a citywide curfew was enacted. The curfew stipulated that all youngsters under the age of 16 were required to be home by 9:00 P.M. Violations of the city ordinance were punishable by fines up to $500.

An editorial in the *Atlanta Constitution* made clear the rationale behind the curfew—to assume the role of the parents who would not properly dispose of their parental obligations: "The target is the parent or guardian who doesn't care enough to take control over people who are too young to make decisions for themselves. The responsible parent is not the target of the curfew."[14] The implication was obvious. Parents who let children wander the streets put them at risk and were irresponsible. Ergo, those who had already lost children to the snatcher were irresponsible and to blame for their murders.

In essence, the issue centered on who was fundamentally responsible for public safety, parents or police. For parents the curfew was just another ploy by the city administration to deflect blame for its inability to apprehend the snatcher. Camille Bell, mother of Yusef, vowed to fight the measure in court, arguing it would be ineffective and unconstitutional and just continued "a trend here for blaming the victims and parents of victims for the streets not being safe." The American Civil Liberties Union agreed and took up the fight against the curfew in the courts. The president of the ACLU, Martha Gains, outlined the reasons for her group's opposition to the measure.

Frankly, we don't perceive the curfew as directly related to the murdered and missing cases. It is the rare child who is reported missing during the hours under the curfew. All the curfew does is pretend we are doing something helpful when we are not.

We're limiting the mobility of young people and, in an oblique kind of way, there is the suggestion that the reason the children have been missing and killed is because of family irresponsibility. I don't believe and the ACLU doesn't believe the case has a thing to do with family responsibility.[15]

The ACLU's efforts to intercede on behalf of the parents caused a great deal of anger. An editorial in the *Atlanta Constitution* opined that the "ACLU should not attempt to interfere with the city's attempts to watch out for youngsters whose parents or guardians can't or won't exercise that obligation for whatever reason."[16] Having conveniently located responsibility with the families of the victims, the paper for one was not about to move it.

In a sense, the newspaper and City Hall were scolding the dead children's families for being bad parents. Other voices joined the chorus. Writing in the *Atlanta Daily World*, Joe Black, vice president of the Greyhound Bus Corporation, took aim at black fathers: "Black males cannot claim that they are Black and proud if they turn their backs on their children."[17] But without question, the supreme insult for the parents occurred when prime suspect, soon to be convicted murderer, Wayne Williams lectured them on proper conduct: "I think you just have a bunch of homicides. I've seen kids in places they don't belong. That is no license to kill. Parents need to tighten up."[18]

Another manifestation of blaming the victims was an implication that the dead children themselves were at fault. This belief found expression in the terms "streetwise" and "hustlers," which were often used to describe the missing children. "Streetwise" was originally used positively to connote a child who was wary of the dangers of city life and not one to be easily duped. For instance, in an early article, columnist Bill Shipp of the *Atlanta Constitution*, describing the murdered children, observed that "all victims were said to be street-wise and not likely to be friendly with strangers."[19]

Over time, the term took on a pejorative meaning, as indicated by this account of the murders that appeared in the same paper on January 18, 1981: "Although they (the victims) were not juvenile delinquents, some of them were streetwise used to being out on the streets until late into the night and often were on their own for long periods."[20] Streetwise had now become synonymous with wild and unsupervised.

The final humiliation for both parents and victims was provided by the Centers for Disease Control. Looking for common denominators among the dead children, CDC epidemiologists attempted to find commonalities in their behavior. After weeks of serious fieldwork, CDC scientists identified three factors all the dead seemed to share: "a certain amount of neglect," "lax parental supervision," and a sense of safety and independence—of being "loose, alone, isolated." The country's top disease detectives had scientifically proven that the parents and the children were at fault.

Just when it seemed that the issue of parental responsibility for the murders was dying down, FBI Chief William Webster blundered and rekindled the controversy. Perhaps trying to pressure local authorities to make an arrest in at least a few cases to show progress in an otherwise unproductive investigation, Webster announced that four cases were "substantially solved," adding "We're satisfied we know the cause and the persons responsible for these killings."[21] For a city desperate to find the killer, the pronouncement hit like a bombshell, implying everything from quick salvation to police malfeasance.

Webster had not directly tied any parents to the murders, but the implication was clear enough. Venus Taylor, mother of Angel Lenair, confirmed what everyone was thinking. "The FBI is telling them I am a suspect,"[22] she said. No indictments were ever brought against the families, but they were forever tainted with presumed guilt.

Aghast at the sheer brazenness of Webster's charge, Mayor Jackson fired off a letter to the FBI chief the next day. As to whether the cases were solved, Jackson wrote, "I am assured positively by Atlanta law-enforcement officials that there is not sufficient evidence in any pending child case to justify an arrest."[23] Then, as if lecturing an ill-mannered boy, the mayor addressed the FBI chief: "Your statements . . . are starting to hurt. We need Washington's help, not more problems. I do not wish to be indelicate, but I respectfully urge that you consider the impact of your casual statements on our local situation, here."[24]

It would have been bad enough if it had ended right there, but as Mayor Jackson's letter was on its way to Chief Webster, Special Agent Mike Twibell of the FBI's Atlanta Office compounded the problem in devastating fashion. Twibell revealed that "some of those kids were killed by their parents" because, he claimed, they were "nuisances." Not only were some parents killers of their own offspring, but now they had been accused of callously murdering to remove an irritant, as if turning off a radio because it was playing too loud. To attack victimized parents on so many levels was outrageous, and Atlanta Public Safety Commissioner Lee Brown asked that disciplinary action be taken against Agent Twibell.

The unfortunate tendency to blame the victims was still not over, however. Throughout the ordeal, especially after Mayor Jackson appealed to the federal government for funds to help the cash-strapped city, donations poured into the city. At times the flow of funds was so overwhelming that it could not be properly accounted for. Making matters worse, the money was often sent to different locations and was earmarked for specific purposes—the investigation, as reward money, and, of course, as help for the families.

The Southern Christian Leadership Conference volunteered to help the mothers of the dead children collect and disseminate funds sent for them, but Camille Bell refused, saying, "I don't intend to accept that from anyone.

No one has the right to collect funds for families or decide what they need."[25] By this time Mrs. Bell and several other mothers had established their own organization, the Committee to Stop Children's Murders. The group and Mrs. Bell were in constant demand throughout the nation, appearing at rallies in Baltimore, Harlem, and Washington, D.C. Camille Bell was even called to testify before the U.S. Senate.

But a backlash was brewing. Collecting funds in the name of dead children had the unpleasant odor of exploitation and profiteering about it. The press criticized the mayor and wondered whether the city too busy to hate should not also be too proud to beg. In the wake of the hue and cry, the state began an investigation into the fund-raising practices of the Committee to Stop Children's Murders. Once again it seemed that the parents were being singled out, and some observers saw the ugly hand of retaliation in the action: "They are being investigated because they are exposing the city's inability to protect black lives. I think the recent attack on them, to get them to open their books, is just another attempt by the government to discredit the mothers and silence them."[26]

A tug of war ensued to try to force the Committee to open its books and disclose how it had used the funds it received. When the organization did, charges were brought for violation of the Charitable Solicitations statute. Although the money had been sought ostensibly to aid summer camps, little of it had been used for that purpose. Of the $40,000 collected, $26,400 had gone for Committee expenses. The victim's families had received less than a thousand dollars apiece.

The mothers turned out to be their own worst enemies. They had stayed in expensive hotel rooms when traveling, and to their embarrassment it was learned that Venus Taylor, mother of Angel Lenair, had used some of the money for cosmetic surgery—a "tummy tuck," to be precise. Critics finally had something for which the victim's mothers were truly at fault. The Committee to Stop Children's Murders quickly faded into oblivion.

A CULTURAL CONSPIRACY

No serial murder case before or since has gained as much national, or for that matter international, notoriety as did the Atlanta child murders. Certainly, part of the reason for the rapt attention was the length of time the case lasted, the number of victims involved, and the fact that most were children. Part of it too was that the dead were poor and black. These characteristics played into a set of preconceived notions about the United States and the condition of black Americans that, in turn, provided off-the-shelf suppositions about who the killer was and what his motives must be.

The national environment also created a context within which the murders would be interpreted and given meaning. Three coterminous circumstances—racial murders, political conservatism, and the resurgence of the

Ku Klux Klan—affected the public's reaction to the child murders. The national political climate and racial violence, real or forecast, created a milieu in which local conditions were amplified and resonated.

International reaction to the murders took it for granted that they were racially motivated. The English suggested that the violence was a continuation of the U.S. Old West mentality, while South Africans assumed the Klan was at fault. Japanese papers suggested that a similar experience could not happen in their country because of its racial homogeneity. In the Soviet Union, Tass concluded that "the Soviet people, like the majority of the world community, would conclude that the Atlanta young people were victims of violent white racism."[27]

Racially motivated murders were just one of several trends facing blacks in the late 1970s. Equally important was the changing political scene. Repudiating the years of stagflation of the Carter administration, the nation was veering sharply to the right. Blacks had visions of a national retreat from hard-won civil rights victories. Reagan's call for spending cuts and reductions in entitlement programs was widely interpreted as antiblack. The great fear was that the budget would be balanced on the backs of the people who could least afford it, black and poor Americans.

Carter, sensing political leverage, hammered home the specter of a Reagan victory. With the election slipping away, he charged that Reagan would divide the country, separating black from white, Christian from Jew, North from South, and rural from urban. An incensed Reagan fired back, stating that Carter owed the nation an apology. Whether or not he did, the fact remained that the president of the United States had confirmed the worst fears of black Americans.

With the election in hand, a newly inaugurated President Reagan was confronted almost immediately with how to deal with the Atlanta missing and murdered children. The city budget was straining under the extraordinary costs of the investigation. Mayor Jackson appealed directly to the president to release federal funds to help offset the costs and for investigative resources from the FBI.

Reagan at first demurred, noting, as other federal officials had before in the John Norman Collins and Son of Sam cases, that federal intervention could only be justified if the children had been transported across state lines or their civil rights had been violated, neither of which seemed to apply. In Atlanta 400 people marched in protest with signs that read "Millions to build killer missiles—Nothing to fight child killers." Reverend Joseph Lowery of the Southern Christian Leadership Conference jibed, "If the President can send $25 million to El Salvador to meddle in the affairs of that nation, he ought to be able to send $2 million to Atlanta to catch the killer of our children."[28]

The president's response was vintage Reagan. He sent George and Barbara Bush to the city wearing green ribbons and released the desired money.

The city was relieved. Mayor Jackson said to the president, "You have not turned your back on Atlanta, and we thank you sincerely for it."[29] But others saw the move as opportunistic and crass; *Atlanta Constitution* columnist Lewis Gizzard wrote: "Ronald Reagan is a smoothie, isn't he? Cut back on this program and that program, but you can always send a couple of guys down to talk to Mayor Jackson. It won't help solve the killings, of course, but it's good ink and all it costs is a couple of airplane tickets."[30]

Although Reagan came through for the city, questions remained about his conservative bent and what that might portend for blacks. The situation was not helped when the Georgia Ku Klux Klan announced that it would disband because Reagan was doing its work for them. While this statement was undoubtedly specious, the threat posed by the Klan was treated as very serious. No less an authority than Benjamin Hooks of the NAACP said that the organization would mobilize 2,000 of its units, consisting of 10,000 members in twenty-four states, to fight the Klan. Continuing, Hooks tied the action to the national political climate: "[A] pattern appears to be emerging that is linked to a growing climate of violence spawning hate. In the black community there is a real and growing sense of frustration, isolation, fear and anger. Black Americans perceive a legitimization of reaction and racism that has made it more 'respectable' to be anti-black and to attack those laws."[31]

The Klan continued to haunt the child murder case and to raise the possibility of pandemic racial conflict. Particularly worrisome was the reaction of black veterans groups to reports that the Klan had set up paramilitary camps throughout the South. Only a few years removed from the Vietnam War, a generation of black men were capable and willing to defend themselves and their families. By some estimates, there were 2.5 million black veterans in the South alone, and their organization, the United States Veterans, sounded the alarm: "The shadow of the KKK is over every black home night and day and an unanswered incident will trigger this riot between blacks and whites."[32]

Some blacks saw a direct connection between the activities of the Klan and the child murders, and believed that the killings were done at their direction. Others, like the head of a U.S. veterans post, saw the influence of the Klan as less direct but significant nonetheless:

We're not saying the Klan is directly responsible for the child killings and other things but we believe they are indirectly responsible. They have created the climate and black people are scared. We are not advocating violence, but we are arming ourselves and will be setting up neighborhood watches in low-income areas where the disappearances and the killings have taken place.[33]

Whether the Klan threat was actual or overblown is somewhat superfluous. For blacks it was a real and present danger, and they were taking steps to counteract it.

Racial murders, political conservatism, the Ku Klux Klan—taken together, created a mind-set among blacks that structured their view of the Atlanta child murders. When looked at in combination, the three warning signs pointed to a much more frightening prospect than did any individually. Jesse Jackson explained, "There is a cultural conspiracy to kill black people. The conspiracy cannot be proven, but it can't be disproven. The present atmosphere in which we're operating has made it open season on black people and poor people."[34]

A FINGER-SNAP AWAY

National events and the changing political climate created a context within which the Atlanta child murders would play out. Local conditions and history, in turn, influenced the form public reactions to the serial murders would take. The Atlanta city government and Police Department had undergone fundamental structural changes in the years preceding the murders, creating fault lines in the community along which public tensions and strain would be expressed.

The core of the city's transformation was a transfer of political power from whites to blacks precipitated by changing urban demographics. In 1973 Maynard Jackson became the first black mayor on the strength of receiving 95 percent of the black vote and 22 percent of the white. The new mayor inherited a police department with a reputation for brutality and bigotry and a police chief, John Inman, not of his choosing. That year police killed nineteen civilians, many of whom were black, including one man who was shot forty times.

The final straw came when mounted patrolmen charged demonstrators led by black leader Hosea Williams. Seizing the opportunity, Mayor Jackson moved to replace Inman. Following an ugly and very public confrontation in which Inman barricaded himself in his office surrounded by a SWAT team, the mayor appointed a friend, Reginald Eaves, public safety commissioner, a new position to which the police chief was forced to report. Outmaneuvered, Inman resigned.

Conflict in the police department was far from over, however. Noting that only 22 percent of police officers were black versus 51 percent of the city population, in 1975 the Afro-American Patrolmen's League brought suit and won a consent decree requiring that police ranks be brought into line with the racial mix of the community. The suit came on top of one brought the year before by the largely white Fraternal Order of Police for reverse discrimination to protest the transfer and demotion of white officers by Eaves.

Commissioner Eaves next became embroiled in a personal scandal. In order to help blacks rise to officer ranks, Eaves condoned, and according to investigators "expressly authorized," cheating on promotional exams. Eaves resigned after the investigative report was made public in 1978.

In his place Mayor Jackson appointed two black men to the top police jobs, Lee Brown as public safety commissioner and George Napper as police chief. Brown was a highly qualified Ph.D. in criminology and a career police officer. A champion of community-oriented policing, Brown had helped draft the National Urban League's position paper on crime in 1972. He was reserved, even stoic, qualities that would serve him well in the coming crisis when he was the focal point for the public's frustration and criticisms.

The years of turmoil in the department had left their mark. Police strength had been reduced by a third to 1,100 officers down from 1,700. Early in the serial murder case, the head of the homicide division, Walter Perry, abruptly resigned over the assignment of child murder cases. Going into the most massive murder investigation in its history, the department found itself with a new, untried leadership team, a depleted force, and a paucity of investigative experience in homicide cases.

Whether the Atlanta Police Department could have apprehended the killer earlier had it not been for its history of dissension is uncertain. What is clear is that past events influenced how the public viewed the department and affected community response to the murders. The department was, for example, held responsible for the rumors that circulated. "The inability of the Atlanta police bureau to apprehend the killer of our youngsters has left the door open for all manner of rumors and speculation namely, that had the victims been white, the reaction from the white community would have been vociferous and sustained until something was settled in the cases."[35]

The most pervasive criticism leveled at authorities was that the city government and police force were not responsive to the tragedy, that they had moved slowly because the victims were poor blacks. The parents of the victims were the first to raise this criticism, but for other members of the black community it found expression in a less direct manner, namely, that things would have been different had the victims been white or middle class. As Roy Innis of the Congress on Racial Equality said, "If this case had occurred around white children—maybe a dozen—the case would be solved right now. If this case had occurred around black middle class children—maybe a dozen—it would be solved by now."[36] George Coleman, contributing poet for the black newspaper, the *Atlanta Daily World*, had his own unique way of echoing Innis's sentiment:

> Why can't we find the killer? Cry the folk
> Why can't the whole town, join in the attack
> Somewhere, in each of us, the truth cries out
> The only children harmed, are just poor blacks.
> Just let a white child come up missing here
> The rage of Joshua will shake this town.

The army and the navy and Marines
Will make Atlanta's walls come tumbling down.[37]

Whites, for their part, did not feel privileged or the beneficiaries of special police protection. Two much-publicized murders in the recent past underscored for whites their vulnerability to urban crime. In one case a white physician attending a convention had been gunned down in his hotel room. In another, a secretary had been shot and killed in an office building. Both victims were white, their assailants black. Columnist Bill Shipp summed up the opinion of many whites: "There is a feeling in much of the white business community that the black city administration was insensitive to criminal acts against the white minority in Atlanta."[38]

Changes in City Hall and conflict in the police department also led to speculation about the motives of the killer and the investigators. Many black citizens assumed as an article of faith that the killer was white. They conjectured that the murders were directed not only at black children but at a black city administration as well. As one man commented, "He is trying to prove that blacks can't head this city. Atlanta is a leader of the black world. It's no accident that this is happening in Atlanta."[39] A variant of this white conspiracy theory was that white officers on the police force were dragging their feet on the investigation, thereby preventing an arrest of the murderer. This would force the administration to call in largely white law enforcement agencies such as the FBI and Georgia Bureau of Investigation, a move that would again discredit the black administration.

Given the political climate in the country and the instances of white on black racial violence in other parts of the country, it was almost impossible for the people of Atlanta not to see the hand of conspiracy in the children's deaths. A small but profound shift in the public's thinking took place. Racial murders became racist murders. *Atlanta Daily World* columnist Charles Price noted: "This linkage of these crimes to race has been due largely to the fact that the scores have been kept in terms of race and age. It does not take a great deal of imagination to link victims as to age and race. And only if one is satisfied that the crimes are being perpetrated because of race or age do these linkages have any real significance."[40]

But that was precisely the problem: the list was kept, only blacks were on it, and that fact was deemed significant. The killings were therefore racially motivated. An article in the *Atlanta Constitution* titled "Black Areas on Edge over Child Murders"[41] explored the depths of these feelings. One person commented, "I think it's a white man 'cause ain't no white children getting killed." Another person saw the murders as well planned and the work of a group of racists. "Well, there haven't been no white children turning up dead. But this is an organization. Ain't no man who can drive a car and snatch a child. And there's money behind it too. They change cars and tags." And if an organization was behind the violence, there was one that immediately came to mind. "I think it's the Klan. They're getting black children—not anybody else."

For prominent blacks and whites, it was a difficult balancing act between the factions in an increasingly polarized city. Black leaders were presented with the dilemma of how to avoid giving credence to racist theories while not losing their own credibility. Reverend Joseph Lowery of the Southern Christian Leadership Conference outlined the problem and his organization's solution to it.

You can't go before the people and say "There's no racial motive behind this" or "What's happening around the country has nothing to do with Atlanta." That's not realistic. It's more inflammatory.

If you don't address the possibility of racial motives, people would think you were shucking and jiving, that you weren't real, that you were a clown. That's why we give these constituencies means of letting people express their outrage. That's why we have a march or a prayer pilgrimage or ecumenical worship service or a motorcade.[42]

Whites were hamstrung by a similar damned-if-you-do, damned-if-you-don't choice. According to one white businessman, "The dilemma for the white politician or civic leader has been that criticism on such a sensitive issue—might be interpreted as racist, while silence might be read as lack of concern."[43] Thus, whites could not take the side of the victims and their families since support might be interpreted as de facto criticism of black city administrators. Most whites wisely chose to keep their opinions, pro or con, to themselves, even though this stance too had its negative consequences. A letter to the editor of the *Atlanta Daily World* from the Ad Hoc Group of Concerned White Atlantans suggested that white neutrality aggravated the local situation: "Our (whites) inaction has contributed to the polarization of Atlanta along racial lines."[44] If for no other reason, the group claimed that the Klan had been emboldened by white silence.

Race riots, started by accident or design, were a very real possibility and were uppermost in the minds of city fathers. Reginald Eaves, reborn after the police scandal as an erstwhile mayoral candidate, offered a sinister scenario of premeditated murder to precipitate racial conflict: "Based on what you hear from folk in the community at this point it could very well be someone trying to divide blacks and whites."[45] In this doomsday view, all it would take to set off a racial Armageddon would be the murder of two or three white children. "The natural reaction on the part of the white community is the black community is retaliating. Then what you have is a clash between the two races."[46] As events transpired, nothing so well planned was needed because a series of instances brought the city to the brink of chaos and violence, the first occurring midway through the murder string.

By October 1980, fourteen children were missing, connections between the victims had been established, and the police department acknowledged the link. Just as the city was coming to grips with the emerging trauma of the missing and murdered children, a second catastrophe struck. A furnace in the Bowen Homes Day Care Center exploded, killing four black three year olds and a fifty-eight-year-old teacher. For black residents of Atlanta, it was prima facie proof of a conspiracy to murder black children.

A subsequent investigation quickly found the cause of the blast to be a poorly maintained boiler, but the sad fact could not dispel hardened beliefs. Inevitably, the Klan was rumored to be responsible. The attitudes of the community were galvanized by the tragedy. Citizens lost faith in elected officials. The mayor and public safety commissioner were booed, and the city "moved within a finger-snap of violence." The day care explosion lingered over the city like a bitter cloud tainting the investigation of the missing and murdered children. Five months later, as an example, a black resident commenting on the murders to a newspaper reporter would say, "Not only have they killed 20 black kids but they have attempted to blow up a whole nursery."[47] The city residents had come within a hair breadth of violence, and they would flirt with it again in the coming months.

One such incident occurred in the Techwood Clark Howell Homes when residents organized "bat patrols," vowing to use their "Hank Aaron crime stoppers" to guard the housing project against "crazed racist killers." According to vigilante leader Chimurenga Jenga, the action was taken because police took too long to answer calls in the area. The police immediately moved in to disband the units, prompting one woman to comment, "The police department is killing these black children. That's the reason they're trying to put us in jail."[48]

Any serious repercussions from the bat patrols were avoided by the quick action of city leaders and the good sense of the project tenants. Mayor Jackson spoke out strongly against the vigilantes, and officially sanctioned youth patrols were set up. The residents meanwhile had no interest in "starting a war" and felt that the patrols were only "rubbing salt in wounds." Jenga lost all credibility as a community activist when it was revealed that he was not even a resident of the projects. The final humiliation was added by the killer, who snatched the next victim from the projects several days later. The movement collapsed unceremoniously.

Nevertheless, tempers remained at a flashpoint; violence could erupt at any moment over any instance, no matter how trivial. A case in point occurred when a black auto parts storeowner saw what he thought were two white men trying to lure a black child into their car. The man gave chase, pulled out a firearm, and began shooting at the white pair. When police were finally able to sort out what had happened, the two white males were found to be innocent and were released, while the black man was arrested for aggravated assault. Neighbors nonetheless considered him a hero.

The incident gave ample proof of how high tensions had risen in the city, how people's attitudes were affected, and how close racial violence was. But overt conflict was avoided until a suspect was arrested a few months later. The fact that the suspect was black did little to assuage the accumulated mistrust. It was difficult to believe the man in custody, Wayne Williams, had committed all the murders or had acted alone. The residue of racial animosity and suspicion remained. Questions about the competence and sincerity of city government were never totally answered. The wounds were old, the scars were fresh.

In the final analysis, the most serious damage wrought by the murders may have been to divide blacks among themselves. Certainly, one effect was for blacks to lose faith in their leaders. A survey of 1,234 black Americans conducted near the end of the crisis demonstrated the pervasiveness and depth of the alienation caused by the murders. Of those contacted, 73 percent said that the police were not paying enough attention to the murders, 58 percent felt that black leaders were not doing enough, and 69 percent indicated that national leaders, black and white, had paid too little attention to the tragedy. Nearly three-quarters of those surveyed felt the murders would have been given more attention if the victims had been white.

Locally, the assumption that the killer was white had been protective since blacks could still feel safe among themselves. But when Wayne Williams was arrested, blacks were forced to confront the possibility that a racial outsider had not been the murderer. One psychologist predicted the outcome would be a lasting suspicion of blacks about other blacks. No longer would parents enjoy the mental freedom that their children were safe among other blacks. A cherished belief had died. "Parents always assumed black children could roam freely and safely in primarily black neighborhoods and that other blacks would look after them."[49] A sense of community belonging, a feeling of security among one's kind was the thirtieth casualty of the serial murderer.

MARTIN'S TOWN

It could have been much worse. The city had come under tremendous stress, nearly ripped apart by tidal forces of history, politics, demography, and beliefs. When threatened, the community began to polarize along these structural underpinnings, the resulting divisiveness finding expression in the behavior of the populace as suspicion, mistrust, animosity, hatred, isolation, alienation, and scapegoating. The principal effect of the killer among us was, therefore, to divide the city along preexisting lines, to deepen divisions already present, and to accentuate and sharpen differences between segments of the population.

Barring forces to the contrary, it is quite possible that the citizenry would have devolved into a fractious collection of warring camps. Lasting damage, perhaps even violence, might have been the result. But there were countervailing forces that held the city together in the hour of crisis. Not surprisingly, the cohesive elements were to be found along the same structural dimensions of history, beliefs, demography, and politics, forming a legacy of positive action that could be called upon when needed. Once the inner strength had been tapped, the city in the end may have been stronger for having gone through the ordeal.

The first and most obvious advantage was that the political power in the city had passed to a generation of competent black leaders. By chance alone, the victims happened also to be black. While the race of the killer remained unknown, it was a constant source of friction, inspiring conspiracy theories, pejorative speculation, and racist conjecture. Until the killer was found, the city, especially the race being victimized, could take solace in the fact that those in charge shared the same ethnicity, cultural heritage, and history.

The police force was also led by black men, Public Safety Commissioner Lee Brown and Chief of Police George Napper. They may have been inexperienced, but they did not crack under the pressure. They refused to be pushed into making frivolous arrests and were always willing to accept help from outside law enforcement agencies. The fact that the leaders of the force were the same race as the victims again served to remove one bone of contention and the most emotionally charged one at that. It was possible then to confront bat patrol vigilantes with a simple, powerful truth. "The police department is on your side, unlike the civil rights days when all of the policemen were white. It's absurd to think that black policemen, including the blacks who head the police department, are part of a conspiracy to do away with our kids."[50] It would certainly have been a very different situation, with undoubtedly a different outcome, had the victims and the city government been different races. That circumstance was due solely to chance and owed nothing to the heads of city government.

Notwithstanding luck, the black leaders of the city had created an environment in which suspicion was minimized because all parts of the city participated in its government and shared political power. City government was viewed as being accessible to all segments of the population such that no group was disenfranchised. The majority of Atlantans viewed the administration as open, sensitive, and caring as a consequence. The power distribution was real and tangible and not cosmetic tokenism. As the *Atlanta Constitution* noted: "Before Jackson, there were only a few blacks and women in city government. The mayor opened real representation of minorities."[51] Andrew Young put the issue more succinctly: "Atlanta is one place where we have made the system work, where representative government is a reality."[52] Moreover, the inequities of past administrations and a history of segregation had been remedied. There were no simmering feuds or old scores to be settled that could be used for political advantage and therefore divide people.

Blacks in City Hall were seen as a testament to Atlanta's progressive attitudes and enterprising spirit. This progress was most clearly evident in the new international airport that had made the city the transportation hub of the new South and that had been a major personal and political triumph of Mayor Jackson. Thus, City Hall was not just a calming influence, but a source of pride for the population. "I am also convinced that had these slayings occurred in a city without this much black leadership that the city would not have been able to hold itself together. Atlanta, with its large group of black professionals, has always put a skew in the charts that paint a bleak picture of black survival,"[53] commented *Atlanta Constitution* columnist Alexis Scott Reeves.

Rather than create jealousies for what had been lost, the representative government produced visible benefits that even whites could appreciate. As a white businessman explained:

City Hall may be something now that is not in my knowledge base. City Hall may be healing wounds. City Hall may be bringing 50 percent of our population into the feeling that they are part of the city, too. Take law enforcement (a generation ago). Police protected the white community and kept the blacks in their black ghetto. From a black perspective, that police force was nothing but an opposing army.

We've come to the point now that we have a police department where I think the blacks really and truly look upon it as law enforcement.[54]

As advertised, Atlanta was operating for the most part as the city too busy to hate.

Outside government, churches provided a second network of organizations to steady nerves and involve the community. One obvious role played by churches was to minister to the spiritual needs of the populace. Appeals to the supernatural are inherently functional and promote social cohesion simply by providing an explanation for the tragedy and an outlet for emotions. By being the conduit for appeals, churches helped manage anxiety and acted as a steadying hand. Furthermore, Atlanta with its generally religious population was more apt to be influenced by churches and church leaders than would other cities in the country with more secular populations.

Churches provided other more worldly assets. Ministers formed a body of nongovernmental leadership. As such, they could be articulate spokesmen for their congregations, which were in a sense political constituencies. Moreover, the facilities of the churches were put to use in programs designed to protect the children. For instance, twenty Methodist churches banded together to offer youth programs in low-income areas. Similarly, seventy churches contributed to Safe Summer '81 in which Atlanta children were given supervised outlets during the school break.

The white population of the city also contributed to the community's general well-being. The missing and murdered children were a black tragedy being handled by black political and spiritual leaders. The white population of the city had the good sense not to interfere. The situation could have been used for political gain or as the rallying cry for an attack on City Hall. Whites for the most part refrained. To the degree that whites did get involved, it was in a positive manner by offering expressions of sympathy and taking part in community activities in support of the children.

Atlantans benefited as well from the memory of their fallen civil rights leader. Dead for more than a decade, Martin Luther King, Jr. had left a legacy that was felt in the transcendent beliefs he espoused and the living leaders he had touched. Many of the community leaders who were to guide the city through the crisis had been with Dr. King in the civil rights struggles of the 1960s. His family, still prominent in the city, was a visible link to the past—Martin Luther King, Sr. at the Ebenezer Baptist Church and Corretta Scott King as president of the Martin Luther King, Jr. Center for Nonviolent Change.

Not coincidentally, it was a product of the civil rights movement, the 1965 Voting Rights Act, that made it possible to have such broad minority representation in local politics and black control of city government. Throughout the ordeal, blacks realized that the conduct of the investigation and resolution of the situation would reflect on their stewardship of local affairs. When a black judge was selected, again by a stroke of good fortune, to hear the case, control was complete. Blacks had a great deal to lose from any disruptions and especially from conflict or bickering among themselves.

With hard-won victories in civil rights at stake, black leaders were unwilling to entertain any dissension in the ranks. Mayor Jackson admonished bat patrol organizers to "lower their voices." Others, including State Senator Julian Bond, businessman John Cox, ACTION Associate Director John Lewis, and State Representatives Hosea Williams, Tyrone Brooks, and Aveda Beale, warned that speculation that the crimes were racially motivated was an invitation for unrest and possibly violence. About the trial, the *Atlanta Daily World* editorialized: "The matter is so serious to the future of the city and the leadership of the Atlanta Black Community, responsible citizens should refrain from expressing an opinion pro or con."[55]

Above all else, the legacy of Martin Luther King provided a method to deal with adversity and effect change through nonviolent means. Recalling the 1966 March Against Fear that Dr. King led to protest blacks being terrorized at the polls in Mississippi, Mrs. King announced a Moratorium on Murder to protest the terrorization of Atlanta's black children. "We are determined to project an assertive, nonviolent alternative to the fear and despair which has gripped our community,"[56] she stated. Local businessman Reginald Swails best summed up the lasting contribution of the civil rights leader. "This is Martin's town—Martin Luther King's town. His old charisma is still out there. We've had 20 bodies and not a word of disruption. Call it pride. Martin's town stands for nonviolence."[57]

In the tradition of Martin Luther King, whenever violence seemed about to break out, the city found a constructive alternative. The most important contributor in this regard was City Councilman Michael Langford. When a wave of vigilantism in the form of bat patrols was sweeping Techwood, Langford through his organization, the United Youth Adult Conference, set up youth patrols as a substitute. Eleventh and twelfth graders were enlisted to monitor black neighborhoods and housing projects.

By far the most significant thing Langford, or for that matter anyone, did was organize searches for the missing children. Parents of the missing children believed that the police department, city government, and other Atlantans were insensitive to their concerns, unheeding of their warnings, and little caring for their children. The searches were a way to demonstrate the opposite. Thousands of townspeople came every weekend to search the woods and vacant lots for the missing children. It was a way to express concern, come together, and help solve the problem. In retrospect, John Bascom of the United Youth Adult Conference assessed the contribution of the searches to the city's well-being. "We probably did more for the city than we did for the children's cases. We brought the entire community together, rich and poor, black and white. Through us, people were able to show their concern for the city and what was happening."[58] The weekend walks shoulder to shoulder through the woods may be as close as Americans have ever come to realizing the dream.

THE ATLANTA SNATCHER

Wayne Williams was born in 1958, the only child of an older couple, Homer and Faye Williams. The parents were both retired school teachers and had moved to Atlanta from Columbus, Ohio. Homer Williams worked part-time as a freelance photographer for the city's black newspaper, the *Atlanta Daily World*. With no other children and little else to occupy their time, the doting parents showered their son with unlimited attention and support, even to their own detriment.

At first, it appeared that their faith in their son was not misplaced. By all accounts, Wayne was highly intelligent, and many considered him to be a child prodigy. Radios fired his imagination from an early age, and by eleven he and two friends had constructed a miniature station, WRAP, and were broadcasting within a few blocks of his house. Wayne acquired all the necessary technical knowledge to build the transmitter by reading books.

His second radio venture was WRAZ, a carrier-current transmission that was sent over house wiring. The station was particularly effective in high-density areas such as housing projects and quickly became a commercial success selling advertising time. Wayne's career hit its apogee in 1974 when he was pictured in *Jet* seated behind his radio equipment with an admiring Benjamin Hooks looking on. The rest of his life he would try to recapture this brief moment in the limelight and his initial financial success.

Self-destructive personality traits were already apparent, however. The spoiled child became a profligate spender. The elder Williamses poured their life savings into WRAZ, and Wayne spent the money on expensive equipment without consulting them. An attempt was also made to obtain venture capital for the station, but a petulant Wayne refused to relinquish control of the business, a requirement for funding. The insolvent station collapsed in 1976, and with it the elder Williamses were forced to declare personal bankruptcy.

Wayne next enrolled in Georgia State University but dropped out before completing a degree. By this point, he had become enamored of other aspects of the entertainment business. His interest in the news led to the acquisition of a television camera, police scanner, and flashing lights for his car. Whether he used any of the equipment to lure children is unknown, but he did learn police procedures from his experiences as an erstwhile reporter. In one chilling instance, he appeared at the site where the body of one of the missing children had been found and volunteered to photograph it for the police.

Wayne also fancied himself a record promoter and spent considerable time, money, and energy trying to put together a singing group he named Gemini. As with his other ventures, it became a frenetic, desperate grasp for riches and fame. But Williams knew little about the recording business, and his efforts were directionless and doomed to fail. On a more sinister level, the recording scheme gave Wayne nearly unlimited access to young blacks. While trying to put Gemini together, Wayne blanketed black neighborhoods with leaflets offering private auditions for children between the ages of 11 and 21. And in an unparalleled example of temerity, Wayne revealed at the trial that he had contacted the missing child task force on three separate occasions to keep them abreast of his recruitment activities among young blacks.

Consistent with his grandiose plans, Wayne demonstrated a penchant to inflate his accomplishments. His resume was filled with positions that did not exist or were aggrandizing titles he assumed in his one-man businesses. During his trial, Wayne asked to be released on bond because he was close to inking a deal with Motown Records and Cap Cities. Representatives of both companies said they knew nothing about it. The child genius had grown up to be a shameless self-promoter and dilettante quixotically looking for quick riches and fame. "He was a promise always about to be fulfilled,"[59] said a friend.

The Atlanta child snatcher appeared to have many of the same needs for publicity and flamboyant tendencies as Williams. While the murder spree was in progress, it was clear that the killer was taunting public figures associated with the case. After Reverend Paulk made a public appeal for the killer to surrender to him, the next body was found within sight of the minister's church. Following the bat patrol incident in the Techwood, the next victim, taken just a few days later, was a resident of the project.

The game continued after his initial questioning until his arrest, and Williams seemed to enjoy matching wits with the police and press immensely. After being questioned by the FBI, Williams became an instant media celebrity. Reporters by the score surrounded his house and kept constant vigil. Papers from around the country and the world were represented. The New York *Post*, as an example, continued the journalistic tradition it had established in the Son of Sam case, describing the events under a banner headline that read "Atlanta Monster Seized."

While other papers were agonizing over the ethics of publishing the suspect's name, Williams called a press conference, announced that he was, in fact, a "prime suspect" and passed out a five-page resume to the assembled throng of reporters. Then, like the boy who asks for mercy after killing his parents on the grounds he is an orphan, Williams petitioned the court to prevent the release of any further prejudicial information since it had already caused him "embarrassment, humiliation and injury" and hurt his business dealings.

Police, too, kept Williams under around-the-clock surveillance, and the suspect took special delight in playing with them. On one occasion, he escaped from his house on the floor of the family car driven dutifully by his father. When police realized Williams was gone, they pursued the errant pair, the ensuing high speed chase ending when the Williamses stopped their car on the lawn of Public Safety Commissioner Lee Brown. Another time, Wayne sent a shiver of anxiety through the force when he sent his father to the airport to inquire into chartering a private plane for a flight to South America.

Wayne Williams was arrested on Sunday, June 21, 1981 and charged with the murder of Nathaniel Cater. A second charge for the murder of Jimmy Payne followed shortly after. The trial was held in Superior Court with the presiding judge chosen at random by a computer, a procedure instituted to eliminate bias and to prevent judge shopping by attorneys in Superior Court cases. By the luck of the draw, the judge selected was Clarence Cooper, the first black elected to the Superior Court in a countywide election. Thus, by a fantastic stroke of chance, the trial would be argued in front of the only black judge on the Superior Court bench.

As fortuitous as the selection appeared for community relations, Judge Cooper was something of an enigma. A poll of his peers did not provide a ringing endorsement. Of the 1,500 lawyers questioned, only 194 thought Judge Cooper to be the best qualified for his position, whereas twice that number, 412, thought him not qualified at all. Equally important, Judge Cooper had limited criminal trial experience and had never been involved with a case as remotely sensitive or potentially explosive.

Race, as expected, entered into the jury selection decisions, with prosecutors tending to avoid blacks and the defense whites. When finally impaneled, the jury was made up of one white male (a former Detroit policeman), three white females, two black males, and six black females. With a black judge presiding and a two-to-one majority on the jury, the black community was well aware of the stakes. An *Atlanta Daily World* editorial chided, "Atlantans, especially blacks who are mostly in control, must show the ability to resolve a difficult situation without delay."[60]

The prosecution's case rested on two types of circumstantial evidence. The first concerned events taking place in the early morning hours of May 22. At about 3:00 A.M, Officer Bob Campbell, on stakeout below a bridge over the Chattahoochee River, heard a loud splash in the water. He alerted the officers watching the bridge above. They, in turn, observed a car that appeared to stop midspan and then proceed on at a slow rate of speed. The car reached the end of the bridge, turned into a liquor store parking lot, changed direction, and retraced its journey across the bridge.

The car was stopped and the driver identified as Wayne Williams. During the in situ questioning that followed, police looked in the car and saw a duffle bag filled with clothes, a pair of black men's shoes, dirty work gloves, and a flashlight. Williams gave a jumbled explanation for his presence on the bridge, many details of which proved to be false on later investigation. FBI agents wanted to arrest Williams on the spot, but the Atlanta Police let him go. Two days later the nude body of Nathaniel Cater surfaced down river from the bridge.

The second circumstantial indication of guilt involved the textile and animal fibers that had been found on the bodies. Experts testified that the fibers matched samples taken from the carpet and bedspread in Williams' home and the family's pet German Shepherd. On the strength of the fiber evidence, the prosecution moved to widen the scope of the trial to present evidence linking Williams to ten other deaths for which he was not on trial. The goal was to show "a plan, scheme, pattern, bent of mind." It was a controversial move that conspiracy theorists would criticize, but the judge allowed it.

To overcome the obvious shortcomings of a case built solely on circumstantial evidence, prosecutors tried to suggest a plausible motive for the crimes. Witnesses testified that Wayne was seething with hatred for his race. One person who worked with him remembered conversations in which his negative views toward blacks were openly uttered. "He said blacks were sorry—the way they lived, the way they acted, leeching off the government."[61] The inference to be drawn by the jury was the hatred for fellow blacks reflected in Williams' inability to accept himself and a deep self-hatred. In this regard, the boys he preyed upon were young versions of himself, ambitious, eager to become famous, to get rich quick, and the most apt to accept a music audition.

The defense counsel predictably presented alternative explanations for the river splash (e.g., it was the slap of a beaver's tail), suggested Officer Campbell may have been drinking at the time, and challenged the conclusiveness of the "thimble full of fibers." With respect to the pattern and connection to past crimes, the defense speculated that the real killer had temporarily stopped so that Williams would be blamed for the murders. A parade of character witnesses testified for the defendant. Then in a self-inflicted coup de grace, Williams was allowed to take the stand.

It started innocently enough with the defendant pointing out: "I'm 23 years old and I could have been a victim. Anyone in Atlanta could have been. I'm not sure it's over yet."[62] But under cross-examination, a different Williams appeared. Pressured about his alleged beating of his father, the defendant completely lost his composure, at one point calling the prosecutor a "fool" and FBI agents "goons." It was a remarkably self-destructive display of petulance and belligerence that might, under different circumstances, be construed as homicidal anger. The prosecutor said simply, "You wanted the real Wayne Williams and you've got him right here."[63]

On February 27, 1982, after hearing nine weeks of testimony and following eleven hours of deliberation, the jury returned a verdict of guilty on both counts. Wayne Williams was then sentenced to two consecutive life terms in prison.

The conviction of Wayne Williams did not close the case for some people. There was a lingering disbelief that a solitary black man, especially the one on trial, could have killed so many children. It challenged credibility on a number of levels: he was not nearly the monster that had haunted their imaginations, how could he have evaded police so long or even committed the crimes without confederates, and most of all that he was black. So when investigators closed twenty-three cases after Williams was convicted, a group of mothers filed suit to have thirteen reopened. The *Atlanta Constitution* articulated the dissonance many were feeling: "[T]he black community remains divided and confused by the fact that the pudgy young man languishing in Fulton County jail is one of their own. Many simply refuse to believe it could be so. Racial pride and cohesiveness have been an integral part of their long struggle."[64]

During the trial, defense attorneys had attacked the idea that a black man could be a systematic predator of his own race. "Have you ever heard, in the history of man, of a black mass killer. It just don't make sense."[65] Others saw conspiracy rather than chance in the selection of a black judge. "With reference to the Black Judge and mostly black jury, the white people wanted to make sure that Blacks had charge so whatever verdict, they (whites) would not be blamed,"[66] commented a speaker at a county Black Republican meeting.

In subsequent years, others took up the mantle of disbelief. James Baldwin in *Evidence of Things Not Seen* wrote an impassioned polemic reprising the conspiracy theory and the evils of white justice. Abby Mann, whose previous credits included *Judgment at Nuremberg*, produced a television docudrama which he admitted was a "crusade" to prove Williams innocent. Atlanta

Mayor Andrew Young called the film distorted and inaccurate and asked advertisers to avoid it. Nevertheless, nearly 20 million households, 31 percent of those with sets on, watched the docudrama when it was broadcast.

All the doubts, reinterpretations of the evidence, books, films, and lawsuits speak to a deeper legacy of the Atlanta child murders. The seeds of mistrust had been planted, the faith of the community shaken. It would be difficult for those who lived through the trauma to view their city or neighbors in the same way again. Always lurking in the background of routine social discourse would be the apprehensions voiced by black poet George Coleman:

> An empty feeling touched my heart
> It did not seem quite right
> I wish that I could be more sure
> Of acts done in the night.[67]

EPILOGUE

In 1985, renowned defense attorneys Alan Dershowitz and William Kunstler took up the defense of Wayne Williams. They petitioned the court to grant Williams a new trial on the grounds that critical exculpatory evidence had been withheld from defense attorneys, specifically that investigators had damaging information that would implicate the Ku Klux Klan in the murders.

The evidence was finally presented in 1991. Although not relevant to the two murders for which Williams was convicted, the new evidence, gleaned from raw investigative reports, was presented to undermine the pattern of behavior that had been used to link the last two deaths to ten previous ones. In particular, police looked into a tip they had received from a convicted car thief, burglar, and forger, Bill Joe Whitaker, who claimed to have overheard another man, Charles Sanders, implicate the Ku Klux Klan in the murder of Lubie Geter.

On the strength of the accusation, police had released Whitaker from prison, set him up in a hotel room wired for sound, and enticed Sanders to a rendezvous. In the subsequent taped conversation, Whitaker is reported to have said, "You killed this Geter kid, didn't you?" To which Sanders is reputed to have replied, "Damn sure did."

Unfortunately for the defense, Whitaker had died, Sanders could not be located, the original tape recordings had been destroyed, and parts of the investigative file misplaced. Of course, the missing evidence only served to validate the beliefs of those who saw the long reach of the Klan behind the murders. And in the interests of their client, defense attorneys kept the divisive conspiracy theory alive, trying to set a convicted murderer free by conjuring ghosts in white sheets.

There All the Time

JEFFREY LIONEL DAHMER
Milwaukee, Wisconsin (1987–1991)

"I hurt those policemen in the Konerak Sinthasomphone matter and shall ever regret causing them to lose their jobs. And I hope and pray that they can get their jobs back, because I know they did their best and I just plain fooled them."
—Jeffrey Dahmer
Statement Before Sentencing, February 17, 1992

In April 1993, the city of Milwaukee was laid low by an outbreak of illness among its residents. As many as a quarter of a million people experienced gastrointestinal distress, nausea, diarrhea, and other flulike symptoms. An investigation revealed the probable cause of the epidemic to be an intestinal parasite, cryptosporidium, which had infected the city's drinking water. As a result, 800,000 people in the greater Milwaukee metropolitan area were forced to drink boiled or bottled water.

City officials, to their shock and dismay, learned that a local group, the AIDS Resource Center of Wisconsin, had detected a high incidence of cryptosporidium infection among AIDS patients involved in a clinical trial for a new antidiarrhea drug five months earlier. Although there had been ample time to avert the subsequent epidemic, the AIDS group had not made known the findings because of their strained relations with public health agencies. Health Commissioner Paul Nannis commented on the implications of not having received the information: "If we had had their study earlier, it would have changed the way we look at what's in the water. It's perplexing and very frustrating that this information wasn't shared with the Health Department."[1] In response, the executive director of the AIDS Resource Center, Doug Nelson, gave his organization's position and reasons for withholding the results: "State and local public health departments really need to listen to and to collaborate with community-based AIDS services and research agencies. Right now the doors are shut."[2]

If there was an unsettling déjà vu feeling about these statements for the people of Milwaukee, it was understandable. For five years, from 1987 to 1991, Jeffrey Dahmer was able to move about the city, murdering sixteen young men with relative impunity, escaping detection over time in no small part because of profound political divisions that separated the city into hostile, uncooperative camps. Nearly two years after Dahmer's bloody deeds were exposed, political animosities were again endangering the welfare of city residents.

And just as factionalized interests were once more contributing to a public menace going unchecked, so too after-the-fact finger pointing must have seemed all too familiar. Public servants were again expressing confusion and a sense of betrayal by the manifest lack of community support, while activist minority groups complained they were not "listened to." Expressions concerning the need for community involvement and support and charges of institutional insensitivity and deafness were constant refrains in the period following Jeffrey Dahmer's discovery when the factions in Milwaukee desperately sought scapegoats and tried to assign blame for the missed opportunities to stop him.

But the Milwaukee experience is by no means atypical. A disturbing fact about serial killers is that most of them should be eminently identifiable. Two-thirds operate within a limited geographic area such as a city or town, and one-third are place-specific killers. That is, they commit their acts of destruction repeatedly in a single place, as John Wayne Gacy did in his house. Serial killers, therefore, give the residents of a community, its police force, and even their neighbors ample opportunity to find them out.

The fact that they do not is attributable to three factors, all of which were operative in the Dahmer case: the characteristics of the victims, the behavior of the killer, and the structural barriers in the social system. Considering the first, victims may be drawn from segments of society that police have difficulty investigating, such as vagrants or runaways, because the cases are so numerous and are likely to resolve themselves or to be inherently unsolvable. Often victims, such as prostitutes, have transient lifestyles, and it is not clear when they have disappeared or have just moved to a new location. Gays, Dahmer's target, may expect harassment and try to avoid police contact. As a consequence, a killer can prey on these populations for extended periods of time without being detected.

Second, serial killers are notoriously ordinary and do not draw attention to themselves. For instance, the one word invariably used to describe Dahmer was "polite." Furthermore, they may have highly developed survival skills, being charming, accomplished, and facile liars. When stalking, the killer may use a simple ruse, such as Ted Bundy's fake arm cast, to inspire trust and ensure victims will be compliant as they are drawn into the trap and are led away to execution. There are no obvious signs, then, that help police pick the killer from the myriad of suspects they are investigating.

Third on a structural level, linkage blindness occurs when a series of murders are not connected and recognized as such because competing political interests act to retard the investigative process or delay the detection and apprehension of the killer. The competing interests need not be exclusively governmental; they can also be those of quasi-official groups or even private citizens when their political outlook blinds them to the true nature of a situation. The Jeffrey Dahmer case is an example of precisely this situation, when a polarized community was so busy acting against itself that it could not recognize the killer among us.

The Jeffrey Dahmer case is the study of how a serial murderer was able to remain invisible, continuing to kill even though his behavior was becoming increasingly risky and overt. Dahmer was there all the time, waiting to be discovered by citizens and public officials alike. That he was not says as much about the internecine struggles in the city as it does about his cunning. Tragically, he was able to slip through the cracks so often because there were so many cracks to begin with.

CITY IN TRANSITION

Like every other case, the Jeffrey Dahmer story is shaped by the city in which the events occurred. Milwaukee is one of the great industrial centers of the northcentral part of the United States—A hard-working, hard-drinking city whose blue-collar work ethic helped fuel the country's industrial dominance that climaxed in the decades immediately following World War II. Since that time, Milwaukee has experienced the same decline in its manufacturing base that other midwestern cities have. As the economic mix of the city changed, so too did the demography of its residents, metamorphosing from a homogeneous population of whites of Northern European stock to a multicultural, multilingual society drawn from all parts of the world.

To illustrate the trend, over the thirty-year time span from 1960 to 1990, the city population declined by 113,300 from 741,300 to 628,000. The white population loss was nearly two and a half times greater, dropping from 667,000 to 398,000, a reduction of 269,000. As a proportion of the total population, whites represented 90 percent of city dwellers at the start of the period, but only 63 percent three decades later.

As whites left the city, their place was taken by a wide range of minorities but primarily blacks. By 1990, Milwaukee was truly racially diverse with a nonwhite breakdown as follows: black—30.2 percent, Hispanic—6.3 percent, Asian—1.8 percent, and Native American—0.9 percent. Non-Hispanic whites represented 60.8 percent of the population. Thus, the racial balance of power had shifted radically from 1960 when the white to minority ratio was 9 to 1 to 1990 when there was one minority for every 1.5 whites in the city.

In addition to the racial composition changing over time, the races in the city were segregated by generation, geography, and standard of living. With respect to generation, adults in the city more closely reflected the earlier racial mix; 70 percent of those eighteen years of age or over were white, while a quarter (24.9 percent) were black. By comparison, for children under the age of 18, whites and blacks were equally represented (45 percent). Hence, whites no longer constituted the majority among children.

The races were, moreover, concentrated in pockets throughout the city that varied widely with respect to economic advantage. For instance, a map of the city and its Aldermanic districts (see Figure 7.1) shows that over half of the city's black residents lived in Districts 1, 6, and 10, with Districts 1 and 10 being more than 90 percent black. Conversely, the southernmost districts were nearly all white with less than 1 percent black residents. The majority of Hispanics (56 percent) meanwhile lived in Districts 8 and 12, with District 12 being more than a third Hispanic.

As well as being divided by age and location, the races differed with respect to their life circumstances. The situation and its influence on subsequent events were described in the report prepared by the Blue Ribbon Commission impaneled by Milwaukee Mayor John O. Norquist to investigate the Sinthasomphone incident. They concluded: "The inner-city districts report the lowest incomes in the City, and a high percentage of housing stock in sub-standard condition or vacant and boarded up. These districts also report the highest crime rates in the City, and therefore the most contact with the Milwaukee Police Department."[3] The cracks in the city's structure were therefore apparent and were made all the more profound by the fact that they overlapped, so that racial lines coincided with divisions in age, neighborhoods, and standards of living.

The Milwaukee Police Department in many ways reflected the wider population it served, but in other respects it resisted the demographic dynamics. It too had once been the virtually exclusive domain of whites. However, in 1976, after legal action by black police and firemen, the city accepted a consent decree requiring a quota system for the hiring of minority personnel. Thereafter, for every five officers hired, two had to be hired from specific minorities including black, Hispanic, and Native American, and one of the five had to be a woman regardless of race.

The consent decree was effective in addressing the racial imbalances in the departmental ranks. As noted in the Blue Ribbon Commission report, "Of those officers hired before the 1976 consent decree and still working, almost 93 percent are white men, just over 5% are men of other races, and 2% are women of any race. Of those officers hired since the consent decree and still working, less than 55% are white men, while almost 28% are men of other races and more than 17% are women of other races."[4] But this racial balance came with a cost. As in the city's civilian population, greater racial diversity led to segregation in the police force on a more subtle struc-

Figure 7.1
Milwaukee Aldermanic Districts and Oxford Apartments Neighborhood

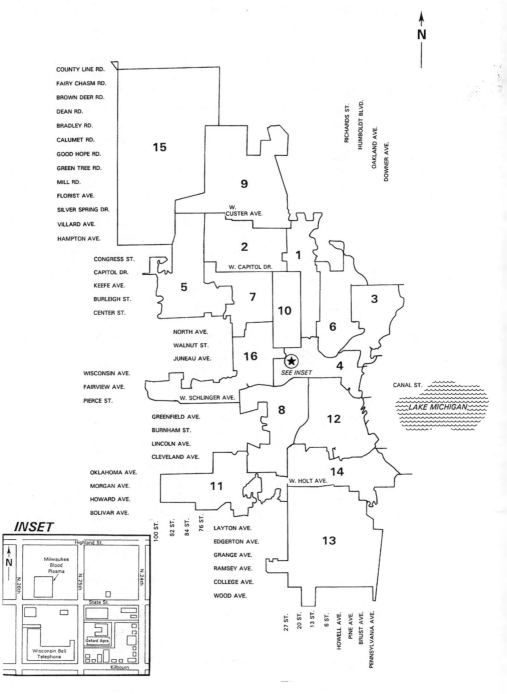

tural level. Again the races were divided generationally. The average white male policeman was 42 years old and had been on the force for eighteen years; comparable figures for minority male officers was 36 years old and eleven years of service. Female officers were even younger, 34 years old on average, and had less seniority, eight years.

Perhaps more important than age and seniority was rank, and on this measure the racial changes were much slower to come. At about the time Jeffrey Dahmer began killing, in December 1986, of the 1,974 sworn personnel on the force, 417 were officers (detective, sergeant, lieutenant, captain, or higher) and of these, 91.8 percent were white males. By comparison, among the remaining 1,557 specialists and police officers, only 75.2 percent were white males. Five years later, in October 1991, two and a half months after Dahmer's discovery, the situation was little changed. The higher ranks were still disproportionately filled by white males, 83.4 percent versus 68.5 percent in the lower levels.

Along with racial insularity came a set of anachronistic attitudes that virtually ensured that departmental personnel would be unprepared to deal with a culturally diverse population. The tone of the department had been set by the former Police Chief Harold Breier whose twenty-year tenure from 1964 to 1984 was characterized by a strong law and order posture and preservation of the status quo. Reacting to the current Police Chief Philip Arreola's proposals to institute community-oriented policing, he clearly summarized his philosophy: "You can take community oriented policing and stick it in your ear. There's no substitute for strong law enforcement. First, a police officer doesn't have the training to take care of all the social ills of the city. And second, he should be so busy maintaining law and order that he doesn't have time for that crap."[5]

Although retired, Breier remained the darling of the force for his strong stand in opposition to reduction in personnel and his staunch defense of patrolmen who came under criticism from the community while he was chief of police. In the aftermath of the Dahmer revelations, his outspoken views on the police administration and its policies became the rallying point for pro-police factions. When the department moved to hire more gay and lesbian officers in the wake of the Konerak Sinthasomphone incident, as an example, the octogenarian Breier announced publicly, "If I were chief of police, I certainly would be opposed. When I was chief, we used to arrest them for sodomy."[6]

Breier's impact on the police department was more subtle and direct than simply his longevity and personal popularity, however, and was evident in one telling statistic. "Approximately three-fourths of the Department including all those in the ranks of Captain and above, joined the Department while Harold Breier was Chief."[7] Thus, his imprimatur and values were indelibly stamped on the rank and file and their officers.

Not surprisingly, the leadership's attitudes sometimes found expression on the streets, leaving the department with a reputation for bias and a legacy of brutality charges. The two most notorious incidents occurred in 1981. One involved a black man, Ernest Lacy, who died while being taken into police custody, possibly as a result of excessive force used by the arresting officers. Although then Police Chief Breier investigated the matter and found no wrongdoing, the Fire and Police Commission disagreed and eventually terminated one officer, suspended three others for forty-five to sixty days, and paid damages to the family.

The second case concerned a white man, James Schomperlen, who was arrested following a complaint of lewd and lascivious behavior lodged by several minors. Apprehended after a car chase, the suspect was later taken to a hospital with facial injuries that police claimed were received when he tripped at the arrest scene. Witnesses told a different story, stating that the police had beaten the man. In this instance, Chief Breier fired the officers for misconduct; two were ultimately found guilty of criminal charges, and the third was acquitted and reinstated to the force.

The same year a survey conducted on behalf of the Fire and Police Commission to study community attitudes toward the police department uncovered a reservoir of alienation and mistrust among minority residents. Although most residents felt that the police were effective in crime control and, regardless of age or race, were willing to call the police in times of need, deep differences separated the races in their perceptions of the force. Blacks were more apt to believe the police would mistreat and use force when dealing with minorities but were less likely to think the police were honest, cooperative, or would act in the best interests of the community.

Little changed over the next decade to ameliorate the strained relations between the police and minority groups in the city. If anything, the department's reputation for bigotry and homophobia increased, not because of additional infamous, high-profile cases, but because of consistent differential treatment given minorities in routine contacts with police. Blacks and Hispanics were particularly vocal in their criticisms of the force for failure to respond rapidly to calls in their neighborhoods, for rude and abusive behavior once officers arrived, and for the frequent use of profanity directed at them. Gays and lesbians felt put upon for similar reasons. Police were accused of being less helpful and informative, less likely to explain legal options fully, and more apt to enforce laws selectively when dealing with gays and lesbians. As if to confirm the public's suspicions concerning police attitudes, one gay policeman described the frequent use of the derogatory terms "dyke" and "fag" by fellow officers and the targeting of gays and lesbians for nuisance crimes like jaywalking. When minorities were victimized, police might suggest that the crime occurred because of a person's race, living condition, or lifestyle. In one often repeated example of the department's orientation, officers responding to a call in a minority neighborhood told the victim, next time "don't call us, call a moving van."

Police enmity toward minorities was returned in kind as interactions with police became disdainful and at times openly hostile. The virtually all-white police force was viewed as "insensitive" to minority concerns and completely incapable of dealing with the city's cultural diversity. And despite the obvious problems, the police were seen as unwilling to take simple steps, such as hiring more minorities or adding translators to the staff, to rectify the situation.

Reciprocal contempt further isolated the department from the population it was intended to serve. A 1991 *Milwaukee Journal* survey of police personnel chronicled the grim statistics of a department under siege. Over half of those responding said they had been shot at, 51 percent, or assaulted, 70 percent, in the line of duty. Nearly half, 47 percent, had fired their gun, and a like figure, 42 percent, felt a high sense of physical danger while on the job. Chronic wariness was manifest as a laundry list of stress-related disorders: 37 percent of respondents drank excessively, 12 percent physically abused family members, 16 percent received counseling for work-related problems, 20 percent were divorced or separated due to job pressures, and 35 percent had been physically ill because of something they had seen while performing their duties.

But for some officers the least comprehensible aspect of their job was the fact that city residents and particularly minorities did not appreciate their position or the public service rendered. As one white sergeant who responded to the survey wrote, "What some members of this community fail to take into consideration is that a majority of the crime is committed by minorities, while minorities also consist of a majority of victims. If this qualifies me for being a racist for doing my job, then so be it. What is forgotten is that for most every minority arrested, another minority (normally the victim) is being helped out by us."[8] A virtually unbridgeable chasm existed between the suspicious, angry, alienated minority groups on the one side and an insular, defensive department that felt betrayed by a lack of community support on the other.

If constant conflict with the community were not enough, the department was also at war with itself. Again, the dividing lines were race and sexual preference. Anonymously commenting on the situation in a *Milwaukee Sentinel* article entitled "Gay Officer Lives in Fear,"[9] a patrolman described repeated incidents of low-level harassment, including derogatory notes pinned to lockers, antigay graffiti on bathroom walls, negative articles about gays posted on bulletin boards, and the time cards of gay officers marked up or otherwise destroyed. Despite what the officer termed "incredible pressure," no official investigation of the harassment complaints had been undertaken.

Blacks, too, had to suffer their share of racist graffiti, but black officers also saw a more insidious and purposeful form of bias designed to undermine the consent decree. The League of St. Martin's, representing blacks on the force, charged that an effort was being made to systematically eliminate minority recruits in the police academy by putting "man-made obstacles" in their path and that any recruit who complained about prejudicial treatment was subject to retaliation.

Then, as if the incipient tensions were not sufficiently crippling, a new police chief was appointed in November 1989, and it is hard to imagine a choice more diametrically opposed to the majority of the force he was hired to lead. Philip Arreola had worked his way up through the ranks of the Detroit Police Department and immediately before coming to Milwaukee had been chief of Port Huron, Michigan, a city one-twentieth the size of Milwaukee. Arreola's philosophy of law enforcement was antithetical to everything the force thought about policing and the way it had operated for decades. He believed the department could be effective only if it was immersed in community life and if it sought and won support from all segments of society. Furthermore, in a department with a history of racial bigotry, it was particularly galling to some that Arreola was Hispanic, or as one observer summarized the situation, "What people don't like to admit is that some of their resistance is due to the fact that Arreola is of Hispanic descent and he's the boss."[10] Arreola was, finally, the first person ever hired from outside the department above entry-level rank. He was an outsider in every way and was resented for it.

Beleaguered by tensions from within and without, the department was like a flawed and brittle gem that was ready to shatter under the slightest pressure. The police power structure reflected a bygone era, and as it grudgingly gave ground to newly emergent minorities, political friction and hostility were the inevitable result. The full extent of these divisions and their potential for civic damage were waiting only for a flashpoint to set off a conflagration of accusation and hatred. Into this tinderbox, on July 23, 1991, stepped Jeffrey Dahmer.

THE MILWAUKEE MURDERER

A great deal has been written about Jeffrey Dahmer's murderous career, and the crimes were every bit as gruesome and grotesque as described in the media. But beyond the incomprehensible specifics of the murders lies a pattern of behavior, a method of acting that took years to develop. The progression of escalating deviance in Dahmer evolved into a personally unique, routine, and replicable killing style.

Generally speaking, Dahmer's actions can be divided into two distinct phases. The initial period was characterized by his testing a variety of different methods to satisfy his aberrant sexual desires and his increasingly frequent and serious conflicts with authority. In a perverse way, Dahmer's single-minded pursuit of the perfect sex partner during this period demonstrates a creative genius for experimentation and trial at the same time as his personal behavior was careening out of control. Dahmer did not often kill during the first phase, and when he did, the murders had an unplanned, spontaneous, and almost haphazard character.

The second stage of activity begins when Dahmer perfected his modus operandi. The murders committed after this point have an ugly sameness about them, differing one from another only in minor detail. During this stage, killings were purposeful, systematic, and committed with increasing frequency. Variations in his behavior were largely confined to his methods of disposal since the rate of murdering quickly outpaced his ability to destroy the remains.

Looking at Dahmer's behavior through the infallible lens of hindsight, it is clear now that many of the behaviors that would find lethal expression in later life were firmly rooted and shaped in childhood. From the earliest days, Dahmer seemed to be fascinated with death and mutilation. As a child, animals, which he tortured, killed, dissected, and displayed as dismembered corpses, provided the outlet for his curiosity. Young Jeffrey even used animal bones, which he called his "fiddle stix," as toys. His aggression against animals at times took on more utilitarian connotations. One incident was seen as particularly significant by a psychiatrist who testified at his insanity trial. Dahmer poured motor oil into a tank containing a friend's tadpole collection; he did so with the knowledge that he was not only killing the animals but would also hurt his companion.

Just as Dahmer's killing and mutilation of animals was indicative of a disturbed personality, his educational career showed marked signs of psychic distress. Although exceptionally bright, Dahmer was a chronic underachiever. In school he became noted for flagrant and outrageous behavior to the point that any serious acting out by other students was known as "doing a Dahmer." Equally important, during his high school years his destructive use of alcohol became apparent. One event is particularly revealing in this regard. Dahmer took a date to the annual prom in one of the rare instances in which he was involved with the opposite sex. Before any personal contact could be made, he fled, obtained alcohol, and drank himself into a stupor. By his senior year in high school, then, he had learned to use alcohol to calm his fears, avoid confrontation, and deal with his inhibitions. Alcohol would play the same facilitating role when he murdered.

Much too has been made of Dahmer's early family environment as a cause, or at least a contributing factor, for his later actions. Parental conflict was commonplace in the Dahmer household, and it would eventually lead to a protracted and acrimonious divorce. The degree of enmity between the parents reached its apotheosis when Jeffrey's father, Lionel, speculated that his abnormal psychological development may have been due to the prescription drugs his mother took while she was pregnant with him.

The constant hostility between his parents seems to have left Jeffrey with a feeling of abandonment. These psychological scars were exacerbated when a second son was born to the couple, and his mother showered all of her affection and attention on his younger brother. If Jeffrey felt abandoned as a child, his worst fears were realized as a teen. As part of the dissolution of their marriage, both parents left their home in Bath, Ohio, his mother taking his brother to live in California and his father leaving with his new wife. No one seems to have made arrangements for Jeffrey or for that matter even informed him of their plans. Jeffrey was left to fend for himself in an empty house where his father found him after several days, almost completely out of food.

These experiences scarred Dahmer for life, and many of his later actions are interpreted as attempts to avoid being left behind again. In fact, fear of abandonment seems to have led directly to his first murder in 1978. With his father already out of the household due to the divorce and his mother and brother visiting relatives, Dahmer again found himself alone for an extended time. Aimlessly cruising the highways in search of companionship, he happened upon nineteen-year-old Stephen Mark Hicks who was hitchhiking home from a rock concert. The pair returned to Dahmer's house, talked, drank beer, and had sex. Hicks, who was to attend his father's birthday party that night, then tried to leave. When Dahmer was unable to persuade him to stay, he first hit Hicks with a dumbbell and then strangled him to death.

Disposal of Hicks's body exhibited many of the characteristics of Dahmer's later killing ritual. The corpse was first dismembered, and the parts were then put in a garbage bag. When the remains began to smell after several days, Dahmer removed them to the backyard and buried them in a shallow grave. Later, whether fearing discovery or driven by guilt, Dahmer disinterred the remains, removed the flesh from the corpse, smashed the bones with a sledgehammer, and scattered them in the woods behind his house. Predictably, Hicks's distraught parents enlisted the aid of a psychic to find their missing son, but the disposal was so thorough no one suspected what lay behind the house until Dahmer confessed to the crime thirteen years later.

After high school, Dahmer enrolled in Ohio State University. He seems to have spent most of his time there drunk and flunked out after a semester. He then joined the army where he trained as an MP but failed to meet the rigorous entry standards. Next he was trained as a medic and was stationed in Germany. Throughout his army experience, Dahmer's involvement with alcohol never slackened, and the most common recollection of those who knew him during this time was Dahmer lying on his bunk, passed out. After three years in the service, Dahmer was prematurely discharged due to alcoholism.

Following his stint in the service, Dahmer settled briefly in Miami but left shortly for Milwaukee. There he lived with his grandmother until his increasingly overt bizarre behavior became too much for her, and he was forced to take up residence in the Oxford Apartments, number 213. Before leaving his grandmother's house, Dahmer was already well established as a serial murderer and had even used the basement to dismember several corpses, once while she attended Easter services.

Dahmer's return to Milwaukee additionally signaled the start of a series of ever more weird attempts to satisfy his sexual desires and progressively more serious contacts with the police for sexual misconduct. It was also a period in which Dahmer would practice and perfect his techniques for attracting and subduing victims, and more importantly doing so without attracting attention or being caught. What he would learn during his first three years in Milwaukee, from 1984 to 1987, would eventually become incorporated in his standard killing practice.

With respect to sexual gratification, Dahmer tried a variety of nonlethal means of achieving his ends. His necrophilia was fully developed by this point, and his actions reflected it. He tried to satisfy his sex drive with a mannequin, attempted to exhume a dead body from a graveyard, and even went to a funeral home when he read about the accidental death of an eighteen-year-old boy. Finally, as if to presage his later cannibalism, while an employee of a plasma center, Dahmer stole a small sample of blood, snuck to the roof of the building, and tasted it. None of these methods proved satisfactory though, and Dahmer was forced to continue to seek live human contact.

But unfortunately for Dahmer and his victims, humans were not as passive as inanimate objects. They had needs of their own and made sexual demands in return. According to one psychiatrist who studied him, Dahmer preferred soft sex consisting of holding, caressing, and foreplay. He disliked rougher forms of sex and had a particular aversion to anal intercourse. Much of his later behavior—quickly subduing the victim, making him compliant, and avoiding confrontation—was motivated by his wish to avoid certain forms of sex.

THE MILWAUKEE MURDERS

By 1987, all the elements were in place that would be needed to turn Dahmer into a killing machine. The forces within his personality coalesced into a pattern that determined how he would achieve sexual gratification, defining in the process the type of victims he would target and where he would seek them out. His experimentation with methods for luring and subduing victims was also finished. And most important of all, he was already a murderer. It seemed only a single event would bring the confluence of forces together to make Dahmer an inveterate killer.

The second murder, that of Steven Toumi, was the catalyst. Based on

Table 7.1
The Victims

Date	Victim	Age	Race
June 18, 1978	Steven Hicks	19	White
September 15, 1987	Steven Toumi	28	White
January 16, 1988	James Doxtator	14	Native American
March 24, 1988	Richard Guerrero	25	Hispanic
March 25, 1989	Anthony Lee Sears	24	Black
June 14, 1990	Edward Warren Smith	28	Black
July 1990	Ricky Lee Beeks	33	Black
September 1990	Ernest Miller	24	Black
September 1990	David Thomas	22	Black
February 1991	Curtis Straughter	18	Black
April 7, 1991	Errol Lindsey	19	Black
May 24, 1991	Anthony Hughes	31	Black
May 27, 1991	Konerak Sinthasomphone	14	Laotian
June 30, 1991	Matt Turner	20	Black
July 5, 1991	Jeremiah Weinberger	23	Hispanic
July 12, 1991	Oliver Lacey	23	Black
July 19, 1991	Joseph Bradehoft	25	White

Source: Abstracted from *The Man Who Could Not Kill Enough*.

Dahmer's recollections, this much is known about what happened. Dahmer met Toumi in a gay bar, Club 219, in November 1987. The couple left the bar and went to the nearby Ambassador Hotel where they drank themselves insensate. From that point on Dahmer's recall is cloudy. He claimed to have awakened the next morning with Toumi dead beside him. Although Dahmer did not remember actually murdering Toumi, the body had strangulation marks around the neck and blood was coming from the mouth.

Fearing discovery, Dahmer left the hotel and purchased a large suitcase. Returning, he stuffed the corpse in the bag, called a cab, and went to his grandmother's house where he was then living, the obliging cabbie helping him to take the heavy suitcase inside. Safe again, Dahmer had sex with the corpse, dismembered it, put the body parts in a plastic trash bag, and threw the remains in the garbage. The disposal was so complete no evidence of the crime was ever recovered, and Dahmer was never charged with the murder.

The killing of Stephen Toumi was Dahmer's personal Rubicon, and after it murders came with increasing frequency (Table 7.1). For example, the number of murders by year was: 1978—1, 1987—1, 1988—2, 1989—1, 1990—4, 1991—8. The only deviation from the ever-increasing tally following Toumi's murder is 1989 when Dahmer spent most of the year in jail for a sexual assault conviction. Toumi's murder was also the last unplanned one, and after it Dahmer sought victims with the intention of killing them. Nevertheless, except for its after-the-fact character, the murder contains all the features of Dahmer's fully mature modus operandi.

The first step in Dahmer's murder ritual was to find an appropriate victim. Dahmer claimed to be attracted only to a particular body type and initially selected targets on this basis. When stalking, he frequented venues in which anonymity was assured; shopping malls and gay bathhouses were his favorite haunts. Next he approached the potential victim with a simple, direct, and brutally effective offer. Sometimes he invited the victim to his house for a drink or to watch pornographic videos. On other occasions, he made a straight cash proposition offering the victim between $50 and $200 to return to his apartment and pose for pictures. Given the nature of the proposition, it is not surprising that several of Dahmer's victims were aspiring models, and two had been previously arrested for prostitution.

Once the victim was secure in his apartment and outside of the public eye, Dahmer proceeded to subdue him and satisfy his own sexual desires. Most often control was gained by offering the victim a drink in which Dahmer had dissolved several tablets of the prescription drug Halcion. The unsuspecting victim quickly became intoxicated and incapacitated. The submission ritual varied only slightly from one time to the next. When Dahmer temporarily ran out of Halcion, he experimented with a rubber mallet, hitting his victims over the head to immobilize them. The only other variation in the ritual was whether or not Dahmer had sex with the victims before he murdered them. On rare occasions he did, but more often he preferred to have complete control over the victim before engaging in sex.

Other expressions of his need for control were evidenced once the victim was drugged. Dahmer attempted to keep the victims in a state of suspended animation, to make them "zombies" always compliant to his sexual demands, and, most importantly for his psyche, never able to leave him. To this end, he attempted crude lobotomies on several victims, drilling holes in their heads and injecting them with hot water or muriatic acid. He consulted with a taxidermist and investigated freeze-drying as ways of ensuring his victims would never leave. Body parts were preserved in a freezer, skulls were kept as souvenirs, and a bicep was fried and eaten as a way of incorporating the dead man into himself.

It is not completely clear how many of the most perverse acts Dahmer actually committed and how many were embellished to assist his insanity plea. Certainly, skeletons and body parts were found in his apartment, as were pictures of victims in various stages of dismemberment. However, his cannibalism has been questioned, as have the lobotomies. For instance, Dahmer claimed to have "drilled" Konerak Sinthasomphone and injected him with acid before he escaped from the apartment and was picked up by the police. However, no person at the scene that night, witnesses, police, or fireman, recalled any wounds to Sinthasomphone's head that indicated his skull had been punctured.

After subduing the victims, Dahmer killed them. Death was not preordained for everyone who entered his apartment, however. On at least one occasion, Dahmer made a personal bond with the intended victim and once personalized allowed him to leave unharmed. More often, Dahmer strangled his victims with a leather strap he purchased specifically for that purpose. In at least one case, Dahmer stabbed his victim to death, and he also maintained that several of the victims succumbed to the lobotomies and subsequent injections. Whatever the mode of death, Dahmer invariably had sex with the corpse.

The final stage in Dahmer's killing ritual was the disposal of the remains. In the early years when the killings were relatively few and widely spaced, disposal was very thorough with little evidence remaining for investigators to find even if they were looking. He first dismembered the body, stripped the flesh, smashed the bones into tiny pieces, and scattered the fragments. This was a laborious and time-consuming process, what one psychiatrist called the "drudgery of disposal," and as the murders became more frequent it was no longer practical. Dahmer switched to dismembering the corpses and throwing the remains in the trash and finally to dissolving the body parts in acid in a huge blue barrel bought for that purpose.

On seventeen terrible occasions, Jeffrey Dahmer proved to be a resourceful and accomplished practitioner of the killer's art. He was always willing to try new methods of luring, subduing, murdering, and disposing of victims. Eventually, he settled on a killing regimen that suited his personality, consisting of a straightforward lure, quick and sure incapacitation, strangulation, postmortem sex, and reduction of the remains.

THERE ALL THE TIME

Over a nineteen-month period, beginning in 1990 and ending the night of July 23, 1991 when he was finally arrested, Jeffrey Dahmer killed twelve times, a rate of once every six weeks. In the final month alone, Dahmer committed four murders, the last just four days before his capture. He was discovered by chance when the soon to be eighteenth victim, Tracy Edwards, though shackled, escaped while an intoxicated Dahmer momentarily lapsed into unconsciousness. Dahmer went undetected for years, despite the mounting body count, and it is likely he could have continued to kill indefinitely had it not been for his own mistakes.

During the killing years, scores of individuals had an opportunity to observe Dahmer's escalating, bizarre behavior at first hand, and yet no one could compute the simple arithmetic of serial murder. In fact, no fewer than seven categories of people, in an official or unofficial capacity, were in a position to realize the magnitude of his crimes and stop him, including the police, the court and its supervisory representatives, medical professionals who treated him and supplied his drugs, his fellow workers at the Ambrosia Chocolate Company, gays upon whom he preyed, neighbors who lived in the same apartment complex, and, of course, his family. No one did until a situation arose that was so out of the ordinary it could not be ignored.

The reasons Dahmer evaded detection for so long offer as many insights into the social construction of everyday life as they do the inner workings of a repetitive killer's mind. Most often he simply remained invisible, below the threshold of attention, not sufficiently abnormal to warrant a second look. Dahmer was uncommonly ordinary, and, not surprisingly, his answers to the Rorschach Ink Blot Test, administered while he awaited trial, were described as "mundane." He also hid behind a mask of social convention; his manners were impeccable; as one person evaluated his behavior, "Some people called him a monster, but he was a polite monster."[11] If anyone had an inkling of suspicion, their imaginations could not stretch wide enough to encompass the horrible reality, and if they challenged him with incriminating evidence, he disarmed them with plausible explanations.

Several of the early murders were committed while Dahmer lived with his family, first in Bath, Ohio and then with his grandmother in West Allis, Wisconsin. Each of these residences was used not only as a killing site but also as an abattoir as Dahmer butchered the corpses, a process so bloody there were signs of the slaughter thirteen years later. Dahmer's grandmother had an opportunity to view a parade of new boyfriends, and one murder was apparently averted when she interrupted Jeffrey as he entered the house with a new prospect. Becoming more suspicious over time, she finally called Jeffrey's father Lionel and asked him to investigate a black substance that was seeping from her trash cans. When confronted with the evidence, Dahmer told his father he had been experimenting with chemicals to remove the skin of dead animals as he had done as a child. His father, a chemist by training, doubted the explanation but let the matter drop. His grandmother was more forthright. Unable to put up with his behavior any longer, in 1988 she asked him to leave. He dutifully obeyed and moved to the Oxford Apartments, carrying the skull of Anthony Sears among his personal possessions.

If for no other reason, Dahmer stood out in his apartment complex because he was the only white in the building. But in addition, his behavior was strange even in a place where unusual was the norm. Neighbors recalled him squeezing through the door of his apartment so onlookers in the hallway were prevented from obtaining an unobstructed view inside. It was his requisite disposal of the murdered remains, though, that brought him closest to discovery. The sound of sawing could be heard coming from his apartment, while near-frantic cats followed him to the dumpster and swarmed over the trash bags he threw in. Most obtrusive of all was the smell that emanated from his unit. On various occasions when confronted, Dahmer explained that it came from spoiled meat, a dirty aquarium, and once simply that he would take care of it. In spite of all this, the building manager, Sopa Princewill, considered making Dahmer a business partner because he was a "nice guy" and kept a clean room.

At the Ambrosia Chocolate Company, where he worked for six years, Dahmer was remembered as a quiet employee who kept to himself. While incarcerated for sexual assault, Dahmer was allowed to continue working at the factory, returning to jail for the night after completing his shift. For anyone who questioned this odd arrangement, Dahmer's ready answer was that he had gotten into trouble propositioning a woman. His employment during this period took on more sinister dimensions when it was later revealed that he kept the skull of one victim in his locker so he could daily relieve the murder and rekindle his fantasies. Never aware of the locker's grisly contents, fellow workers, like everyone else who ever met him, described Dahmer only as "very polite."

In the final months before his arrest, Dahmer's behavior became more erratic as his personal life spiralled downward toward infamy. With his absenteeism growing apace, the management decided to fire him. Even after being told of his termination, Dahmer's behavior never broke form. He simply cleaned out his locker, shook hands with the man who fired him, said good night, and left the building.

Throughout his years in Milwaukee, Dahmer was thoroughly immersed in the gay subculture. Gay bars and bathhouses were populated with young men, many of whom fit the body type that conformed to Dahmer's image of the ideal sex partner and, hence, figured so prominently in his killing calculus. The anonymity and live and let live lifestyle also suited his purposes perfectly. Frequent and brief liaisons made it easy to pick up victims, while providing numerous opportunities for him to perfect his killing methods.

As if on a practice run on his way to becoming an efficient serial killer, Dahmer began around 1986 to experiment seriously with drugs to subdue unsuspecting victims. By the second murder in 1987, Dahmer had been kicked out of one gay bathhouse for drugging another patron to the point the man could not be revived, had to be taken to a hospital, and took a week to recover. On another occasion, Dahmer drugged and sexually assaulted two men in the Ambassador Hotel, a site he would use again for more deadly purposes. Despite these and other incidents, when called to investigate, police were unable to find anyone who was willing to press charges, and Dahmer was allowed to escape with his newfound knowledge.

The druggings were to continue in 1988 and thereafter, but fewer young men were able to escape with their lives. Those who did often had nothing more than a twist of fate to thank for their good fortune, like a man who was not killed because Dahmer thought he was too big to be disposed of easily. Along with the murders, near misses kept accumulating, leaving a trail of outrageous conduct that was never called to account by the gay community.

In one truly inexplicable encounter, Dahmer attacked a partner with a rubber hammer, then attempted to strangle the man, but was unable to overcome him. Following the attack, the two men talked, had sex, and once personalized, Dahmer allowed the erstwhile victim to go free. In 1988, Ronald Flowers was given a mug of drug-filled coffee and later came to in a hospital. A year later, Flowers saw Dahmer outside a gay bar in conversation with another potential victim. Flowers confronted the pair, shouting hysterically that Dahmer was crazy and should be avoided. Unaware of the irony, Dahmer responded that he really did not remember Flowers but suggested they go for a cup of coffee to discuss their differences.

On several occasions, Dahmer was seen with victims just before they disappeared. Anthony Sears was in the company of Jeffrey Connor when picked up by Dahmer. Connor even drove the couple to within several blocks of Dahmer's grandmother's house where Sears was killed later that night. After being approached, Jeremiah Weinberger asked a friend if he thought it was safe to go with Dahmer. Once reassured, Weinberger went quietly to his execution. In spite of what can only be regarded as two extraordinarily curious disappearances, neither incident came to light until Dahmer was arrested.

In the face of incidents such as these, Dahmer began to develop a reputation in the gay community as being dangerous. Self-described "street minister" Jean-Paul Ranieri, who spoke with Dahmer during this period, was particularly impressed with the threat. In conversation, Dahmer's antigay attitudes came across clearly; he hated all gays for their "bizarre and perverse" behavior and especially found "black queens disgusting."[12] Struck by the obvious projected self-loathing, Ranieri warned members of the community to avoid Dahmer.

More than any other group then, gays had the most direct evidence of Dahmer's deviance as he periodically culled their number. He did so repeatedly, often using Club 219 as a stalking ground. The relative silence of the gay community when presented with a growing menace is a feature of the Dahmer case that virtually cries out for explanation. No doubt, the homophobic reputation of the Milwaukee Police Department was a contributing factor, such that gays were more willing to provide for their own security with informal warnings than invite the scrutiny of a hostile force. But part of the explanation too must lie with the lifestyle of the community. Tolerant, nonjudgmental, and at times "anything goes" attitudes put Dahmer's behavior, albeit on the fringe, within acceptable limits.

Another factor was that theirs could be a perilous existence, causing gays to become inured to predators, of which Dahmer was only one. Indeed, while he was stalking victims, Dahmer once became one. On Thanksgiving Day 1989, in an instance that would give the families of his own victims a sense of perverse satisfaction, Dahmer was sexually molested. Awakening from an intoxicated state, he found himself hog-tied and suspended from the ceiling, while his attacker repeatedly violated him with a candle.

Dahmer's abnormal sexual needs and his callous attempts to satisfy them inevitably brought him into conflict with the law. But even before coming to Milwaukee, he had a history of police contacts in Bath, Ohio. In 1978, he was questioned by the police in the theft of a watch, radio, and $120. Also that year, in one of the endlessly mysterious episodes that dot the landscape of serial murder cases, Dahmer was stopped by the Bath Police while driving with trash bags holding the remains of Steven Hicks. Like serial killer Edmund Kemper who found himself in an identical situation, Dahmer talked his way past the oblivious officers. Also before leaving Bath, Dahmer was arrested for disorderly conduct.

In Milwaukee, his offenses took on a decidedly sexual intent. In 1982, he was fined $50 for lowering his pants in front of a crowd of people, including women and children, at the Wisconsin State Fair. Four years later in 1986, Dahmer was arrested for masturbating in front of two twelve-year-old boys. He denied the charge initially, saying he was simply relieving himself against a tree when spied by the boys, but later admitted to masturbating publicly five times in the preceding months. He was given a sentence of one-year probation and court-ordered therapy.

Then in an incident that would be an eerie harbinger of things to come, Dahmer picked up a young Laotian boy, Keison Sinthasomphone, in September 1988. The 13 year old was taken to Dahmer's apartment and given a drink laced with the powerful sedative Halcion. Despite being intoxicated, Keison escaped and alerted police. Dahmer was arrested for sexual assault and enticing a child for immoral purposes. Dahmer tried at first to explain the situation away by saying that he had actually prepared the drink for himself and Keison had mistakenly drunk from the wrong cup; he did, indeed, have a prescription for the drug. In January 1989, he pleaded guilty to the charges and was sentenced to one year in jail, for which he served ten months and five years probation.

The Keison Sinthasomphone incident was a fleeting glimpse into the future and not simply because Dahmer would kill Keison's younger brother, Konerak, three years later under strikingly similar circumstances. Although prosecutors would argue for a much stiffer sentence, Dahmer was given a relatively light one in part because no one from the Sinthasomphone family appeared in court to ask for a harsher judgment. For their part, the family claims never to have been notified of the trial. At a critical juncture, the administrative apparatus of the judicial system had broken down allowing Dahmer to go free after a short time behind bars. The mistake would have devastating consequences for the Sinthasomphone household, a dozen other families, and Milwaukee generally.

After release from jail, Dahmer came under the supervision of the State Division of Probation and Parole and, as part of his rehabilitation, court-ordered therapy. Several psychiatrists and psychologists treated Dahmer, and interestingly, as a group, they were among the only people to register a negative opinion of him. In the assessment of one therapist, Dahmer was a difficult patient, his prognosis for alcoholism was dim, and his participation in a court program for sex offenders was likely to be unsuccessful and therefore pointless. For his part, Dahmer used the therapists as a ready source of Halcion and at one time had prescriptions for the drug from three doctors. One of those who treated him even warned Dahmer that he might become addicted to the drug, but by that time he already had a much more deadly use for it.

Meanwhile, his probation officer, Donna Chester, was required to meet with him twice a month to monitor his progress. Normally, probation would also entail home visits, but in Dahmer's case she was excused from the responsibility because his neighborhood was so dangerous. Given the killing site his apartment was to become and the ghastly secrets that were hidden there, a significant opportunity was missed to force open his twisted inner world. Nevertheless, Ms. Chester appears to have been diligent in her efforts to help Dahmer, but with a caseload in excess of 120 he was lost in a tower of probation files.

Thus, the Circuit Court system missed three chances to stop Dahmer by not imposing a stiffer sentence for his sexual assault conviction, not monitoring his deepening involvement with psychotropic drugs and cutting off his supply, and not providing closer supervision and especially conducting home visits while he was on probation.

Close calls and police contacts continued while Dahmer was on probation. In 1990, police questioned a fifteen-year-old Hispanic boy who had been assaulted with a rubber mallet. Dahmer escaped detection yet again because the teenager could only recall that his assailant's name was Jeffrey. Once the smell from Dahmer's apartment became so overpowering that police were called to investigate, but in another example in a long list of tragicomic mistakes, the police kicked in the wrong apartment door, just two away from the unit that held the partially completed reduction of one more serial murder victim. Dahmer was also questioned in 1991 in connection with the murder of a man who lived above him in the Oxford Apartments. The police even briefly entered his apartment, but finding nothing amiss, quickly left.

In just under four years from September 1987 until July 1991, Jeffrey Dahmer killed sixteen young men in the city of Milwaukee and its suburb West Allis. Over that time he had at least seven contacts with police, was arrested three times, was put on probation twice, and was jailed once. It is worth considering in some depth then, why it was that until his arrest, the police department, and for that matter the city of Milwaukee, was totally unaware that a serial killer was on the loose.

Part of the reason undoubtedly is the staggering crime statistics of a major metropolitan area. Milwaukee actually has a relatively low crime rate and ranks forty-fourth out of fifty-two cities with populations over 300,000. Even so, in a typical year there is one murder, rape, or aggravated assault for every 100 residents. In addition, personal crime was on the rise in Milwaukee. Coinciding with Dahmer's killing years, the homicide rate in the city jumped 95 percent, from 86 in 1988 to 168 in 1991.

Beyond the most serious crime is a level of community chaos that puts heavy demand on Milwaukee's law enforcement resources. No fewer than 1 million calls per year, or 2,600 calls a day, are fielded by 911 operators. In the average year, police officers are dispatched on over a half a million calls or roughly 1,500 per day. The sheer volume of activity creates a level of background noise that obscures the truly serious incidents, let alone connections between them or an emergent pattern. Furthermore, the city of Milwaukee has between 6,000 and 7,000 missing persons cases a year, three for every person on the police force, and of these approximately 400 are never resolved. If these figures were not enough to disguise the deeds of a serial killer, one more fact is telling. The police force of the nation's seventeenth largest city, nearly 2,000 men and women, had never in its history investigated a serial murder case.

By May 1991, Jeffrey Dahmer had survived a series of incidents any one of which might have been enough to stop the murder string. His family suspected something was wrong but consistent with their track record, left Jeffrey to his own devices rather than delve too deeply into his life. With his fellow workers at the Ambrosia Chocolate factory and at the Oxford Apartments, he hid behind a mask of passivity, social distance, and good manners. A growing reputation as a homosexual whose self-hatred threatened other gays was not sufficient—whether because of mistrust and animosity toward the police or the freewheeling lifestyle of its members—for the gay community to surrender him to authorities. An overburdened court system was too busy processing cases to pay much attention, and a series of mistakes and all too human oversights allowed Dahmer to slip repeatedly through the fingers of the police in three cities. Then, as the city of Milwaukee was preparing for a long weekend and the beginning of summer, the police would get one last chance.

MAY 27, 1991

There is little doubt that John Balcerzak and Joseph Gabrish were experienced, brave, and competent police officers or that they were representative of the police force with respect to attitudes toward minorities and homosexuals. There can also be no doubt that between 2:00 A.M. and 3:00 A.M. on the start of Memorial Day weekend 1991 they would make the misjudgment of a lifetime. By not reading the situational cues accurately and trusting their own instincts and professional judgment, while dismissing the streetwise concern of several minority witnesses, they would deliver a naked, incoherent Laotian boy into the hands of a serial killer. When the truth became known, their careers would be ruined, the political factions in Milwaukee would fly apart in a centrifuge of recrimination, and worst of all, four more young men would be dead.

The facts surrounding the events that night were straightforward—the interpretation of them anything but. Five black, young adults, Tina Spivey, Nicole Childress, Sandra Smith, Johnnie Jones, and Ted Robertson, observed a naked Asian male, Konerak Sinthasomphone, stagger across the street, fall and hit his head on a sewer cover, lie back, and moan. On closer inspection, they noticed his eyes "flipping back," and since he did not appear drunk they assumed he had taken drugs. They also noticed blood around his buttocks, testicles, and pubic hair.

Subsequently, according to the witnesses, a white male, Jeffrey Dahmer, appeared, pretending initially not to know the Asian boy. When Tina Spivey told Dahmer that the police had been called, his demeanor changed. He picked Konerak up and tried to pull him into an alley, holding him in what one witness called a "full Nelson." During this time, Dahmer called Konerak by several different names. Witnesses also heard Konerak say "no" several times when approached by Dahmer.

First to answer the 911 call was a fire department emergency crew who wrapped Konerak in a blanket. About 2:06 A.M., officers John Balcerzak and Joseph Gabrish arrived on the scene, followed by a second squad car carrying Richard Porubcan and Peter Mozejewski, who would have little role in the events or their aftermath. Tina Spivey identified herself as the caller and tried to explain the situation to the policemen. Dahmer interrupted, told the officers Konerak was his roommate, and that he was taking him home. Spivey, in turn, told the officers that Dahmer did not know the boy's name and that they should look at "his butt." The officers told her to be quiet and let Dahmer give his side of the story.

The witnesses tried again to contradict Dahmer's version of the events. At this point, the officers reputedly told them to "shut the hell up" and to "get lost." One officer supposedly told a witness that he had been on the force for ten years and did not need an amateur to tell him how to do his job. Dahmer then invited the officers to his apartment. The police told the fire department crew that it was a "false alarm" and to "pick up," which they did as the policemen accompanied Dahmer to his apartment.

As Konerak sat on the couch mumbling unintelligibly, Dahmer explained the situation in what Balcerzak would later describe as "a calm, clear voice." He stated that Konerak was 19 or 20 and had been drinking. To prove their relationship, Dahmer produced snapshots of Konerak posing in black bikini underwear and then simply said "everybody has to be into something." The officers did acknowledge an unpleasant odor in the apartment but said later they thought it was from a bowel movement; it was in actuality the decomposing remains of Anthony Hughes killed three days earlier. Otherwise, "Ba-

Table 7.2
Witness Reports of Konerak Sinthasomphone's Age and Injuries

Witness	Age Estimate	Injury Assessment
Spivey	16 - 17	Eyes flipping back, blood in genital area
Jones	18 - 19	Convinced someone tried to have anal sex with Konerak
Robertson	19 - 20	Thought injuries resulted from fall
Childress	about 12	Blood on buttocks
Smith	11 - 12	Scrapes on knees, buttocks, shoulders-- darker blood on inner thigh running from buttocks
Firefighter Linscott	13 - 16	Bruised, puffy cheek, did not look below waist

sically, it was a well-kept apartment. It was neat,"[13] Balcerzak said. They then told Konerak they were going to leave, but he was unable to respond. Dahmer was warned that he would be in trouble if Konerak was seen on the street again that night. Having made the determination, as Gabrish would later say in a chilling summary of their mistake, "We were convinced all was well,"[14] the officers left. The entire call, alley to apartment, took sixteen minutes.

Questions eventually raised about the officers' legal culpability revolved around two issues: Konerak's age and the extent of his injuries, while the political ramifications centered on their handling of the minority witnesses. With respect to age, the officers were legally obligated to take Konerak into protective custody if he was determined to be a minor, that is, under 16 years old, or if he was in need of medical attention. Table 7.2 summarizes the observations of the key witnesses that night.[15] Three of the six thought he was not a minor, two thought he was, and one placed him in both categories. There is more unanimity of opinion with respect to his injuries. All of the witnesses saw the minor injuries Konerak received when he fell, and four of the five who looked thought they observed evidence of a sexual attack. The police officers saw no indication of sexual molestation, but, of course, by the time they arrived, Konerak was wrapped in a blanket. Even so, they apparently made no effort to check.

Six weeks later, when the consequences of the officers' actions were known, Milwaukee County District Attorney E. Michael McCann requested that the office of Wisconsin Attorney General James E. Doyle investigate the incident to determine whether any criminal statutes had been violated. The report of the Division of Criminal Investigation, known as the Doyle Report, concluded: "Considering all the available evidence, we do not believe it could be proven beyond a reasonable doubt that the officers not only believed Konerak Sinthasomphone was a victim of sexual intercourse or sexual contact with an adult, but also that they believed he was under the age of 16."[16] A preliminary investigation by the U.S. Attorney General's Office also exonerated the officers of any civil rights violations.

Legal liability is one matter, but judgment lapses are another, and it is again instructive to review the factors that caused the officers to so mortally misconstrue the situation. As for what happened on the street, Dahmer was white, calm, and polite. Like the officers, he wanted to get Konerak off the street and out of public view. The witnesses were black, young, and emotional. They interrupted the officers, shouted at them, and backed the policemen into a corner from which they lashed out. A cultural gulf existed between the witnesses and the officers that was embedded in race and expressed as styles of personal conduct. Unable to intellectually or affectively bridge the divide, the officers took the word of the contrite, white killer.

Another factor certainly was that in the normal course of their daily job activities, the event did not stand out as either serious or dangerous. Balcerzak and Gabrish had come on duty at twelve o'clock and in the two hours preceding the Konerak Sinthasomphone incident, they handled eight calls, two in which gunshots were fired, another for a man with a gun, three domestic disturbances, and one injured person report. They would handle five more before the night was through. The unfortunate fact was that, although the events seemed extraordinary to witnesses, in the course of normal police work they were not unusual. Again, as the Doyle Report concluded:

At the time the contact occurred between the officers and Dahmer, there was nothing in particular that set the incident apart from the multitude of incidents that the officers responded to that night. In each of the many situations that the officers were assigned to handle, they repeatedly exercised discretion and judgement. While in hindsight we wish that the officers had handled the encounter with Dahmer differently, we are firm in our belief that they cannot be criminally prosecuted for their actions.[17]

Alone with the officers, Dahmer was able to turn on his psychopathic charms. As Gabrish recalled, "He gave us no reason to suspect anything of him at all. He was very cooperative with us."[18] He did not hesitate to let the officers into the apartment, he did not act drunk, and he spoke in a clear, coherent manner. Konerak, by comparison, could not talk and appeared intoxicated. There was no sign of a struggle, indeed, just the opposite. Konerak had apparently posed for seminude photos. The apartment was neat, and when the officers inspected Konerak's clothes, stacked on the couch, they could find no indication of his age. As an anguished Officer Gabrish later characterized the situation, "We're trained to be observant and spot things. There was just nothing that stood out, or we would have seen it. I've been doing this for a while, and usually if something stands out, you'll spot it. There just wasn't anything there. I run this through my mind, I wish there would have been. There just wasn't."[19]

If that was all there was to it, the community might have come to terms with what happened and, if not forgiven, at least understood how the officers could have made such a mistake. But they would put themselves beyond redemption forever with one brief transmission to their dispatcher and an equally short telephone conversation with a relative of two of the witnesses. In the process, officers Balcerzak and Gabrish would confirm the public's deepest fears and doubts about the racial bigotry and homophobia of the Milwaukee Police Department.

At 2:22 A.M., the officers radioed the dispatcher and between audible laughs said they had returned "the intoxicated Asian naked male to his sober boyfriend." Without the laughter even this might have been acceptable, but then Balcerzak added, accompanied by more background laughter, "my partner's gonna get deloused at the station." The pejorative remarks left little doubt about how the officers viewed homosexuals, and when they were reported nationwide weeks later, there was no place for the officers on the department to hide.

At roughly the same time, Sandra Smith and Nicole Childress went to the apartment of Glenda Cleveland, respectively, their mother and aunt. Hearing what transpired, Cleveland, at the request of the two witnesses, called the Milwaukee Police Department to find out how the case had been resolved. The call was transferred several times, and finally a policeman, Balcerzak, answered and identified himself as one of the officers on the scene. He assured Cleveland that it had been an affair between boyfriends, one of whom was intoxicated. Cleveland continued to press the issue of Konerak's age:

Caller: Well how old was this child?

Officer: He was more than a child. He was an adult.

Caller: Are you sure?

Officer: Yup.[20]

It is entirely likely Konerak Sinthasomphone was dying as they spoke.

Although rebuffed, Cleveland pursued the matter with perseverance that bordered on the heroic. A newspaper article showing Konerak's picture and mentioning his disappearance prompted a second call to the police. Although she was assured someone would get back to her, no one from the department followed up the call. On the third call about a week later, she spoke to a homicide detective, who said he was busy on a murder case but would have someone contact her; no one did. In the interim, Cleveland made several anonymous calls to the Sinthasomphone family to make sure he had not returned home. Her fourth call, about a week and a half after May 27, was to crime reporting number "800 We Tip," who suggested she call the FBI. When called, the FBI said they would look into the matter but did not visit her until after Dahmer was arrested. Finally, in desperation she called two local television stations but was told to call the police. Having come full circle, she made no more attempts. But by then Dahmer's discovery was just days away.

Thus, the events that occurred on the night of May 27 and the efforts of Glenda Cleveland in the weeks following represented the last, best chance to stop Dahmer. On the street, attitudinal myopia prevented two seasoned and decorated officers from believing the right people and forming correct conclusions. In the apartment, the officers misread the seemingly open and cooperative behavior of a serial killer who was secure in the knowledge that he could lie without contradiction. Having made the original determination that Konerak was an adult, it is little wonder that Officer Balcerzak confirmed it when challenged by Glenda Cleveland. Less readily explicable is the succession of failures to investigate later calls. Since law enforcement agencies and private parties alike fell short in this regard, it suggests less a breakdown in administrative procedures or apparatus than a tendency of people, whether acting officially or not, to expect the commonplace and hence be unable to distinguish truly serious matters from pedestrian ones.

In the same neighborhood six weeks later, Officers Rolf Mueller and Robert Rauth would be presented with a remarkably similar set of circumstances. This time a young, handcuffed black man ran up to their squad car with a wild story about a man who attacked him in a nearby apartment. The officers were initially dismissive. Suspecting a homosexual quarrel, they told the man, Tracy Edwards, to have his boyfriend remove the handcuffs. After further appeals by Edwards, they agreed to accompany him to Jeffrey Dahmer's apartment.

Inside, the events of May 27 could have easily recurred. Dahmer was conciliatory, polite, and had a glib answer for every question. Unlike Konerak Sinthasomphone, however, Edwards was not incapacitated and could act in his own defense by insisting that the officers check the rest of the apartment. Only when it became clear that he could not prevent the policemen from entering the adjacent bedroom, where evidence of carnage was in plain sight, did Dahmer finally lose control and struggle with the officers. Nevertheless, again in the early morning hours of July 23, 1991, for the same reasons as before, Jeffrey Dahmer came within a hair breadth of perpetuating his deception.

SACRIFICIAL SCAPEGOATS

The public was caught completely unaware by the discovery that took place on July 23 at the Oxford Apartments. As more facts became available almost hourly, the pall over the city deepened and each new revelation set off a wave of reaction. When it was learned that Dahmer sometimes smashed and scattered the bones of his victims, bones began to turn up everywhere. Thirty-five people asked city officials to investigate their findings; none were human.

As always tips came in from across the country, and for a time Dahmer sightings eclipsed those of Elvis. He was reported to have been seen at a highway rest stop in South Dakota, a waitress in San Diego was sure she had served him, and one woman in Arizona reported that Jeffrey Dahmer had lived in her apartment before she occupied it. She was correct but identified another man with the same last name. In all, the leads filled 4,000 pages of police records.

Dahmer became an instant celebrity and the hero of the lunatic fringe. In jail he received sixty letters a day from all over the world, including South Africa, England, Israel, and Saudi Arabia, one of which was a fan letter sent from a convicted satanist and was written in blood. Two teenage vandals were caught painting walls with racist epithets, satanist symbols, and pseudopolitical ravings such as "David Duke for President" and "Free Jeffrey Dahmer." Some simply needed to bask in his fifteen minutes of fame, as did the man who claimed to have been in Dahmer's apartment before he was captured and while there had seen body parts. The desperate sycophant was arrested when his story proved false.

But almost immediately, public reaction took on ominous political overtones. Dahmer became a strawman for anyone with an agenda. He was likened to mob figure Sammy "The Bull" Gravano. Vegetarians placed ads that compared his cannibalistic habits to the consumption of animal meat. Abortion protestors accused physicians of being serial murderers and told women entering clinics that they were no better than Dahmer. An editorial appeared in the *Milwaukee Journal* that decried the preoccupation with Dahmer's tally of seventeen murders when no one was prepared to speak out against the wholesale slaughter of Iraqis by the U.S. arsenal of "smart bombs"; paraphrasing Stalin, the article noted that the death of one person is murder, while 100,000 deaths are foreign policy.[21]

The public directed its most vitriolic attacks against groups, no matter how hapless or innocent, who had been in contact with Dahmer and who, in the rapidly hardening public mind, should have realized the enormity of his crimes. Observing this disturbing trend, local psychiatrist Basil Jackson saw clearly the psychological and sociological mechanisms behind it. He noted that political factions in the city were trying to push their own agendas while the community was vulnerable, so that the police and institutionalized racism rather than Dahmer were blamed for the murders. The all-out effort to assign blame and find scapegoats was due, in his view, to collective anxiety and feelings of guilt over what had happened. Milwaukee, Dr. Jackson believed, was experiencing "post-traumatic stress disorders on a community wide level."[22]

As it became clear what had happened in his unit and what Dahmer had hidden there, his neighbors at the Oxford Apartments became an obvious and easy outlet for the outraged community. They were overrun by news-hungry reporters, received bomb threats, snipers took shots at the building, and residents received hate mail claiming they should have known what Dahmer was doing. Guilt, publicly ascribed or self-generated, was tremendous, and the personal toll devastating. Nightmares of people screaming or being cut to pieces were commonplace, drinking problems developed, at least one man was fired because he could no longer concentrate on his job, several were given therapy, and thirty of the forty-nine occupants relocated immediately.

The presumed culpability of the residents was succinctly summarized by Dahmer's next-door neighbor Shelia White: "Society itself made us victims. It is like people think there wasn't anything that happened to us, that all of us together with Jeffrey Dahmer had something to do with what happened there. How can you blame somebody for living in a place we call home?"[23] In a show of solidarity, Reverend Jesse Jackson came to Milwaukee and held a demonstration outside the apartment complex, pleading for the city to embrace the residents rather than blame them and recognize that they were victims too. Eventually, with all the residents gone, the building itself became an unwelcome reminder and a barrier to community healing. Nothing short of complete eradication was sufficient; it was razed as if to expunge forever what took place there.

After it was revealed that Dahmer killed while on parole for the sexual assault of Keison Sinthasomphone, public ire zeroed in on Circuit Court Judge William Gardner, who passed sentence in the case. Judge Gardner came under immediate criticism for staying Dahmer's original sentence of eight years in prison and instead having him serve one year in jail followed by five years on probation. The *Milwaukee Sentinel* brought suit to have Dahmer's confidential presentencing investigative report unsealed, arguing the public had a right to know the criteria on which Judge Gardner based his decision. The request was denied when Circuit Court Judge Michael Guolee ruled that release of the documents would create a dangerous precedent and have a "chilling effect" on those charged with preparing the reports in the future.

The State Division of Probation and Parole equally came under fire for its handling of Dahmer in the wake of the Sinthasomphone sentence. An editorial in the *Milwaukee Journal* railed at the system's inability to rehabilitate offenders like Dahmer.[24] Leonard Sargent, a friend of victim Tony Hughes, was more focused in his attack, demanding that the entire probation and parole program be reviewed and calling for disciplinary action against Dahmer's parole officer and her immediate supervisor. As she often did,

Dorothy Slaughter gave voice to the feelings of the families and the community: "If he was insane when he committed these murders, what does that say about the people from probation? He was on probation when this all happened. They were supposed to be supervising him."[25]

Then in an attempt to determine the prescribing physicians, police subpoenaed Division records when it became known that the sedative Dahmer used to overcome his victims had been given to him while he was on parole and under court-ordered therapy. One of the physicians involved, Dr. Carrol R. Olson, reported a backlash from his patients who wondered how he could have been involved with Dahmer and have treated him without recognizing his peculiarities. Olson also received calls from strangers requesting the drug, in one instance, because the caller wanted his girlfriend to sleep with him. And when Prosecutor McCann mispronounced the doctor's first name in court, an unfortunate and unrelated Dr. Carl Olson began to receive calls from his patients, making sure he was not involved with Dahmer too.

The impact on the gay community was more complex, with some positive developments but enough negative ones to make people question how much had really changed. Gays charged that hate crimes increased in frequency and seriousness after Dahmer's arrest. However, calls to a hotline run by gays reporting bias attacks declined by 50 percent from 1990 to 1991. Queer Nation demonstrated against the police, once staining a building with red palm prints they said were symbolic of the blood that was on the hands of the department. The police department, for its part, hired a consulting firm from Washington, D.C. to institute a sensitivity training program for its employees and moved to recruit more gay and lesbian officers. Nevertheless, spokesmen for the gay community maintained that homophobia directed at gay officers remained rampant on the force.

Gays were forced to fight subtle forms of bias, the perpetuation of stereotypes and their own fears. They objected when Dahmer's behavior was labeled "homosexual overkill" and had to listen as defense lawyers asked prospective jurors if they could remain impartial after hearing descriptions of gay lifestyles. In an obvious antigay reference, critics of Chief Arreola made fun of his "girlish" handwriting. Phillies Manager Jim Fergosi even got in the act, insulting a Milwaukee sportswriter with the following: "I thought that Dahmer guy took care of the sportswriters up there."[26]

Ultimately, on the level of personal interaction, there was a diminution in the quality of life, or as Terry Boughner, executive editor of a gay newspaper, *The Wisconsin Light*, stated, "People are a little more chary about who they meet, a little more cautious. Dahmer is still remembered. He came across like anybody else in the bar."[27]

Perhaps most disappointing was a lack of support, both official and private, for gay issues. An effort to improve the environment in Milwaukee public schools for gay students by providing sensitivity courses, information on gay lifestyles, and student counseling was met with a demonstration by 700 people who invoked the will of God to justify their protest. The fact that many protestors were black and should have had common cause with gays was doubly cutting. The School Board eventually reduced the scope of the initiative. No representatives of the gay or lesbian community, estimated to be between 60,000 and 100,000 people or one-tenth the population of the city, were appointed to the Blue Ribbon Commission empaneled by Mayor Norquist to investigate police actions surrounding the Konerak Sinthasomphone incident. And when the mayor subsequently vetoed a $5,000 city appropriation for the annual Gay/Lesbian Pride Parade, he was accused of "queer bashing for votes."

Gays attempted to distance themselves from Dahmer and prove he was not representative of their group. Tracy Boughner again expressed the sentiment of gays: "I would hope that people would realize that Dahmer is not typical of the gay community. He's not typical of the straight community. Face it, he's not a typical human being. The bottom line is that what he did had nothing to do with sexual orientation."[28] Conversely, blacks were at pains to show that Dahmer's actions were racially motivated. They were particularly incensed when psychiatrist and noted serial murder expert Park Dietz testified that Dahmer was unaffected by the victim's race or sexual orientation but instead had chosen targets based on certain "aspects of masculine physiques." In the view of the black community, the very fact that most of Dahmer's victims were black was prima facie evidence of the centrality of race in his murderous ideation.

Blacks also tended to interpret events in the context of what they perceived as a national climate of racial discrimination. Citing such diverse examples as the Rodney King verdict, the Charles Stuart case in Boston, and President Bush's refusal to allow Haitian boat people to enter the country, blacks saw a pattern of institutional prejudice that threatened their welfare. Locally, they charged that Dahmer was able to continue killing only because the majority of victims were black and society cared less for the safety of minorities. And, of course, the murder of Konerak Sinthasomphone provided the most obvious example of institutional bias since it could be directly attributed to the police believing one white rather than five blacks.

Some blacks saw racism too in the way Dahmer was treated by authorities. Milwaukee rapper Top Dog expressed it best:

> My name is Top and I don't like that sucker Jeff
> Live by the sword, die by the sword, why ain't he dead yet?
> 'Cause he's white, they'll never treat that man rough
> If he was black they'll beat him down with
>   handcuffs.[29]

> A black man goes to court, his security is deep;
> but a white man goes to court, they give him something
>   to eat.

You want to know why I use so much profanity
They're gonna free that fool on temporary insanity.[30]

In response, blacks insisted on a greater role in the legal process. Black politicians demanded that a black psychiatrist evaluate Dahmer, called for more blacks on the jury, and complained about the treatment families of the victims received. Rita Isbell, sister of victim Errol Lindsey, carried the argument to the extreme, contending that blacks alone should judge Dahmer's insanity plea.

Racial debate quickly focused on police handling of minority witnesses on the night of May 23 and was fought in the arena of political conflict that had been simmering in the department. Chief Arreola immediately seized on the incident as a means to push his community-oriented policing program. Three days after Dahmer's arrest, before any investigation was completed, Arreola suspended officers Balcerzak, Gabrish, and Porubcan. Evaluating their conduct, he stated, "What did they do? They didn't do anything. They didn't fill out a field investigation card, they didn't take names of witnesses. There was virtually nothing in their memo books regarding the incident. They spent less than 16 minutes total on the investigation. Frankly, I have problems with the evaluation of witnesses in the report."[31] Officer Porubcan, after an abject apology from him for what happened that night, was reinstated.

Arreola then earned the lasting enmity of the force with several precipitous moves. Despite being cleared of criminal wrongdoing by the Wisconsin Attorney General's Office, the officers were cited with seven violations of departmental procedure since, as former police officer and professor of criminal justice David Barlow explained, "If the officer is following procedure, then the complaint is against the department. If the police department can show this is an aberration and not part of its policy, then it doesn't look so bad."[32] Balcerzak and Gabrish eventually pled guilty to one charge of failing to conduct a proper investigation but not before Arreola had fired them summarily and publicly on television.

Ultimately, Arreola drew the battle lines on race. At a community rally he appeared on the podium with Reverend Jesse Jackson and confirmed that racism was present on the force. If these statements seemed hypocritical and self-serving to some listeners, it was because Arreola had not been a champion of racial issues before Dahmer's arrest. In fact, just the week before on July 17, Arreola had been criticized in a letter from Lenard Wells as head of the League of St. Martin's for ignoring racial problems at the police academy. Nevertheless, throughout the crisis Arreola enjoyed the unqualified support of the minority community.

The rank and file on the force and their union representatives reacted with equal alacrity and anger. A petition was filed with the Wisconsin Employment Relations Committee, and officers threatened Blue Flu and a procedural work slowdown. "Dump Arreola" T-shirts cropped up, followed soon after by shirts saying "Thank You Chief." A thousand people attended a pro-police rally at which former Chief Breier was a featured speaker. As if to symbolize the cultural and demographic differences that separated the police from the community, it was held at the Serb Memorial Hall. More revealing still, no black officers attended.

A survey of police officers quantified the extent of ill feeling. Fully 78 percent of the department took the trouble to respond, and of these, nearly all, 98 percent, felt that the officers should not have been suspended prior to the completion of a thorough investigation. Turning to the chief, 92 percent rated Arreola's performance as below acceptable or poor. A similar percentage, 93 percent, said they did not have confidence in Arreola's ability to run the department. The "no confidence" vote immediately became a cause célèbre and was roundly vilified, creating yet one more division between the police and minority community.

Solidarity among the officers was not complete, however. Black officers, in particular, tried to straddle the rapidly shrinking middle ground between their race and occupations. Keeping a low profile, the League of St. Martin's resolutely pressed for change in the department's hiring and training policies. But the voices of reason were being drowned out by racial rhetoric, and when the opposing sides clashed at a Fire and Police Commission meeting, one person commented, "This is no longer a right or wrong issue. It is becoming a color issue."[33]

The mayor and city administration supported Chief Arreola without hesitation, and, like gays, police representation was conspicuously missing from the Blue Ribbon Commission. Its orientation having been made clear in advance, the Commission's opinion was hardly surprising: "Our conclusion is that good relationships and effective policing are best fostered by community-oriented policing with appropriate training, in a Department which values both its own diversity and the community's."[34] Chief Arreola and the League of St. Martin's had won.

CASHING IN

If some members of the community used the Jeffrey Dahmer tragedy to push their political positions, the motives of others were even more crass. Serial murder is big business, and there seems to be an unflagging fascination with the motivations and actions of serial killers and no end to the number of people who are willing to exploit the public's thirst for lurid details. For some, the Jeffrey Dahmer case provided a once in a lifetime opportunity to share in a windfall profit, and they jumped at the chance. While this is not unusual, the Dahmer case represents a disturbing trend in how far people are willing to go to satisfy the voyeuristic predilections of a mass market.

Dahmer artifacts were immediately valuable. Souvenir hunters stole anything they could get their hands on, including the numbers from his apartment door and finally the door itself. Two police officers guarding Dahmer while he awaited trial obtained his autograph, which experts speculated was worth $1,000 if auctioned; they were subsequently reprimanded and given six months probation. One enterprising machine operator even attempted to acquire Dahmer memorabilia with the expressed intention of opening a crime museum. The demand was so great that the Milwaukee Police were forced to devise a plan to store and eventually destroy trial evidence, including the infamous freezer and blue barrel, to keep it out of the hands of collectors.

Nevertheless, Dahmer material did make it to market or was fit into existing products. A Louisiana firm sold Dahmer's confession for a mere $13 plus $2 for shipping and handling. Eclipse Enterprises, Inc. announced plans to include Dahmer in its series of 110 true crime trading cards, while another company prepared to introduce a 55-card set of serial killers and mass murderers with Dahmer upstaging Ted Bundy as the "star" card. Even conservative Time-Life Books got into the act by offering a volume entitled *Serial Killers* as the first installment in their Library of True Crime Series, while British publisher Marshall Cavendish added the Dahmer story to its series of Murder Casebooks under the title *Murder and Mutilation*.

A comic book appeared titled *Jeffery Dahmer: An Unauthorized Biography of a Serial Killer*. It was apparently produced in such haste that publisher Hart Fischer of Boneyard Press did not even check the correct spelling of Dahmer's name. The excessively graphic contents infuriated the victims' families, and they traveled in a "Caravan of Love" to confront the publisher at his home in Champaign, Illinois. Not to be outdone, NBC-TV arranged and broadcast a publisher-family confrontation on the program, "A Closer Look with Faith Daniels."

Observing the rush to cash in, Dennis McCann of the *Milwaukee Journal* captured the essence of the phenomenon:

Dreck is Dreck, but enough people love it that there will always be a market. You can't aim too low to make money. No matter how offensive Dahmer comics and trading cards and probably action toys, too, you can be sure they will find buyers. Just as no matter how good (unlikely) or bad (count on it) the . . . TV movies turn out to be, millions of people from coast to coast will watch anyway.

Deplore it, but don't expect to stop it. This is America, and that's free enterprise. Anyway, the worrisome part isn't the supply. It's the demand.[35]

He was prophetic. Despite being priced at $2.50 a copy, comic book sales rose commensurate with the increase in publicity.

Comic books and trading cards were just the beginning. Almost immediately after the depth and details of the tragedy were revealed, Dahmer biographers began to appear. The potential financial rewards were immense, with disproportionate proceeds likely to go to the first book in print. The competition was fierce, therefore, and otherwise respected scholars were caught up in the mad dash for riches. One expert on serial murder, Dr. Joel Norris, who had previously written a serious academic book, *Serial Murder*, released a popular work on Dahmer that was so riddled with typographical errors that it seemed not to have been proofread.

At times it seemed that anyone remotely associated with Dahmer or his trial wrote or contemplated writing a book. Several would-be authors particularly outraged the families of the victims who thought others were trying to use their special proximity to the events to profit from their misfortune and grief. A howl of protest was raised when it was rumored that Judge Gram, who presided over the insanity trial, might be writing a book. A flurry of lawsuits were initiated when it was learned that Lionel Dahmer had received a $150,000 advance to write a book to be called *My Son*.[36]

The electronic media were no less immune. Everyone it seems had a proposal to make a Jeffrey Dahmer movie. An NBC executive noted that the network had received numerous proposals for television movies about Dahmer but had refused all offers because the subject matter was "too weird and repulsive." Few others showed such restraint.

Of course, tabloid journalists, whether print or broadcast, had a field day. Dahmer himself brought one such example to court and displayed the headline of the supermarket checkout paper that screamed "Milwaukee Cannibal Killer Eats His Cellmate"; Dahmer was segregated from other prisoners at the time. Meanwhile, Geraldo Rivera on "Now It Can Be Told" suggested that Dahmer was part of a violent gay underground. More respectable programming settled for interviews with key players in the drama who, in turn, basked in instant celebrity status. Tracy Edwards was a favorite guest, and his story of escape became more grandiose with each appearance.

News coverage of the events and trial was equally intense. At the trial alone, 400 reporters from ninety-five news organization around the world covered the proceedings. Reporters camped out on the doorstep of the victims' families' houses, invaded their homes, and climbed on furniture to get photographs. In the pursuit of news, the media modified it. Participants changed and embellished their stories so much that Anne Schwartz, the *Milwaukee Journal* reporter who was first on the scene the night the murders were discovered, later observed about the witnesses: "I believe their comments the first night were the last honest feelings they expressed before all the sensationalism got in the way."[37] County Executive David Schultz saw the media coverage in a more negative and sinister light: "In their ghoulish fascination with this hideous occurrence, they (the media) have literally run the danger of precipitating collective community psychic suicide."[38] In its headlong pursuit to provide information to the public, the media became part of the unfolding story, and in so doing manufactured a reality that was potentially detrimental to the citizens of Milwaukee.

The more people and organizations seemed to profit from the events, the more disgruntled the families of the victims became. They complained about the supposed special privileges Dahmer received in jail and about the preferential treatment the media received at the trial. In response, they demanded special seats, a private place to eat, free meals, and even a clothing allowance. And, characteristic of members of a litigious society, in the end they sought redress in the courts.

Some of the suits brought were substantive, addressing issues of true loss, while others were frivolous and more indicative of a plaintiff's avarice and a barrister's creative interpretation of the law than real grievances. Whether trivial or material, however, the suits were numerous, and each took time and taxpayer expense to resolve.

Tracy Edwards sued the city for $5 million, claiming police officers sent him back to Dahmer's apartment to have his handcuffs removed, thereby violating his constitutional right to equal protection under the law. The case was summarily dismissed. Hart Fischer and Boneyard Press were sued for using the names and likenesses of the victims in the Dahmer comic book, the premise being he had violated Wisconsin's Right to Privacy Law. One family sued a funeral home for emotional distress when the remains of the victim were returned without being embalmed and were mistakenly shipped in a box marked as a compact copier.

In another action, Martha Hicks, the mother of the first victim, sued Dahmer's parents for $50 million, claiming they were negligent in raising him and that they should have known he was deviant and would almost certainly cause injury to others. Commenting on the case, Dennis McCann of the *Milwaukee Journal* summed up what must have been the reaction of many: "Maybe Hicks came up with this on her own. Maybe some lawyer sold her a bill of goods. But however real her grief and anger, this thing is a real reach."[39]

The family of Konerak Sinthasomphone filed suit against the city, stating that the city had an unwritten policy of discrimination against minorities and that this policy led to the death of their son. Similar suits were brought by the families of victims killed after Sinthasomphone, the argument being that the racially biased attitudes prevalent in the Milwaukee Police Department had prevented the police officers from apprehending Dahmer on May 27. Had they done so, the suits alleged, their family members would not have been murdered. The judge in the case disagreed, ruling that the murders of Joseph Bradehoft, Matt Turner, and Oliver Lacy were too remote from the Konerak Sinthasomphone incident to establish liability. The cases were dismissed.

And finally, the Dahmers, Jeffrey and Lionel, were sued to prevent them from profiting from any resultant publicity of the events. Most of the actions were directed at Jeffrey Dahmer, with the plaintiffs seeking $3 billion per family in damages. Ultimately, the families were awarded $10 million each.

Reacting to the verdict, Janie Hagen, Richard Guerrero's sister, left little doubt about the motives behind the suits. "Ten Million? That's better than nothing I suppose. The judge did a little justice. At least we may get something because a lot of people are making money out of our brother's death and they're not sharing it with us."[40] Given Dahmer's limited prospects for future earnings, it was a hollow victory.

EPILOGUE

On November 27, 1992, after fifteen days of testimony and thirty hours of deliberation, the Milwaukee Fire and Police Commission refused, by a vote of 4 to 1, to reinstate officers Joseph Gabrish and John Balcerzak. Commission Chairman M. Nicol Padway explained that the officers' conduct had been deemed to be grossly negligent and could not be excused as an error in judgment. In rebuttal, Ken Murray, attorney for the officers, vowed to appeal the decision, charging that the two men "were being made 'scapegoats' for a police administration that did not have the guts or courage to take the heat over the Dahmer affair."

Cryptosporidium was again found in the city's water supply on October 17, 1993. This time, however, the Health Department determined the contamination was not sufficiently severe to warrant a public alert or the wholesale boiling of water. Subsequent tests failed to find any evidence of the parasite in the water supply. Meanwhile, AIDS activists maintained that at least fifty people with the disease died prematurely as a result of the original infestation six months earlier.

Jeffrey Dahmer was given fifteen life sentences to be served consecutively, nearly a thousand years of confinement. In prison, he was put in solitary confinement, segregated from other prisoners for his own safety. Prosecutor McCann provided an epitaph for Dahmer's living death: "He was desolately lonely to do the things he did. Now he's desolately lonely forever."[41] For Jeffrey Dahmer forever came quickly. Despite precautions, he was beaten to death by a fellow inmate on November 28, 1994.

The Classic Case

JACK THE RIPPER
London, England (1888)

"Something like a panic will be occasioned in London today by the announcement that another horrible murder has taken place in densely populated Whitechapel."

—*Pall Mall Gazette*, September 8, 1888

It is widely believed that serial murder is a uniquely American phenomenon whose incidence has been increasing rapidly in recent years. This seems unlikely, however. It is more probable that knowledge and technology have only lately become available, enabling seemingly disconnected crimes to be linked. Certainly, reactions to serial murder are stable, with regular forms of response and characteristic adaptations emerging wherever a serial murderer threatens the populace.

The preceding chapters have sought to illustrate a set of responses common to communities that have a serial killer within them. Several of these responses—rational explanations, supernatural appeals, and transference—are closely coupled cognitive processes that threatened people use to contain fear and make sense out of inherently incomprehensible events. Other responses—ordinary obscurity, media circus, and social dissolution—speak to the impact of the killer's presence on social life.

These psychological defenses and social consequences are an integral part of the human condition and the construction of everyday experience; hence, they have a certain verisimilitude about them that transcends modern American society. To demonstrate this universality, one more case will be considered, the Whitechapel murders perpetrated by Jack the Ripper in 1888. All the stages of reaction and social processes observable in contemporary America were evident in the public record left by Victorian England.

In 1888, the East-end of London was home for 900,000 people; 80,000 of them lived in the Whitechapel district, a seething slum of destitute men and women and Jewish immigrants. The poverty of the residents was appalling, the housing stock deplorable. It was estimated that 11,000 were homeless and completely without means of survival and another 100,000 were continually on the verge of starvation. Work when it could be found was highly seasonal. Newborns stood a less than equal chance of reaching adulthood, 55 percent dying before the age of 5. Four thousand houses in Whitechapel were condemned as uninhabitable; 8,500 people lived in 233 houses, with some rooms holding 80 beds. By one estimate, one in every sixty units was a brothel, and one in every sixteen women a prostitute.

The East-end and Whitechapel were embarrassments for Victorian Britons, a rotting core in the capital of the richest, most powerful empire in the world. The better classes of London wished nothing more than not to be reminded they existed. While half-hearted efforts had been made to clean up the squalor, it was Jack the Ripper who brought the conditions of the poor into the harsh glare of public scrutiny, or as George Bernard Shaw so aptly put it, "Whilst we conventional Social Democrats were wasting our time on education, agitation and organization, some independent genius has taken the matter in hand."

THE WHITECHAPEL MURDERS—EIGHT IN TWELVE MONTHS

Like so many other serial murder cases, what the public believed to be the murder count differed from the number ultimately attributed to the killer. Table 8.1 gives the roll call of murders as it appeared in the *Pall Mall Gazette* the day after the corpse of Mary Jane Kelly was discovered. Ironically, the article was titled "Eight in Twelve Months and More to Follow," but her violent death would mark the end of the murder spree.

The first three murders were quite clearly acts of isolated violence and in retrospect are not normally associated with Jack the Ripper. The first woman to die had an iron stake thrust so deeply into her vagina it fatally ruptured internal organs. Emma Smith died as a result of injuries suffered during a gang rape. Shortly before her death, Martha Turner was seen in the company of two soldiers and was later found stabbed to death, a bayonet having caused some of the wounds.

While each of the first three murders was undoubtedly sexually motivated, what distinguishes the Jack the Ripper murders was mutilation of the corpse. Beginning with Mary Anne Nichols, the defilement grew progressively more horrible with each event. Of the last victims only the murder of Elizabeth Stride, during which the killer was thought to have been disturbed before he could finish, did not demonstrate gratuitous damage to the corpse secondary to death. Because of the interruption, it was believed, the killer struck again that night to complete his ghoulish mission.

Table 8.1

The Whitechapel Murders: Eight in Twelve Months and More to Follow

Title	Date	Victim	Description
No.1 - Impaled With An Iron Stake	At Christmas 1887	Unidentified	A certain grim horror distinguished it from ordinary murders by the the fact that an iron stake was thrust into her person.
No. 2 - Outraged to Death by a Gang	Easter Tuesday April 3, 1888	Emma Smith	The gang seemed to have been animated by plunder and passion. They stayed long enough to kill the woman by every imaginable atrocity.
No. 3 - Stabbed with Thirty-nine Wounds	August 7, 1888	Martha Turner	The woman when found presented a shocking appearance, her body being covered with stab wounds to the number of thirty-nine, some of which had been done with a bayonet.
No. 4 - The First Disembowelled	September 1, 1888	Mary Anne Nichols	Murdered under circumstances of the most revolting character. Her throat was cut from ear to ear, and her body ripped up from the abdomen almost to the bone, while a second cut gashed the left thigh.
No. 5 - The First Missing Portion	September 9, 1888	Annie Chapman	The lower part of her body had been horribly mutilated. The throat had been cut so deeply that the head was nearly severed from the trunk. On examination it was found that the uterus had been removed.
No. 6 and 7 - Two in One Night	September 30, 1888	Elizabeth Stride	The woman's head was nearly severed from her body and her blood streaming down the gutter.
		Catherine Eddowes	The woman's throat had been cut from the left side, the knife severing the main artery and other parts of the neck ... the weapon had been thrust into the upper part of the abdomen and drawn completely down, ripping open the body, and, in addition, both thighs had been cut across. The intestines had been torn from the body, and some lodged in the wound on the right side of the neck.
No. 8 - The Latest and Worst	November 9, 1888	Mary Jane Kelly	Hacked to pieces.

Source: Abstracted from the *Pall Mall Gazette*, November 10, 1888, pp. 2–3.

The last murder, that of Mary Jane Kelly, was especially gruesome. It occurred in the victim's room. Off the street, with no fear of detection or interruption, the killer had ample time to indulge his compulsions. The body, found lying on a bed, evinced the psychotic limits his grotesque fantasies could reach. The victim's ears and nose were cut off, her face slashed beyond recognition, the stomach and abdomen split open, breasts, heart, and kidneys removed and placed on the table beside the bed, the genital area mangled, and the liver excised and placed on the right thigh. The violence was so extensive, the damage so extreme, that the *Pall Mall Gazette* trying to describe it was at a loss for words—"Hacked to pieces" was all it could muster.

It is, therefore, mutilation that defines the Jack the Ripper murders, and in this regard the string began and ended in a brief two-month period. However, in terms of public reactions, the murders extended over a full year. Moreover, the pace increased over the final months, when five women were killed in ten weeks of terror; the savagery of the murders also increased, the tempo and violence causing a crescendo of anxiety in the last months of 1888.

Along with mutilation, the populace recognized a number of common denominators. All the women were destitute, surviving by prostitution. Killings invariably occurred on weekends, causing people to speculate that the killer's occupation might take him outside London during the week. He might, for example, be a hop-picker or a sailor on a regular run. The murders were perpetrated in a tight geographic area, and great significance was given to the location of the corpses, as if the killer were trying to draw a picture with dead bodies. The public and press alike spent untold hours trying to discern the pattern in the crimes.

The public was only too willing to help find the Ripper, and as would happen again and again, the outpouring of public support put a crushing burden on the police: "Since the two above-mentioned murders, no fewer than 1,400 letters relating to the tragedies have been received by the police, and although the greater portion of these gratuitous communications were found to be of a trivial and even ridiculous character, still each one was thoroughly investigated."[1]

There was no end to the ideas the public had for catching the killer. Among other things, they suggested: pardoning accomplices, making everyone in Whitechapel report before going to bed, dressing police as women, arming prostitutes with pistols, putting police in rubber shoes so they could sneak up on the killer, allowing police to stop and search anyone on the street for knives, using handwriting experts, and putting "baby-faced pugilists" in women's clothes so they could pummel would-be attackers.

The police for their part beefed up patrols in Whitechapel, conducted house-to-house searches, questioned "polyandrous women," made dozens of arrests, and read Ripper letters to constables before each watch. Bloodhounds were brought in to assist the search, setting off a spirited debate in the papers on the relative merits of bloodhounds, a "lowly breed," versus the more noble retrievers for such work. Subsequently, when the bloodhounds were lost mid-search, the press howled with ridicule and derision, "Who will track the trackers?"

Defensive measures taken to protect against the lurking danger were commonsensical and would be repeated in case after case for the next hundred years. Rewards were offered. Women carried whistles, walked in groups, and devised a signaling system to summon help if need be. A Vigilance Committee was established, and volunteer patrols were organized. Finally, in desperation, 5,000 women of Whitechapel petitioned Queen Victoria, requesting that she "suppress the moral disorders" and close the "bad houses" in which "such wickedness is done and men and women ruined in body and soul."

Although the murders were confined to a tight area, fear quickly spread throughout the city and across the country. Drunks confessed regularly but did so at their own peril, often having to be rescued from angry lynch mobs. A man traveling in the mining region of the country was accosted by a group of suspicious workmen who screamed he was Jack the Ripper, apparently for no other reason than he was unknown in the region. A note from the killer, almost certainly apocryphal, claimed he had moved his operation to Glasgow, setting off paroxysms of fear in that city when it was published. The fear was real, palpable, ubiquitous, and lethal in its own right. "On Tuesday afternoon Mrs. Burridge, a shopkeeper of the Blackfriars-road, was reading an account of the Whitechapel murder and she was so affected thereby that she fell down in a fit and died."[2]

THE POWER OF REASON—THE SCIENTIFIC SOCIOLOGIST

Victorian England prided itself on the pursuit of knowledge through the application of the scientific method. It was an era in which the natural world held endless fascination and every country squire was an amateur naturalist; a time during which the farthest reaches of the planet, particularly the darkest regions of Africa, were explored, and when great theories of life processes like evolution through natural selection were formulated. A society so accustomed to scientific observation was quick to describe the causes for the killer's aberrant behavior in quasitechnical terms.

The mind of a madman could be as readily classified as the natural world, therefore, and the resulting categorization reflected the class-conscious culture and its acceptance of the doctrine of evolution. Thus, it was noted that killers had brains of the "low-type." One theory had it that "the murderer is a victim of erotic mania which often takes the awful shape of an uncontrollable taste for blood." Another theory held that the killer was seen to be an example of retrogression in the march of evolutionary improvement, an atavistic creature suffering from homicidal mania. "Professor Benedikt, of Vienna, has developed a theory that the brains of murderers resemble in their conformation those of ferocious beasts. They have, he contends, a special likeness to the brains of bears."[3]

An interesting twist on the theme of rational explanations present in the Jack the Ripper case was not only that scientists could solve the crimes but, in fact, that the killer was himself a scientist. One popular speculation, which neatly encapsulated the dual themes of rational explanation and xenophobia, suggested that an American anatomist had hired the Ripper to obtain organs that would then be submitted along with a technical manuscript for publication in a scientific journal. The bloody bounty for the specimens was reputed to be 20 pounds.

As incredible as this belief might seem in retrospect, it received considerable credence until completely debunked by the *Pall Mall Gazette*. The paper contacted the subcurator of the Pathological Museum, who quoted the prevailing rates for body parts used for scientific purposes:

The following are the prices which we are paying at present for anatomical subjects

For one corpse complete	£3.50
For one thorax	£0.50
For one arm, leg, one head and neck, and one abdomen, net	£1.50

In summation, he noted: "These prices refer to pickled dissecting-room subjects. The organs removed by the murderer can be had for the asking at any post-mortem room twelve hours after death."[4]

Another variation on the scientist as killer motif was the argument intricately reasoned in the press that the murders were being committed by a "Scientific Sociologist," who was conceptualized as a social reformer gone berserk.[5] According to this view, the conscience-stricken crusader was reacting rationally to the misery of the slums and the lack of concern shown by "Parliament, police & press," or as the paper reasoned for the Ripper:

If these cesspools of brutalized humanity were not to become a permanent source of poisonous miasma, it was necessary something should be done that would at once rouse public attention, create universal sensation, and compel even the most apathetic and self-indulgent to admit the first postulate of the Socialist's faith, that the luxury and the wealth of the West must be employed to mitigate the squalor and crime of the East. The only question was what the means should be.

What to do? The Scientific Sociologist, being a rational man, would seek to obtain the maximum effect for the minimum expenditure of money and life and seize, in Bismarck's terminology, the "psychological moment" to deliver a decisive stroke. Following this train of thought to its conclusion, no ordinary killing would do since it would not impress the public. There had to be something so shocking it could not be ignored. Mutilation was therefore an absolute necessity. Summing up the presumed homicidal ratiocinations of the killer, the paper continued:

We must presuppose in our scientific Sociologist such a supreme devotion to the welfare of the community, that he cannot for a moment hesitate in sacrificing a few worthless lives in order to attain his end. This is exactly what he seems to have done. The victims belonging to the class which of all others, suffers the most hideous and tragic fate in the human lot. None of them found life worth living. All were drunken, vicious, miserable wretches, whom it was almost a charity to relieve of the penalty of existence. He took them to the very centre of the plague spots to the existence of which he was desirous of turning the public attention. There he seems to have killed them with the merciful painlessness of *science*, so that suffering was reduced to a minimum, and death came as a welcome release from the insupportable miseries of existence. After killing his victim he mutilated her, well knowing that a knife's slit in a corpse makes more impression on the vulgar mind than the greatest cruelties, moral or even physical, inflicted on the living. Then he seems to have waited to see if his actions would have the desired effect.

In the name of science and with the use of its methods to achieve his ends, the image of the murderer had become a malignant cross between Jane Addams and Dr. Jekyll. "What then is more reasonable than to suppose that these horrors may have been produced in this scientific sensational way to awaken the public conscience?," the paper wondered. The logic was airtight.

SUPERNATURAL APPEALS—SEVEN HUMAN SACRIFICES

Strong supernatural undercurrents enervated the public's reaction to Jack the Ripper and animated public discussions about the crimes. As usual, references to ghosts, spirits, and the occult were used to explain the killer's actions, suggest how he might be captured, and even predict the site of the next slaying. As would become de rigueur in serial murder cases for the next hundred years, those reputed to have extrasensory powers were entreated to catch the killer.

Typical of the reactions, Jack the Ripper was seen initially as inhumanly bloodthirsty; his crimes were termed "Red Indian Savagery"—he was "The Savage of Civilization," a Sioux "bathing his hands in blood." For others, he was a religious fanatic on a God-given mission to rid the slums of prostitution. It only stood to reason, then, that if the killer were driven by devilish cruelty or conversely divine inspiration, the agent of his destruction would also have otherworldly gifts. Not surprisingly, letters to the editor of the *Pall Mall Gazette* suggested that spiritualists, the turn-of-the-century equivalent of psychics, be called in to solve the case. The paper, whose most famous serialized novelist Sir Arthur Conan Doyle was himself an ardent proponent of spiritualism, took up the public's challenge. Appealing to the psychic detectives of the day, the paper asked, "Where are Messrs. Stuart Cumberland and Irving Bishop?"[6]

Following a conspicuous silence from the extrasensory set, the paper raised the stakes further[7] by noting:

There is some sense . . . in the suggestion that the Whitechapel murders afford the practitioners of occult science (or religion) an unexampled opportunity to prove and advertise the genuineness of their pretensions. If spiritualists, clairvoyants, and thought readers all "lie low and say nuffin," we may at least conclude that whatever spirits may be present at their seances, public spirit is notably absent.

Taunting the believers once more, the paper continued:

Interviews with Carlyle and Shakespeare may be all very interesting, but a short conversation with one of the six spirits so recently sent to the long abode . . . would for practical purposes be worth more than a volume of trans-Stygian Carlylese. Clairvoyants . . . might set to work upon "Jack the Ripper's" letter and determine whether it is genuine or a hoax. Why does the Society for Psychical Research stand so ingloriously idle?

The gauntlet lay where it was thrown, for no spiritualist answered the mocking challenge.

In an article entitled "The Whitechapel Demon's Nationality and Why He Committed the Murders," signed By One Who Thinks He Knows, the author again saw the dark hand of evil behind the Ripper's actions and threw in a bit of Francophobia for good measure.[8] Examining the syntax and grammar of one of the messages left at a crime scene, the writer concluded that the killer was French. Besides, he noted, "in France, the murdering of prostitutes has long been practiced and had been considered to be almost peculiarly a French crime."

Having established the continental origins of the threat, One Who Thinks He Knows went on to demonstrate that the murders were essential ingredients for the black magic rituals practiced by the killer. Spells were cast using, among other things, "skin of a suicide, nails from a murderer's gallows, candles made from human fat, the head of a black cat which had been fed forty days on human flesh, the horns of a goat which has been made the instrument of an infamous and capital crime, and a preparation made from the body of a *harlot*." It was, the author noted, "This last point . . . that first drew my attention to the possible connection of the murderer with the black art."

Equally critical were human sacrifices and "the profanation of the cross and other emblems considered sacred." And it was in this regard, the author suggested, that Jack the Ripper demonstrated an evil genius. Locating six of the murders on a map conveniently provided for the illustration, One Who Thinks showed that they did indeed form a crude cross. Only the murder site of Mary Jane Kelly had to be eliminated to make the point—perhaps it was sampling error. Having come inexorably to his inferences, One Who concluded, "Did the murderer, then, designing to offer the mystic number of seven human sacrifices in the form of a cross—a form which he intended to profane—deliberately pick out beforehand on a map the places in which he would offer them to his infernal deity of murder? If not surely these six *coincidences* (?) are the most marvellous event of our time."

A week later, this preposterous suggestion elicited a response.[9] In his letter to the editor, the author said, "I am myself engaged in preparing a diagram by which I hope to prove that the crimes were really the work of a Unionist who is gradually marking out in the East-end of London an exact reproduction of the lines of the Union Jack." The letter, written in flawless English, was signed simply "A Frenchman."

TRANSFERENCE—NOT ONE MAN IN A THOUSAND

The process of transference is an outgrowth of fear and mystery. Fear inspires a search for meaning, while mystery virtually assures that none will be found. Most often the murders are accompanied by inexplicable circumstances either in the behavior of the victims such as Karen Sue Beineman's infinitely incomprehensible trust in a stranger or in the modus operandi of the murderer. Whatever the source of the mystery, the public eventually seeks the cause of it in the special character, personality, or skills of the killer.

In the case of the Whitechapel murders, the abiding question for the public was how the killer could have caused such unspeakable violence without having come to the attention of anyone nearby. It was after all a teeming slum in which unrelated people lived four to a room, where streets were filled day and night, and police patrols had been constantly increased throughout the terror. Nonetheless, the victims, as often repeated in testimony at the Coroner's inquests, were never heard to cry out, and there was no evidence that they struggled.

Puzzling too was how the killer could have escaped the scene without attracting notice. Such extreme violence and mutilation were accompanied by extensive bleeding; one expert even has suggested that severing the arteries in the neck would have caused blood to shoot as much as three feet. The murder of Annie Chapman was committed in the early evening between 5:30 and 6:00 P.M. when it was still light. But the presumably blood-soaked killer was able to walk away, through crowded streets, in broad daylight without causing one iota of suspicion.

Of course, explanations for each of these mysteries could be found in simple physical realities. Neck wounds as deep as those on the victims would have made crying out impossible. An attack from behind would have limited the amount of blood spilled on the killer, as would mutilation after the death blow had been delivered. But while medical professionals at the time appreciated these facts, they failed to convince the general population.

Answers to these perplexing questions were found in the killer's extraordinary capabilities, which varied depending on the suspect who was in favor at the moment. For instance, about one suspect, John Pizer, aka Leather Apron, it was said: "But the most singular characteristic of the man is the universal statement that in moving about he never makes any noise. His uncanny peculiarity to them is that they never see him or know his presence until he is close by them."[10] He could, in short, materialize out of thin air.

When it was thought that a Malay had run amok and killed the prostitutes out of vengeance for having been robbed by one of their number, a Manchester resident, writing to the editor of the *Pall Mall Gazette*, noted that Malays were "vindictive, treacherous, and ferocious" and, more importantly, *"These vicious attributes are hereditary and apparently ineradicable"* (author's italics).[11] Thus not only was uncontrollable rage a special trait of the Malay killer, but it was a defining quality of his race, bestowed at birth in his genetic makeup, to be carried ever after.

In some quarters, even the remains of the victims were thought to have special powers:

Much the most gruesome contribution to the Whitechapel horrors is that which appears in the *Standard* to-day from its Vienna correspondent. According to Dr. Bloch, a Galician member of the Reichsrath, there is no more inveterate superstition among German thieves than the belief that a candle made from the missing portions of the victims in Whitechapel will throw all those upon whom its light falls into the deepest slumber. Such candles are, therefore, invaluable to burglars.[12]

Dissection of the corpses and removal of organs also seemed to set the killer apart. The mutilations appeared to be so deliberate and premeditated that it was assumed the killer knew precisely what he was doing, where to look for the desired organs, and how to excise them with "no meaningless cuts." This was taken as proof of "considerable anatomical skill and knowledge"; as one newspaper put it, "His anatomical knowledge carries him out of the category of a common criminal, for that knowledge could only have been obtained by assisting at post-mortems, or by frequenting the post-mortem room."[13] All this was believed despite the fact that one physician who examined the body of Annie Chapman testified before the Coroner's inquest that the killer possessed no special training or expertise. Nevertheless, this solitary voice of reason was ignored. The public chose to believe instead that "Not one man in a thousand could have played the part of Annie Chapman's murderer."[14]

MEDIA CIRCUS—SO MANY STORIES HAVE BEEN INVENTED

The Whitechapel murders were a source of limitless fascination for the residents of London. After the double murders of Elizabeth Stride and Catherine Eddowes, hundreds, and by some estimates thousands, of gawkers queued up, patiently waiting hours for a chance to view the murder site in spite of the fact that the bodies had been removed the day before and the street washed clean of blood in the interim. Local residents trying to capitalize on the windfall traffic set up refreshment stands to cater to the curious.

The press similarly went to great lengths to satisfy the voyeuristic preferences of the public. One reporter, never to be outdone by his modern counterparts, dressed as a woman and roamed the streets of Whitechapel hoping to be attacked by the killer, risking death for the scoop of a lifetime. At one point, popular speculation reasoned that the killer was, in fact, an "enterprising newspaperman" because "the amount of 'copy' produced by the expenditure of this moderate sum (the murders) is practically unlimited."

While no one suspected for long that a reporter was the murderer, the conjecture did touch a sensitive nerve. Newspapers did have a considerable stake in perpetuating the story and publishing the horrors. Fear, quite simply, sold papers. Editors therefore found it in their financial interest to publish the most ghastly details of the crimes and the most outlandish theories about the murderer.

A variety of structural factors in Victorian society and its economy had combined to spur dramatic growth in the newspaper industry. In the mid-nineteenth century, liberal reformers attacked "taxes on knowledge" and repealed several laws that made newspapers prohibitively expensive. Duties on paper were eliminated, as were taxes on advertising and newspapers themselves. Furthermore, the Public Education Act passed in 1870 mandated compulsory education for all citizens. By 1888, a generation of Englishmen had come to majority since the law was passed, and its effect was obvious— 98 percent of the population was literate.

Newspapers were cheaper to produce and sell, bringing their cost within reach of the average man, while at the same moment in history, the average person was sufficiently well educated to read the product. The dual forces drove newspaper demand skyward. In 1840, there were 14 papers in the city. The number grew tenfold to 150 by 1880 and would more than double over the next decade, during which 180 new titles appeared.

With such significant competition, a shakeout in the industry was inevitable, and as fate would have it, the Whitechapel murders occurred in the midst of the resulting circulation war. Reporters swarmed over the East-end with the often repeated effect that their presence began to modify the interpretation of events they were supposed to describe. According to one paper, "so many stories have been invented for the sake of gain by people who live in the locality since these murders became the sensation in the newspapers that it is difficult to ascertain at once whether they are accurate or otherwise."[15]

Newspapers did whatever they could to keep public interest alive. If need be, they would fan the flames of controversy, lead the attack on the police, publicize the wildest theories about the identity of the killer, and give voice to rumors and superstition on which the edifice of anti-Semitism was built. Ultimately, in the drive for circulation, the press may have gone beyond the bounds of reporting news to the manufacture of it.

On September 26, the Central News Agency reported that it had received a communication from a man who claimed to be the killer. In the letter, the self-proclaimed killer taunted the police, "I have to laugh when they look so clever and talk about being on the right track." He wrote about his motivation, "I am down on whores and I shan't quit ripping them." He spoke in chilling terms of his pride and pleasure in murdering: "Grand work that last job was. I gave the lady no time to squeal. I love my work and want to start again." He warned that he would strike again, and he graphically described what he would do when he did: "The next job I do I shall clip the lady's ears off and send them to the police officers just for jolly. . . . My knife is nice and sharp I want to get to work right away." The letter was signed "Jack the Ripper," which the author referred to as his "trade name."

The letter when released to the public was an unqualified sensation. In an era when everyone was given a nickname, both suspects—John Pizer "Leather Apron"—and victims—Elizabeth Stride "Long Liz," Mary Anne Nichols "Pretty Polly," Annie Chapman "Dark Annie"—the killer had chosen to reveal his, to make himself one of the lads. Like Son of Sam, the name personalized the killer, making the threat real and present for countless women. More importantly, for the papers it was a shorthand reference to the killer's persona, a sobriquet they could sensationalize. And for future generations, it ensured that a slum predator would never be forgotten, and therefore it was the first step in myth making.

But was it genuine? The initial letter and all the later communications supposedly written by the killer have been scrutinized by Ripperologists ever since. The consensus is that the first letter was undoubtedly a fake, as were all but one of the subsequent notes. Even at the time, police were reputed to have known the letter had been sent by "an enterprising journalist" but refused to reveal his identity.

The overwhelming reaction to the first communique inspired a series of subsequent letters, notes, and telegrams. The Ripper wrote to newspapers, the police, the head of the Whitechapel Vigilance Committee, even to Sir Charles Warren, the Home Secretary. Letters were sent to papers outside

London such as one received by a Belfast paper claiming the Ripper had moved his operation there. The net effect was to spread the Ripper terror throughout the Kingdom. Crude fakes appeared, such as two written by a woman in Bradford, for which she was arrested. There was even one sent to the Nottingham Press from "Jack the Ripper's Pal," who said he had been "mesmerized" by the killer into being his accomplice.

Perhaps most intriguing of all, the fictitious letters may have provided the impetus for the true killer to write. A letter received by George Lusk, the leader of the Whitechapel Vigilance Committee, on October 16 is the only communique experts believe to be authentic; it read:

From Hell

Mr. Lusk Sir.

I send you half a kidne I took from one woman prasarved it for you tother piece I fried and ate it was very nise I may send you the bloody knif that took it out if you only wate a whil longer

Catch me when you can Mishter Lusk

The letter contained part of what examining doctors called the "ginny Kidney" of a forty-five-year-old woman, which seemed to fit the description of Catherine Eddowes, from whom it was presumably taken.

Could it be that the press in its desperate scramble for readers crafted fictitious letters from the killer, created copy, and in the process prodded the real killer to break his silence? We, of course, will never know, but one thing is certain. Ninety years later an unknown postal worker longing for attention would be captivated by the case and try to recapture the public relations coup by sending his letters not "From Hell" but "From the Gutters of New York."

COMMUNITY DISSOLUTION—THE JUWES ARE THE MEN

Fear, ever present, began to wear away the fabric of the community, dissolving the connective bonds that held it together. First to disappear was trust in one's fellow man, accompanied by a reciprocal rise in suspicion. As one newspaper commenting on the situation observed, "It seemed at times as if every person in the streets were suspicious of everyone else he met, and as if it were a race between them who should first inform against his neighbor."[16]

Next came the search for scapegoats, and in this regard the Jewish population of Whitechapel was a convenient group against which the public could vent its frustration and hate. Having emigrated to England to escape the pogroms in Eastern Europe, Jews were shocked when suddenly confronted by a new wave of persecution. Without provocation, Jews were attacked in the streets. One of the first men accused of the crime, John Pizer, was a Jewish shoemaker known by the nickname Leather Apron. Pizer was arrested for suspicion, interrogated, but much to the chagrin of the public who was convinced he was guilty, completely exonerated and released.

The third stage in the cresting wave of fear and hate was the resurrection of an ancient calumny that murder and human sacrifice were required under Jewish law. One paper explained, "Among certain fanatical Jews their [sic] exists a superstition to the effect that if a Jew became intimate with a Christian woman he would atone for his offense by slaying and mutilating the object of his passion. Sundry passages of the Talmud are said to sanction this form of atonement."[17]

Speaking for the community in an article titled "The Whitechapel Murders and the Blood Accusation,"[18] the *Jewish World* pointed out that the source of the attack was "a superstition which has pursued Jews through the ages." Continuing the defense, the paper argued that no Jews had ever committed such an atrocity and that the recent trial of Ritter in Austria, where the same charge was leveled, proved beyond doubt that no prescription requiring human sacrifice existed among the Jews. The *Jewish World* concluded, "Who can foresee to what terrible consequences such a superstition might lead, when the people frantic with rage and terror, get hold of it and wreak vengeance on innocent men?"

A week later, in an editorial titled "Panic and Prejudice,"[19] the *Jewish World* turned its attention to the other papers that helped promulgate the rumor and kept it alive. "We venture to utter this warning note at the present moment, not because we think there is any immediate cause for alarm, but because the thoughtless sensationalism of some of our evening contemporaries shows a tendency to run in channels which may easily lead to combustible material."

Hoping to quash the Blood Accusation rumor and quell the internecine unrest in his district, the Member for Whitechapel, Samuel Montague, spoke out vehemently on behalf of his constituents. "I cannot see how the atrocious acts of one man should affect a class,"[20] he wrote, but few were willing to heed the simple truth of his statement.

Despite the best efforts of the *Jewish World* and the Whitechapel MP to defuse the situation, it seemed at times as if the killer were deliberately trying to incite the anti-Semitic hatred of the masses. Near the body of one victim police found a piece of apron clearly left there by the murderer. John Pizer, Leather Apron, was identified in the press as the prime suspect when the suggestive swatch was found. Then on a wall above the sprawled and mutilated body of Catherine Eddowes, written in white chalk, was the most inflammatory clue of all. "The Juwes are the men that will not be blamed for nothing," it read. The message was so potentially explosive that the Home Secretary, Sir Charles Warren, personally ordered it erased before news of it set off anti-Semitic rioting.

Cooler heads began to wonder whether the well-placed clues were not just a bit too good to be true, whether the apron fragment and scrawled message had not in reality just been a transparent ruse to throw off the police. Why, they asked, if the killer were Jewish had he written Juwes? The answer appeared almost immediately in the papers; Juwes was the Eastern European spelling of the word, it was claimed. In response, Jews pointed out that anyone of their group from the continent would have used the word Yid or Yiddish, and hence no real Jew would have written Juwes.

But the matter simply would not die. In an attempt to maintain the fiction, a correspondent to the *Pall Mall Gazette* pointed out that the word, perhaps written in haste, could have been misinterpreted by the police. Instead of Juwes, it might really have been Juives, the French spelling for Jews. The paper meanwhile, by its choice of words, left little doubt about its position concerning the minority immigrants of Whitechapel. It wrote of Juwes, "This the police consider a strong indication that the crime was committed by one of the numerous foreigners by whom the East-end is infested."[21]

ORDINARY OBSCURITY—NOT MARKEDLY DIFFERENT

During the Ripper terror, there was never a shortage of suspects, self-identified, picked up by the police or pointed out by the public. Arrests for "suspicion" were commonplace, but in every instance the detainee could account for his actions and was quickly released. There was also no dearth of theories about who Jack the Ripper might be. Depending on the deductions of the speculator, he was a Malay, a sunstroked physician, a cattle drover, an employee of a slaughterhouse, a Frenchman dabbling in the occult, an American anatomist, or a Scientific Sociologist. The list went on and on, limited only by the imagination of the theorist and rarely hindered by fact.

In the century following the murders, the search for Jack the Ripper's identity has been unflagging, and the suspects named and the rationale for their guilt have been no less creative, or at times any less farfetched, than they were at the time. Table 8.2 lists the most popular candidates for the dubious honor of being Jack the Ripper as well as the basis for their presumed guilt. Generally speaking, a good Ripper suspect must satisfy three criteria: (1) demonstrate a homicidal nature or malevolence toward women, (2) provide some reason for his ability to avoid detection, and (3) offer a basis to explain why the murders stopped so abruptly. Consequently, choosing a favorite Ripper candidate approximates a projective test completed by filling in the blanks of motivation, evasion, and remission.

There is something that does not ring true about the list of suspects, however. Most are infamous criminals or well-educated men from the upper classes whose lofty status, even noble birth, presumably insulated them from

Table 8.2
The Usual Suspects

Suspect	Rationale
George Chapman	A Polish barber born Swerm Klosowski convicted of poisoning three wives and upon whose hanging in 1903, head of the Ripper investigation Inspector Abberline was heard to remark, "You've got Jack the Ripper at last."
Dr. Neill Cream	Poisoned four prostitutes with strychnine, earning him the sobriquet the "Lambeth Poisoner." When hanged in 1892, he reputedly called out "I am Jack the ..." just as the trapdoor was sprung. Was imprisoned in Illinois from 1881 to 1891.
Frederick Demming	Murdered two wives and four children. Confessed to being Jack the Ripper while awaiting execution in 1892, but was in prison at the time of the murders.
Dr. William Gull	Physician to the royal family who, depending on the conjecturer, became homicidal after suffering a stroke or executed the women to cover up a blackmail plot against the heir to the British throne, Prince Albert Victor. Died in 1890.
Prince Albert Victor	The Duke of Clarence and second in line to the British throne. Dim-witted and sometimes assumed to be mad, the Prince was thought to be able to escape arrest because of his high birth. Died of pneumonia in 1892. Was probably out of London when at least one murder was committed.
James K. Stephen	Oxford don and tutor of Prince Albert Victor who wrote virulent antifemale poetry. It has been suggested that Stephen and the Prince were homosexual lovers, and no less an authority than Dr. David Abrahamsen has proposed that the two men killed in tandem. Died of syphilis in 1892, hopelessly mad and locked in an asylum.
Montague J. Druitt	Teacher and sometime barrister, who bore a stunning physical resemblance to Prince Albert Victor. Druitt's presumed guilt rests on two foundations: one, he was identified as the most likely suspect by head of Scotland Yard CID Sir Melville Macnaghten in a confidential memorandum (Macnaghten claimed Druitt was a doctor), and two, he committed suicide in November 1888.

discovery. On a practical level, it may be that only the notorious or prominent members of Victorian society left enough documentation about their lives that could be mined for clues. Given the findings of recent systematic studies of serial murder, however, it seems doubtful that anyone on the list was actually Jack the Ripper.

By comparison, armed with the latest psychological profiling techniques, the FBI's Center for the Analysis of Violent Crime reviewed what was known about the murders and formulated a description of the killer. According to the FBI, Jack the Ripper was a highly intelligent 28 to 36 year old who lived in the area, probably in the vicinity of the first murder in Bucks Row. He was unmarried and had a domineering mother with whom he had an ambivalent relationship. With respect to personality traits, he was fastidious and orderly, but also suffered from poor self-esteem as a result of a real or perceived physical defect. Socially detached and a loner, he was timid and shy. Prostitutes were chosen as victims then, because they initiated contact, something he would never have had the courage to do on his own.

As for the more flamboyant behaviors attributed to Jack the Ripper, the increased damage done to the corpses as the killings progressed was evidence of his growing confidence. The FBI concluded that the Whitechapel murderer would not have drawn attention to himself by writing letters to the press, and it was very unlikely in their view that he would have committed suicide. "In short, Jack the Ripper was a young resident of Whitechapel, not markedly different from anyone else, though perhaps perceived by his family as a little strange."[22]

EPILOGUE—ON THE OUTLOOK IN NEW YORK

Although the murder of Alice McKenzie in Whitechapel on July 17, 1889 is sometimes attributed to Jack the Ripper, it was sufficiently distant in time and different in commission so as to make its link to the other murders quite unlikely. Thus, for most Ripperologists and certainly for the public at large, the gory reign of Jack the Ripper ended with the butchery of Mary Jane Kelly. Indeed, the progression of cruelty seemed to reach some gruesome zenith with the extreme barbarity of her disfigurement. As one newspaper observed, "Short of absolutely skinning the next victim from head to heel, it is difficult to see what fresh horror is left for him to commit."[23] The flaying of the corpse was so depraved that some speculated that the killer, seeing the enormity of his crime, committed suicide shortly after.

For others, the assumption was that Saucy Jack, as he intimated in one of his notes, fled Whitechapel because it "Got rather too warm there. Had to shift." Many believed he returned to America from whence he came to begin with. As reported in the *Pall Mall Gazette* on the last day of 1888,

Inspector Andrews, of Scotland-yard, has arrived in New York. . . . It is generally believed that he has received orders from England to commence his search in the city for the Whitechapel murderer. Mr. Andrews is reported to have said that there are half a dozen English detectives, two clerks, and one inspector employed in America in the same chase. The supposed inaction of the Whitechapel murderer for a considerable period and the fact that a man suspected of knowing a good deal about this series of crimes left England for this side of the Atlantic three weeks ago, has . . . produced the impression Jack the Ripper is in that country.[24]

With that, having established the benchmarks by which other serial murder cases would be judged in the future, Jack the Ripper walked out of the East-end fog and into the equally murky realm of legend.

Epilogue

Richard Valenti, Albert DeSalvo, John Norman Collins, David Berkowitz, Wayne Williams, Jeffrey Dahmer, and Jack the Ripper. Seven examples of serial murderers. Killers of men and women, young and old, black and white. Executioners armed with guns, knives, garrote, club, and hands. Separated by decades of history, by continents and oceans, by race, culture, and life circumstance. Yet identical in psychological ideation, motivated by fantasies of murder and the need to replenish the images with new acts of violence. Their behavior rigid and ritualized, encapsulated in a repeated modus operandi, codified in a choreography of death.

Seven men infamous and obscure, convicted and uncaught, guilty and perhaps innocent, but symbols all. Each the personification of personal vulnerability immanent in social life. Identical too in their ability to strike irrational and inordinate fear in the hearts and minds of others. When confronted with their perceived threat, no matter how remote the true risk of peril, a community of individuals is galvanized into a single being, an entity evincing a unified, albeit collective, psychology and behavior as stylized and ritualized as that of the provocateur.

This collective adaptation is based on the need to understand—to combat fear by knowing—and to contain the threat by apprehension and acceptance. This understanding is founded on plausible explanations for the presence of the threat and the behavior of the killer, whether it be rational reasons, supernatural explanations, or the special traits of the killer that set his actions apart from the rest of society.

This collective adaptation is also evidenced by characteristic reactions of segments of the community toward other groups. A community will attempt to contain the threat by attributing it to an outsider or someone from another part of society, or by ultimately finding the victims themselves responsible for their own misfortune. Social distancing, finding fault, and laying blame are a community's classic defense. Ritualized behavior is also apparent on an institutional level, occurring when the protectors of society are unable to apprehend a killer despite repeated chances because of inexperience, governmental boundaries and barriers, a mountain of information, the strategies used to cull the roster of suspects and process the myriad bits of factual detail, and, possibly most important of all, an inability to recognize abnormal behavior disguised by the conventions of everyday life and when the patterned behavior of the media whose commercial interests in reporting the news transform into the making of it.

These seven killers and cases have been chosen to illustrate the stages of collective psychological adaptation and ritualized group and institutional response. Each case was used to demonstrate one aspect of community reaction, but, as the Jack the Ripper case was intended to show, all elements are present in every serial murder experience. Also, serial murder was chosen as a unique form of threat to social order, the collective reaction to which is extreme and disproportionate. It remains to be seen how representative the reactions described here are to those exhibited as a result of other forms of unusual social behavior, for example, martyrdom, or other outpourings of collective emotion such as that associated with the onset of war, the occasion of economic panic, or a mass tragedy like a plane crash. Undoubtedly, means of collective psychological defense and characteristic group and individual response are present to be documented.

Notes

CHAPTER 1

1. As retold by Folly Beach Police Chief George Tittle during interview, November 11, 1992.

2. *Charleston Evening Post*, April 19, 1974, p. 1–B.

3. *Ibid.*

4. *The News and Courier*, April 17, 1974, p. 1–A.

5. *Ibid.*, p. 2–A.

6. *Ibid.*, April 19, 1974, p. 2–A.

7. *Ibid.*, April 18, 1974, p. 1–A.

8. *Charleston Evening Post*, June 26, 1974, p. 2–A.

9. *Ibid.*, April 18, 1974, p. 1–A.

10. *Ibid.*

11. *Ibid.*, April 19, 1974, p. 1–B.

12. *Ibid.*

13. *Ibid.*

14. *The News and Courier*, June 27, 1974, p. 1–A.

15. *Ibid.*

CHAPTER 2

1. *Time*, July 27, 1987, p. 61.

2. R. Holmes and J. DeBurger, *Serial Murder* (Newbury Park, Calif.: Sage Publications, 1988), pp. 24–25.

3. S. A. Egger, "Linkage Blindness: A Systemic Myopia," in S. Egger (ed.), *Serial Murder* (New York: Praeger, 1990), p. 164.

4. E. W. Hickey, *Serial Murderers and Their Victims*. (Pacific Grove, Calif.: Brooks/Cole Publishing Co., 1991), p. 20.

5. *New York Times*, July 26, 1991, p. A12.

6. R. Doney, "The Aftermath of the Yorkshire Ripper: The Response of the

United Kingdom Police Service," in S. Egger (ed.), *Serial Murder* (New York: Praeger, 1990), p. 102.

7. A. E. Schwartz, *The Man Who Could Not Kill Enough* (New York: Carol Publishing Group, A Birch Lane Press Book, 1992), pp. 26–27.

8. *Ibid.*, p. 176.

9. J. Conklin, *The Impact of Crime* (New York: Macmillan Publishing Co., 1975), p. 9.

CHAPTER 3

1. *Boston Herald*, March 8, 1964.

2. *Herald Advertiser*, September 2, 1964.

3. *Boston Record American*, January 13, 1964.

4. *Boston Traveler*, September 12, 1962.

5. *Boston Record American*, January 13, 1963.

6. *Boston Globe*, September 9, 1962.

7. *Boston Record American*, February 8, 1963.

8. G. Frank, *The Boston Strangler* (New York: The New American Library, 1966), p. 26.

9. *Boston Record American*, January 13, 1964.

10. *Ibid.*, January 24, 1963.

11. *Boston Traveler*, January 17, 1967.

12. *Boston Record American*, January 9, 1963.

13. *Ibid.*

14. *Herald Advertiser*, January 20, 1963.

15. *Boston Record American*, January 24, 1963.

16. *Ibid.*, February 8, 1963.

17. *Boston Herald*, January 12, 1964.

18. *Boston Record American*, January 9, 1963.

19. *Boston Globe*, September 2, 1962.

20. *Boston Herald*, September 2, 1962.

21. *Boston Traveler*, January 17, 1967.

22. *Boston Globe*, March 6, 1963.

23. *The Traveler*, March 20, 1963.

24. *Boston Record American*, July 30, 1964.

25. *Boston Globe*, August 18, 1964.

26. *The Traveler*, February 6, 1964.

27. *Ibid.*, February 8, 1964.

28. *Boston Record American*, August 25, 1966.

29. *Ibid.*, September 8, 1966.

30. *Ibid.*

31. *Herald-American*, January 28, 1973.

32. *Boston Globe*, January 15, 1967.

33. *Daily News*, February 28, 1967.

34. R. Granger (ed.), *Murder Casebook: The Boston Strangler* (London: Marshall Cavendish, Ltd., 1991), p. 178.

35. *Ibid.*

36. *Daily News*, February 28, 1967.

37. *Boston Herald*, June 14, 1987.

38. The most recent illustration of the never-ending debate concerning Albert DeSalvo's authenticity as the sole murderer is provided by Susan Kelly in a newly published book, *The Boston Stranglers*. Kelly, again, makes the case the eleven killings attributed to the Boston Strangler were not all connected and were committed by several murderers, none of whom was Albert DeSalvo.

CHAPTER 4

1. *Eastern Echo*, October 22, 1968, p. 2.

2. *Ibid.*, January 9, 1968, p. 4.

3. *Detroit Free Press*, July 28, 1969, p. 1–A.

4. *Michigan Daily*, July 29, 1969.

5. Reproduced from a map appearing in the *Detroit News*, July 28, 1969.

6. *Ypsilanti Press*, April 21, 1969, p. 1, Byline: John Cobb.

7. *Ann Arbor News*, April 16, 1969, p. 1–A.

8. *Ibid.*, June 11, 1969, p. 1–A, Byline: William B. Treml.

9. *Ibid.*, June 12, 1969, p. 5–A, Byline: Gene Goltz and Tom Ricke.

10. *Michigan Daily*, June 14, 1969, p. 2.

11. *Detroit Free Press*, July 30, 1969, p. 1–A, Byline: Glenna McWirter.

12. *Ann Arbor News*, April 4, 1969, p. 4.

13. *Ibid.*, April 6, 1969, p. 4.

14. *Eastern Echo*, February 28, 1969.

15. *Detroit Free Press*, August 11, 1969.

16. *Ypsilanti Press*, April 17, 1969.

17. *Ibid.*, April 21, 1969.

18. *Ann Arbor News*, June 21, 1969, p. 8, Byline: Roy Renolds.

19. *Ibid.*, June 13, 1969, p. 1, Byline: William B. Treml.

20. *Ibid.*, June 14, 1969, p. 1, Byline: William B. Treml.

21. *Ibid.*

22. *Ibid.*, June 20, 1969, p. 4.

23. *Detroit Free Press*, August 2, 1969, p. 2–A, Byline: Walker Lundy.

24. *Ann Arbor News*, June 17, 1969, p. 17.

25. *Ibid.*, June 17, 1969, p. 4.

26. *Ypsilanti Press*, July 29, 1967, p. 3.

27. *Ann Arbor News*, July 28, 1967, p. 1, Byline: William B. Treml.

28. *Detroit Free Press*, July 6, 1969, p. 10–A, Byline: Arnold Rosenfeld.

29. *Ibid.*

30. *Ann Arbor News*, March 27, 1969, p. 31, Byline: William B. Treml.

31. *Ypsilanti Press*, July 12–13, 1965, p. 1.

32. *Ann Arbor News*, July 16, 1965, p. 25.

33. *Ibid.*, July 12, 1969, p. 8.

34. *Traverse City Record Eagle*, July 23, 1969.

35. *Ibid.*

36. *Ann Arbor News*, July 24, 1969, p. 25, Byline: Dennis Chase.

37. *Michigan Daily*, July 25, 1969, p. 1.

38. *Ypsilanti Press*, July 24, 1969, p. 2.

39. *Ann Arbor News*, July 22, 1969, p. 15, Byline: Dennis Chase.

40. *Ypsilanti Press*, July 28, 1969.

41. *Detroit Free Press*, August 12, 1969, p. 3–A.

42. *Ann Arbor News*, July 23, 1969, p. 23.

43. *Ypsilanti Press*, June 13, 1969, p. 1.

44. *Detroit Free Press*, April 17, 1969, p. 4–A.

45. *Ann Arbor News*, June 11, 1969.

46. *Ypsilanti Press*, July 28, 1969.

47. *Detroit Free Press*, April 21, 1969, p. 1–A, Byline: Curtis Haseltine.

48. *Ibid.*, July 21, 1969.

49. *Detroit News*, July 28, 1969, Byline: Ronald L. Russell and William Connellan.

50. *Ibid.*, July 31, 1969, Byline: Al Blanchard.

51. *Detroit Free Press*, August 1, 1969, p. 2A.

52. *Michigan Daily*, August 6, 1969, p. 7.

53. *Ibid.*, August 2, 1969, p. 3.

54. *Detroit News*, August 19, 1969, Byline: Armand Gebert.

55. *Ann Arbor News*, January 5, 1972, Byline: William B. Treml.

56. *Ibid.*

57. *Detroit Free Press*, February 28, 1982, p. 1–B, Byline: Jim Neubacher.

CHAPTER 5

1. *New York Times*, November 8, 1993, p. B2.

2. D. Abrahamsen, *Confessions of Son of Sam* (New York: Columbia University Press, 1985), p. 11.

3. R. Ressler and T. Shachtman, *Whoever Fights Monsters* (New York: St. Martin's Press, 1992), p. 69.

4. Like many facts in the Son of Sam case, the number of women attacked is in doubt. Laurence Klausner in *Son of Sam* (New York: McGraw-Hill, 1981) says two, based on statements by Berkowitz. However, Berkowitz changed his story on many occasions. According to author Maury Terry in *The Ultimate Evil* (New York; Bantam Books, 1987), Berkowitz later denied the first attack on the unnamed woman.

5. Klausner, *Son of Sam*, p. 16.

6. *New York Post*, June 28, 1977, p. 14, Byline: Edmund Newton.

7. Typical of this approach is Elliott Leyton, who, in his book *Compulsive Killer: The Story of Modern Multiple Murder* (New York: Washington Mews Books, 1986), proposes that serial murders are hypersensitive about their social standing, are class conscious, and obsessed with status, class, and power. Because they feel alienated (in Berkowitz's case by his illegitimacy) from society, their motivation is to "wreak vengeance upon the established order," and they select targets from the social class immediately above their own. For this reason, Leyton maintains, Berkowitz attacked in the Bronx and Queens where young people slightly better off than he predominated. As interesting as this purely sociological explanation of serial murder and Berkowitz is, it does not seem to square with the facts of the case, most notably the strong and lasting attachment between David and his adoptive father and the loyalty shown him by his mother Betty Falco.

Other explanations of Berkowitz's actions tend to be heavily influenced by when they were written and what was known at the time. The first pseudobiography, *.44* by Jimmy Breslin and Dick Schaap, makes no pretense of objectivity, is a novelization of the events, and portrays Berkowitz as a slobbering madman.

Son of Sam by Laurence Klausner is based on transcripts of interviews with Berkowitz while he was in prison awaiting trial. It accepts uncritically the frequent allusions to demons and devils and concludes that Berkowitz was insane and believed he was driven to kill by the blood lust of a 6,000 year old man, Sam. At the time, however, Berkowitz was using the demon possession story as the basis for his insanity plea, and the statements are essentially self-serving. When he heard that Klausner was writing the book, he publicly recanted, stating that the ravings about demons were apocryphal and played no role in the murders.

Psychiatrist Dr. David Abrahamsen had access to Berkowitz and examined him on behalf of the prosecution in the attempt to decide his mental competence to stand trial. Abrahamsen never believed the stories about Sam and stated categorically that Berkowitz was legally sane. After the trial, Berkowitz and Abrahamsen communicated extensively, and the correspondence became the basis for the book *Confessions of Son of Sam*. As a psychoanalyst, Abrahamsen was most apt to attribute Berkowitz's behavior to his early emotional development and therefore considered the meeting with Betty Falco as very important and precipitory.

A darker hypothesis was forwarded by Maury Terry in *The Ultimate Evil*. Using as a springboard the facts that witness descriptions of the killer varied widely, Terry produced four very different composite drawings. The police once believed the killer wore a wig and that some shootings were ruthlessly efficient while others were amateurish. The author develops a complex and well-documented scenario that Berkowitz was involved in satanism and belonged to a coven that committed murders from coast to coast. Stranger still, Terry suggests that Berkowitz had accomplices, including John and Michael Carr, sons of Sam Carr (Son of Sam in the notes), both of whom died violently shortly after Berkowitz was arrested, and that the coven was associated with Charles Manson. In Terry's view, the religious terminology in the notes are satanic references.

8. *New York Times*, May 17, 1978, p. 84, Byline: Howard Blum.

9. Abrahamsen, *Confessions of Son of Sam*, p. 195.

10. *New York Times*, October 22, 1977, p. A22, Byline: Max Seigel.

11. *Daily News*, March 11, 1977, p. 5, Byline: Thomas Pugh and Wilham Neugebauer.

12. *Ibid.*, August 4, 1977, p. 33, Byline: Bob Kappstatter.

13. *New York Times*, August 1, 1977, p. A34, Byline: Eric Pace.

14. *Ibid.*, August 7, 1977, Section 4, p. 6, Byline: Howard Blum.

15. *Daily News*, July 28, 1977, p. 3, Byline: Jimmy Breslin.

16. *Ibid.*, August 5, 1977, pp. 3, 15, Byline: William Federici and Richard Edmonds.

17. *Ibid.*, p. 3.

18. Klausner, *Son of Sam*, p. 130.

19. Ibid., p. 146.

20. Abrahamsen, *Confessions of Son of Sam*, p. 209.

21. *Daily News*, April 19, 1977, p. 3.

22. *New York Post*, April 28, 1977.

23. *Daily News*, June 5, 1977, p. 51, Byline: Jimmy Breslin.

24. Abrahamsen, *Confessions of Son of Sam*, p. 4.

25. *Daily News*, July 28, 1977, p. 69, Byline: Jimmy Breslin.

26. *New York Times*, August 5, 1977, p. B3, Byline: Deirdre Carmody.

27. *Ibid.*, June 28, 1977, p. 28, Byline: Francis X. Clines.

28. *Ibid.*, August 5, 1977, p. B3, Byline: Deirdre Carmody.

29. Klausner, *Son of Sam*, p. 263.

30. *Ibid.*, p. 264.

31. *Daily News*, July 29, 1977, p. 16, Byline: Richard Edmonds.

32. *Ibid.*, August 11, 1977, p. 1, Byline: Owen Moritz.

33. *New York Post*, October 28, 1977, p. 25, Byline: Sidney Zion.

34. *New York Times*, October 29, 1977, p. 27, Byline: Max H. Seigel.

35. R. Ressler and T. Shachtman, *Whoever Fights Monsters* (New York: St. Martin's Press, 1992), p. 67.

36. *Daily News*, August 12, 1977, p. 67, Byline: Kay Gardella.

37. *New York Times*, August 4, 1977, p. 137, Byline: Richard F. Shepard.

38. *Ibid.*, August 18, 1977, p. 20.

39. *Ibid.*

40. *New York Post*, August 29, 1977, p. 6.

41. *Ibid.*, September 2, 1977, p. 6.

42. *New York Times*, August 22, 1977, pp. 1, 38, Byline: Carey Winfrey.

43. *New Yorker*, August 15, 1977, pp. 21–22.

44. *New York Times*, August 16, 1977, p. 24, Byline: Marcia Chambers.

45. *Ibid.*

46. *Ibid.*, April 10, 1979, p. 6, Byline: David Bird.

47. *Ibid.*, April 18, 1979, p. 21.

48. *Ibid.*, November 20, 1979, p. B8, Byline: Joseph P. Fried.

49. *Ibid.*, November 22, 1979, p. B3, Byline: Joseph P. Fried.

50. *Ibid.*, September 1, 1977, p. C3, Byline: Marcia Chambers.

CHAPTER 6

1. *Ebony* 36, No. 2(1980): 136.

2. *Atlanta Constitution*, August 22, 1980, p. A22, Byline: Brenda Mooney and Gail Epstein.

3. *New York Times*, March 15, 1981, p. 32A, Byline: M. A. Farber.

4. *Atlanta Constitution*, July 17, 1981, p. 4C, Byline: Jerry Schwartz.

5. *Ibid.*, June 14, 1981, p. 1D, Byline: Jack Tarver.

6. *Atlanta Daily World*, March 3, 1981, p. 6.

7. *Ibid.*, October 30, 1980, pp. 1, 6, Byline: George Mason Coleman.

8. *Ibid.*, February 22, 1981, p. 4.

9. *Atlanta Constitution*, February 1, 1981, p. 1C, Byline: Frederick Allen.

10. *New York Times*, January 26, 1981, p. 12A, Byline: Reginald Stuart.

11. *Ibid.*, March 22, 1981, p. 24, Byline: Wendell Rawls, Jr.

12. *Atlanta Constitution*, December 25, 1980, p. 23A, Byline: Gail Epstein.

13. *Ibid.*

14. *Ibid.*, April 22, 1981, p. 4A.

15. *Ibid.*, March 30, 1981, p. 1C, Byline: Brenda Mooney.

16. *Ibid.*, April 9, 1981, p. 4A.

17. *Atlanta Daily World*, April 23, 1981, p. 9, Byline: Joe Black.

18. *Atlanta Constitution*, June 7, 1981, p. 14A, Byline: Greg McDonald and David B. Hilder.

19. *Ibid.*, August 8, 1980, p. 4A, Byline: Bill Shipp.

20. *Ibid.*, January 18, 1981, p. 12A, Byline: Chet Fuller.

21. *Ibid.*, April 14, 1981, p. 1A, Byline: Andrew J. Glass.

22. *Ibid.*, April 16, 1981, p. 19A, Byline: Brenda Mooney.

23. *Ibid.*, April 15, 1981, p. 14A, Byline: George Rodrigue and Ken Willis.

24. *Ibid.*

25. *Atlanta Daily World*, March 6, 1981, p. 6.

26. *Atlanta Constitution*, June 11, 1981, p. 2, Intown Extra, Byline: David Secrest.

27. *Atlanta Daily World*, June 16, 1981, p. 6, Byline: Raymond H. Boone.

28. *Atlanta Constitution*, March 10, 1981, p. 1C, Byline: Joe Brown.

29. *Atlanta Daily World*, June 26, 1981, p. 1, Byline: Mark Mayfield.

30. *Atlanta Constitution*, February 2, 1981, p. 1C, Byline: Lewis Gizzard.

31. *Ibid.*, April 16, 1981, p. 5A.

32. *Ibid.*, November 2, 1980, p. 6B, Byline: Chet Fuller.

33. *Ibid.*

34. *Ibid.*, March 9, 1981, p. 10A.

35. *Atlanta Daily World*, June 5, 1981, p. 6.

36. *Ibid.*, April 24, 1981, p. 1, Byline: Charles Taylor.

37. *Ibid.*, February 1, 1981, p. 1, Byline: George Mason Coleman.

38. *Atlanta Constitution*, August 8, 1980, p. 4A, Byline: Bill Shipp.

39. *Ibid.*, March 22, 1981, p. 14A.

40. *Atlanta Daily World*, February 8, 1981, p. 4, Byline: Charles Price.

41. *Atlanta Constitution*, March 22, 1981, p. 1, 14A.

42. *Ibid.*, p. 7C, Byline: Dallas Lee.

43. *Ibid.*, May 10, 1981, p. 7C, Byline: Dallas Lee.

44. *Atlanta Daily World*, May 22, 1981, p. 6.

45. *Atlanta Constitution*, January 29, 1981, p. 2C, Byline: Linda Field.

46. *Ibid.*

47. *Ibid.*, March 22, 1981, p. 14A.

48. *Ibid.*, March 21, 1981, p. 4A, Byline: Ken Willis and George Rodrigue.

49. *Atlanta Daily World*, October 1, 1981, p. 8.

50. *Atlanta Constitution*, March 25, 1981, p. 5A, Byline: Ralph Wayne Wright.

51. *Ibid.*, July 30, 1981, p. 4, Intown Extra.

52. *New York Times*, January 3, 1982, p. 16, Byline: Wendell Rawls, Jr.

53. *Atlanta Constitution*, October 30, 1980, p. 3, Intown Extra, Byline: Alexis Scott Reeves.

54. *Ibid.*, May 10, 1981, p. 7C, Byline: Dallas Lee.

55. *Atlanta Daily World*, July 21, 1981, p. 6.

56. *Atlanta Constitution*, February 26, 1981, p. 8A.

57. *Ibid.*, March 15, 1981, p. 11A, Byline: Ron Taylor.

58. *Ibid.*, May 17, 1981, p. 6B, Byline: Clem Richardson.

59. *Ibid.*, June 28, 1981, p. 14A, Byline: Ron Taylor and Clem Richardson.

60. *Atlanta Daily World*, October 23, 1981, p. 4.

61. *Atlanta Constitution*, July 31, 1981, p. 10A, Byline: Gail Epstein and Ken Willis.

62. *New York Times*, February 23, 1982, p. 12A.

63. *Ibid.*, February 25, 1982, p. 18, Byline: Wendell Rawls, Jr.

64. *Atlanta Constitution*, September 20, 1981, p. 21, Atlanta Weekly, Byline: David Nordan.

65. *New York Times*, February 27, 1982, p. 7, Byline: Wendell Rawls, Jr.

66. *Atlanta Daily World*, March 7, 1982, p. 1.

67. *Ibid.*, March 4, 1982, p. 4, Byline: George Mason Coleman.

CHAPTER 7

1. *New York Times*, April 10, 1993. Section: National, p. 6, Byline: Michail deCourcy Hinds.

2. *Ibid.*

3. The Mayor's Citizen Commission on Police-Community Relations, "A Report to Mayor John O. Norquist and the Board of Fire and Police Commissioners," October 15, 1991, p. 4.

4. Ibid., p. 9.

5. *The Milwaukee Journal*, August 29, 1991. Section: News, p. A1, Byline: Katherine M. Skiba.

6. *Ibid.*, June 11, 1992. Section: News, p. A1, Byline: Tom Vanden Brook.

7. Mayor's Citizen Commission, "A Report to Mayor John O. Norquist," p. 9.

8. *The Milwaukee Journal*, September 22, 1991. Section: News, p. A1, Byline: Joe Garofoli.

9. *The Milwaukee Sentinel*, April 2, 1992. Section: News, p. A1, Byline: Crocker Stephenson.

10. *The Milwaukee Journal*, August 9, 1991. Section: News, p. 5b, Byline: Joe Garofoli.

11. *The Milwaukee Sentinel*, March 12, 1992. Section: News, p. 5A, Byline: William Janz.

12. *Ibid.*, January 27, 1992. Section: News, p. 1A, Byline: Jan Uebelherr.

13. *Ibid.*, February 12, 1992. Section: News, p. 1A, Byline: David Doege.

14. *Ibid.*

15. Wisconsin Department of Justice, Division of Criminal Investigation, "Milwaukee Police Department Re: Jeffrey Dahmer; May 27, 1991," August 23, 1991.

16. *The Milwaukee Sentinel*, September 7, 1991. Section: News, p. 1A, Byline: Rick Romell.

17. *Ibid.*, August 30, 1991. Section: News, p. 1A, Byline: Amy Renaid; Tom Held.

18. *Ibid.*, February 12, 1992. Section: News, p. A1, Byline: Jim Stengl.

19. *The Milwaukee Journal*, August 25, 1991. Section: News, p. A1, Byline: Katherine M. Skiba.

20. *New York Times*, August 2, 1991. Section: National, p. A10.

21. *The Milwaukee Journal*, May 12, 1992. Section: OPED, p. A6, Byline: Barbara Markoff.

22. *The Milwaukee Sentinel*, August 13, 1991. Section: News, p. 5A, Byline: Lisa Sink.

23. *The Milwaukee Journal*, February 7, 1992. Section: News, p. A6, Byline: Celeste Williams.

24. *Ibid.*, September 27, 1991. Section: OPED, p. A8, Byline: Lawrence M. Venture.

25. *The Milwaukee Sentinel*, January 14, 1992. Section: News, p. 1A, Byline: David Doege.

26. *The Milwaukee Journal*, March 1, 1992. Section: Sports, p. C2.

27. *Ibid.*, July 19, 1992. Section: News, p. J3.

28. *Ibid.*, January 20, 1992. Section: News, p. B1, Byline: Tom Vanden Brook.

29. *Ibid.*, January 28, 1992. Section: News, p. A6, Byline: Tim Cuprisin.

30. *The Milwaukee Sentinel*, October 7, 1991. Section: News, p. 5A, Byline: Crocker Stephenson.

31. *The Milwaukee Journal*, September 9, 1991. Section: News, p. A1, Byline: Kevin Harrington and Anne Bothwell.

32. *The Milwaukee Sentinel*, October 10, 1992. Section: News, p. 5A, Byline: Tom Held.

33. *The Milwaukee Journal*, September 15, 1991. Section: News, p. B1, Byline: Joe Garofoli.

34. Mayor's Citizen Commission, "A Report to Mayor John O. Norquist," p. i.

35. *The Milwaukee Journal*, May 15, 1992. Section: News, p. B1, Byline: Dennis McCann.

36. Eventually published as *A Father's Story* by William Morrow.

37. A. E. Schwartz, *The Man Who Could Not Kill Enough* (New York: Carol Publishing Group, A Birch Lane Press Book, 1992), p. 141.

38. *The Milwaukee Sentinel*, February 7, 1992. Section: News, p. 8A.

39. *The Milwaukee Journal*, September 2, 1992. Section: News, p. B1, Byline: Dennis McCann.

40. *The Milwaukee Sentinel*, August 15, 1992. Section: News, p. 5A.

41. *Ibid.*, March 23, 1992. Section: News, p. 1A, Byline: William Janz.

CHAPTER 8

1. *The Times*, November 12, 1888, p. 6.

2. *Pall Mall Gazette*, September 13, 1888, p. 8.

3. *Ibid.*, October 6, 1888, p. 2.

4. *Ibid.*, October 1, 1888, p. 1.

5. *Ibid.*, September 19, 1888, p. 1.

6. *Ibid.*, October 3, 1888, p. 3.

7. *Ibid.*, October 4, 1888, pp. 4–5.

8. *Ibid.*, December 1, 1888, p. 2.

9. *Ibid.*, December 6, 1888, p. 3.

10. *Ibid.*, September 8, 1888, p. 8.

11. *Ibid.*, October 10, 1888, p. 1.

12. *Ibid.*, October 9, 1888, p. 4.

13. *Ibid.*, September 27, 1888, p. 10.

14. *The Times*, October 1, 1888, p. 6.

15. *Pall Mall Gazette*, November 10, 1888, p. 8.

16. *The Times*, October 8, 1888, p. 6.

17. *Pall Mall Gazette*, October 2, 1888, p. 7.

18. *The Jewish World*, October 5, 1888, p. 6.

19. *Ibid.*, October 12, 1888, p. 5.

20. *Pall Mall Gazette*, October 15, 1888, p. 6.

21. *Ibid.*, October 8, 1888, p. 8.

22. R. Granger (ed.), *Murder Casebook: Who Was Jack the Ripper?* (London: Marshall Cavendish, Ltd., 1991), p. 40.

23. *Pall Mall Gazette*, November 10, 1888, p. 1.

24. *Ibid.*, December 31, 1888, p. 10.

Selected Bibliography

Abrahamsen, D. *Confessions of Son of Sam*. New York: Columbia University Press, 1985.
———. *Murder and Madness: The Secret Life of Jack the Ripper*. New York: Donald I. Fine, Inc., 1992.
———. *The Murdering Mind*. New York: Harper & Row, 1973.
Baldwin, J. *The Evidence of Things Not Seen*. New York: Henry Holt & Co., 1985.
Breslin, J. and D. Schaap. *.44*. New York: Viking, 1978.
Browning, N. L. *Peter Hurkos: I Have Many Lives*. New York: Doubleday, 1976.
———. *The Psychic World of Peter Hurkos*. New York: Doubleday, 1970.
Cahill, T. *Buried Dreams: Inside the Mind of a Serial Killer*. New York: Bantam Books, 1986.
Conklin, J. E. *The Impact of Crime*. New York: Macmillan, 1975.
Cullen, R. *The Killer Department*. New York: Pantheon Books, 1993.
Dahmer, L. *A Father's Story*. New York: William Morrow and Company, 1994.
Davis, D. *The Milwaukee Murders: Nightmare in Apartment 213: The True Story*. New York: St. Martin's Paperbacks, 1991.
Doney, R. "The Aftermath of the Yorkshire Ripper: The Response of the United Kingdom Police Service." In S. Egger (ed.), *Serial Murder: An Elusive Phenomenon*. New York: Praeger, 1990.
Egger, S. A. "Linkage Blindness: A Systemic Myopia." In S. Egger (ed.), *Serial Murder: An Elusive Phenomenon*. New York: Praeger, 1990.
———. "Serial Murder: A Synthesis of Literature and Research." In S. A. Egger (ed.), *Serial Murder: An Elusive Phenomenon*. New York: Praeger, 1990.
Federal Bureau of Investigation. *Law Enforcement Bulletin* 54, no. 8 (1985).
Ford, D. A. "Investigating Serial Murder: The Case of Indiana's 'Gay Murders.'" In S. A. Egger (ed.), *Serial Murder: An Elusive Phenomenon*. New York: Praeger, 1990.
Frank, G. *The Boston Strangler*. New York: The New American Library, 1966.
Granger, R. (ed.). *Murder Casebook: Who Was Jack the Ripper?* London: Marshall Cavendish, Ltd., 1991.

Hickey, E. W. *Serial Murderers and Their Victims*. Pacific Grove, Calif.: Brooks/Cole Publishing Co., 1991.

Holmes, R. M. *Profiling Violent Crimes*. Newbury Park, Calif.: Sage Publications, 1989.

Holmes, R. M., and J. DeBurger. *Serial Murder*. Newbury Park, Calif.: Sage Publications, 1988.

Jeffers, H. P. *Who Killed Precious?* New York: St. Martin's Paperbacks, 1991.

Kelly, S. *The Boston Strangler*. New York: Carol Publishing Group, A Birch Lane Press Book, 1992.

Keppel, R. D. *Serial Murder: Future Implications for Police Investigations*. Cincinnati, Ohio: Anderson Publishing Co., 1989.

Keyes, E. *The Michigan Murders*. New York: Readers Digest Press, 1976.

Klausner, L. *Son of Sam*. New York: McGraw-Hill, 1981.

Levin, J., and J. A. Fox. *Mass Murder: America's Growing Menace*. New York: Berkley Books, 1985.

Leyton, E. *Compulsive Killers: The Story of Modern Multiple Murder*. New York: Washington Mews Books, 1986.

Malcolm, J. *The Journalist and the Murderer*. New York: Vintage Books, 1990.

The Mayor's Citizen Commission on Police-Community Relations. "A Report to Mayor John O. Norquist and the Board of Fire and Police Commissioners." October 15, 1991.

Norris, J. *Jeffrey Dahmer*. Canada: Pinnacle Books, 1992.

———. *Serial Killers*. New York: Doubleday, 1988.

Ressler, R., and T. Shachtman. *Whoever Fights Monsters*. New York: St. Martin's Press, 1992.

Rumbelow, D. *Jack the Ripper: The Complete Casebook*. New York: Berkley Books, 1990.

Schwartz, A. E. *The Man Who Could Not Kill Enough*. New York: Carol Publishing Group, A Birch Lane Press Book, 1992.

Smith, C., and T. Guillen. *The Search for the Green River Killer*. New York: Penguin Books, 1991.

Terry, M. *The Ultimate Evil*. New York: Bantam Books, 1987.

Wisconsin Department of Justice, Division of Criminal Investigation. "Milwaukee Police Department Re: Jeffrey Dahmer; May 27, 1991." August 23, 1991.

Index

About the Author

JOSEPH C. FISHER (Ph.D., Tufts University) is President of InterData, Inc., a research firm specializing in advertising evaluation studies and marketing investment analysis. His previous books include *Advertising, Alcohol Consumption, and Abuse* (Greenwood, 1993) and *Advertising, Alcohol Consumption, and Mortality* (Greenwood, 1995). He is also the author of several works in criminology including a study of the relationship between the availability of firearms and homicide rates.